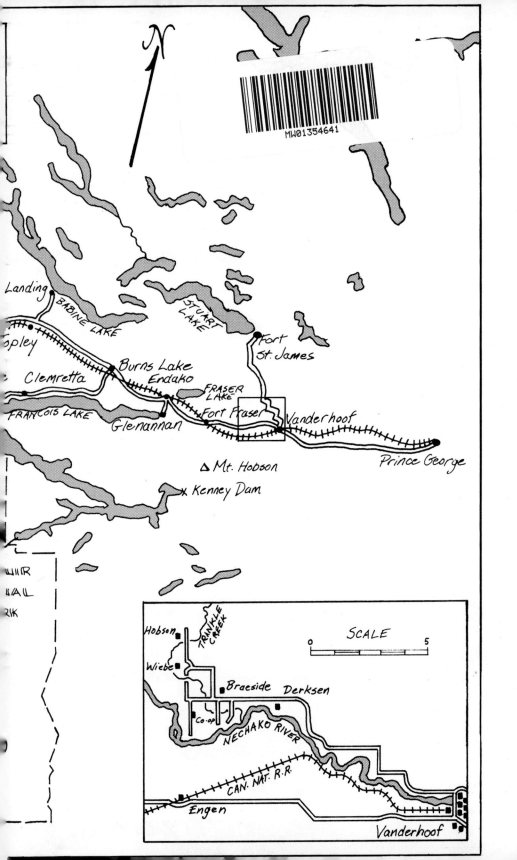

Chinked with Oakum

For Roger... one of my
good friends... who
also likes adventures
Eve

Eve Hobson
December 1986

Chinked with Oakum

Eve Hobson

Illustrations by Eve Hobson

Admont Corporation of Staunton, Virginia

Copyright © 1986 by Admont Corporation

All rights reserved. No part of this work may be reproduced or transmitted in any form or by any means, electronic or mechanical, including photocopying and recording, or by any information storage or retrieval system, except as may be expressly permitted by the 1976 Copyright Act or in writing from the publisher.

Requests for permission should be addressed to: Admont Corporation, Post Office Box 3148 Staunton, Virginia, 24401.

First Edition

Library of Congress Cataloging-in-Publication Data

Hobson, Eve,
   Chinked with Oakum.

    1. British Columbia--Description and travel.
2. British Columbia--Social life and customs.
3. Hobson, Eve,   --Journeys--British Columbia.
I. Title.
F1087.H768 1986   917.11'044   86-20619

ISBN 0-939421-00-3

Printed in the United States of America

Endpaper map by Marsha Vayvada

For George

Acknowledgements

Before my wilderness adventure was finally written many of my friends had prodded and encouraged me. I give my thanks to Victoria Hobson, Cynthia Foote, and Sarah Deane for their editorial help and to Sally Chapman for typing the final copy.

To my husband George, who cheered me on in the whole process, my especial thanks for his advice and support.

Contents

Acknowledgements - vi
List of Illustrations - ix
Introduction - xi
1 - Ten Minutes Early - 1
2 - The Jeep - 16
3 - Prospectors, Trappers, & Loggers - 23
4 - Little Creek Ranch - 32
5 - The Nechako Dam - 48
6 - The Western Novel - 56
7 - Wedding in the Poplar Grove - 68
8 - Pack Rats - 83
9 - Frontier Living - 95
10 - Frozen Nose - 114
11 - "Bossy is Bald!" - 123
12 - Moose and the Porcupine - 133
13 - Bears, Pigs, and Pullets - 144
14 - Teeney and Friends - 153
15 - Nature's Messages - 160
16 - One-Room School - 175
17 - Baths I Have Been In - 189
18 - Mud and the Visiting Inspector - 203
19 - Fishing Summer - 215
20 - Cattle Roundup - 228
21 - Change is in the Air - 234
22 - Ranch for Sale - 245
23 - Goodbye Little Creek—
Farewell to the North Country - 258
Epilogue - 273

List of Illustrations

Cabin chinked with oakum - iii
The Jeep - 20
"Bumpy" - 38
Fireweed - 69
Pack Rat - 86
Porcupine - 141
The New Piglets - 149
Chickens - 173
Canadian Geese - 275

Introduction

Had I not been passing through British Columbia in the early 1950s there would have been nothing to write. There I saw geese gather on broad rivers, white goats scramble on snow-capped mountains, moose feed on willow tips in rich bottom lands and Indians trade their furs on landings in lakes.

Fascinated, I stayed on sharing more of the wealth of the Central Interior—the old pioneers who had come in by boat, fighting their way in on foot or by pack train at the turn of the century—and the young men to whom the pioneers had handed on their heritage. They told me their personal stories, dreams they had held on to and the illusions they had lost.

The land also shared its history, old overland telegraph buildings, rusting machinery used in gold-seeking days and the remains of an Indian village. And always jack pine and blue spruce pointed multitudes of green fingers to the sky scenting the air with spicy fragrance—a place of magic and mystery.

Against this backdrop while journeying through this land of mountains, lakes and wild hay meadows I met my man. With him and with my other love—the land—I lived on an isolated cattle ranch in a cosy log cabin, chinked with oakum, at the end of a dirt road swallowed up in the wilderness. This is my story.

E. H.

ONE

Ten Minutes Early

I pushed aside the small piece of wood covering the one-inch hole drilled for ventilation in the rough wooden frame of the storm window. Cold air filtered through the small space into my overheated room in the small hotel in the Central Interior of British Columbia, Canada. I breathed deeply of the bracing night air—snow! It's strange how one can smell snow. It was mingled with the acrid scent of wood—the pungency of burning sawdust piles in the local sawmills. How I loved wood, "a substance with a soul," as William Penn said. I had arrived by train, and an hour before had registered at the Vanderhoof Hotel in the village of the same name on the fifty-fourth parallel. The little frontier community clung tightly to the lifeline of this part of the province— the Canadian National Railway.

I was working for the *Prince Rupert Daily News* and had come to Vanderhoof to get information about Richmond Pearson Hobson, Jr., whose book, *Grass Beyond The Mountains*, had become a bestseller. The author was a rancher who lived fifty miles south of Vanderhoof.

The book lay on the bed. In the back-cover photograph, the author was wearing a moosehide jacket, chaps, and an old cowboy hat. He was riding a horse called Nimpo, one of the nine horses, "conquerors of the silent, lonely trails," to which he had dedicated his book.

Rich Hobson had been in this part of the Canadian wilderness since the early 1930s. His hope had been to find extensive wild hay meadows near the headquarters of the Blackwater River beyond the Itcha, Algak, and

Fawnie Mountain ranges and to start a cattle ranch there.

He was the son of Admiral Richmond Pearson Hobson, who, as a young navy lieutenant during the Spanish American War, had won fame by sinking the collier Merrimac across Santiago Harbor to bottle up the Spanish fleet.

During the Great Depression, Rich Hobson had left a lively social life in New York and headed west. He found work as a roughneck in the oil fields of Texas. Later, he met Panhandle Phillips, a cowboy, and together they made their way to British Columbia to find these wild hay meadows.

I had met men earlier in the year—loggers, trappers, and miners—who also had dreams, and had answered in their various ways, the alluring call of this fascinating yet ruthless wilderness where some dreams were found and others faded.

I, too, had heard its call. In the previous summer, from June until September, with a woman companion from Port Credit, Ontario, I had driven a ton-and-a-half Anglican Mission van belonging to the Diocese of Caledonia. We drove along the unpaved dusty road between Prince Rupert and Prince George, down narrow logging trails, and around lonely lakes, to visit isolated Indian and white families. We slept in the van wherever we happened to end the day. I swam naked in mysterious loon-haunted lakes. I washed my dust-impregnated clothes in them and spread them to dry on tall, blueberried Saskatoon bushes.

I walked over to the bed and leafed through the book again; we had common ground for talking. I knew what "jack-pine forests," and "lonely loon-haunted lakes" were. I had gazed at "mountains that split the sky," and had seen white goats scramble there. I, too, knew the power of a mountain, had reverence for water and a mystical feeling for trees. I understood what the author meant when he wrote, "It's a land that drew me like a magnet into its soul."

But what were "dish-faced, short-backed bays?" I supposed they were horses. I closed the book. The cold air filtering through the hole in the window frame had made me hungry. I must eat and then go on to my appointment with Grizelda Hobson, the mother of Rich Hobson, with whom I had made the appointment earlier from the office of the *Nechako Chronicle*, the Vanderhoof newspaper. I could not visit the author at his Rimrock Ranch as I had no car. Grizelda Hobson expected Rich to come in that night. I checked my watch; just time to eat and arrive on time for the eight o'clock appointment.

I glanced at myself appraisingly in the full-length mirror. The black gabardine suit an expert tailor in Perth, Western Australia, had made for me a few years previously, was wearing well, except for the frayed cuffs. I slipped on my flat English walking shoes; pulled on a jockey-type felt hat over my blonde hair and drew myself up to my full five feet seven-and-a-half inches. I took another look at myself: not bad-looking for forty—still trim—and completely broke, I admitted to myself wryly.

Picking up my heavy, Harris-tweed coat which enveloped me like an Indian blanket, I headed out. A small zippered black Moroccan leather case held my notebook and pencil. In better times it had contained an elegant enameled mirror and brush-and-comb set given to me on my twenty-first birthday. As is usually the case with such milestone gifts, the outside covering had outlasted the contents, and it was too good to throw away. It looked rather snappy, I thought.

"From the cut of her and her walk, I'll bet she's an Englishwoman." The speaker, like the others gathered at the entrance to the hotel, wore a bright logging shirt and a battered cowboy hat. Their voices were loud, although the beer-hall night was still young.

"I wonder how he knows I am English," I mused, as I passed the group. "It must be the long strides I take. Or perhaps it's this big, bulky coat." I rounded the corner by the drugstore, nearly tripping over the store step, which stuck unusually far out. A plump, middle-aged, bespectacled little man clothed in white—the pharmacist, I assumed, turned out of the drugstore right across my path. Like a white leghorn hen seized with an extreme eagerness to reach the other side of the road, he hastened across the narrow main street and vanished head first into a small restaurant, scattering a knot of oriental-looking Indians of all ages gathered around the entrance. I followed him in. I had eaten here in the summer. At that time a station wagon was parked outside. On top of it, tethered to a spare tire, a peregrine falcon had been tearing at its lunch of raw chicken. Its owners were inside the restaurant, hungrily fingering their chicken, fried. When I asked the men, who turned out to be from Seattle, about the bird, they replied they were on the way to the Queen Charlotte Islands to take young feathered peregrine falcons out of their nests to train them in Seattle for hunting. The bird I had seen was probably a female, larger and more ferocious than the male, with whom she mates for life, and probably twice as strong. I ate and left for my appointment.

I strode along in the middle of the snow-scraped dirt street, passed a few miscellaneous stores on either side and turned right on to the boardwalk. A few yards farther on was the frame house, Frontier House. I was ten minutes early for my appointment. Little did I think then that this habit of mine of arriving early was to change my life. I rang the bell; the door opened.

"Come in, won't you"—a man whom I couldn't see spoke from the inside.

I stepped through the doorway from the screened porch into a cozy, knotty-pine paneled living room. On the right, a bright fire burned in a large hearth, and near the opposite wall stood an upright barrel heater and a large supply of pine logs.

"May I take your coat?"

I turned to the youthful-looking man who had greeted me and who now held out his hand. He was about forty, handsome, of medium height, slim and beautifully proportioned from what I could see of the form concealed under the old, red-plaid wool logging shirt open at the neck. He wore incredibly dirty patched jeans turned up about a foot at the bottom. Was this Rich Hobson? He certainly didn't look like the photo in his book.

And his feet! How could they be so large? Not wanting to stare, I raised my eyes to his expressive face. He had a fantastic amount of curly, prematurely gray hair; it couldn't have been cut for several months. He leaned slightly forward to take my coat, held out a strong, well-shaped, but somewhat dirty hand, and smiled a devastatingly attractive smile, even though several of his front teeth were missing.

A good-looking gray-haired woman came in, holding out her hand graciously to greet me. She was petite, with the proud posture of a little queen.

"This is my youngest son, George. He is in from his ranch," she said, as if apologizing for her son's rugged appearance. "Rich has not arrived yet."

I wondered how big George's ranch was. I had always thought of a ranch as being gigantic like those in Texas or the Frontier Cattle Company ranch Rich Hobson had originally formed and written about. My recent travels in the van had taught me, however, that in that part of the country, a small piece of land with a few beef cattle could be called a ranch.

Grizelda Hobson drew her flaming-red stole closely around her shoulders and led me to a settee facing the fire. The contrast in outward appearance between the roughly-clad man and the exquisite, elegantly-dressed older woman was striking.

Opposite where I sat and above the fireplace hung a large portrait in oils of a young man with the same straight eyebrows as the young rancher I had just met, and who was now sitting in a comfortable armchair to one side of the portrait. But the hair was raven-black in the picture, not gray.

"That's George when he was twenty-one, painted during Tennis Week in Newport, Rhode Island," said his mother.

I looked at the gray-haired man with the young face. He was still as handsome as in the portrait. I looked again intently at the unusually large rubber boots, the tops of which vanished under the turned-up jeans.

"Oh! I've got two pairs of boots on," he volunteered, smiling. "Can't afford a new pair now. The holes in each pair don't match anyway, so they'll keep most of the snow out until I sell the calf crop. He stretched out his legs in front of him and surveyed them with no displeasure. His scheme made sense, I thought, although such an idea was new to me.

"It's wonderful to be in a real home again, Mrs. Hobson," I remarked enthusiastically, taking out my notebook and feeling very comfortable. I gazed around at the walls and tables covered with family photos and mementos and thought of the home in Australia I had left a few months before. How far away it now seemed! But what was I doing in someone else's home with a notebook in my hand, talking to a man who wore two pairs of boots and had only a few front teeth?

"My husband, Admiral Richmond Pearson Hobson, wrote, too, you know," Mrs. Hobson continued, "about all kinds of subjects including his life at Annapolis, which he entered at the age of fourteen. *The Sinking of the Merrimac* in the Spanish American War was the best known. Later, he was given the Congressional Medal of Honor for this deed."

"Now Mother, we're supposed to be talking about Rich and his book," George protested, as I paused in taking notes.

"Then of course there's Lucia, my daughter, who's married and in the East, and George, my youngest," she continued, not heeding George's remark. "He joined Rich on his ranch after the war and now he has his own ranch twenty miles north of here. He's been here six years. He was a paratrooper with the Office of Strategic

Services during the war and jumped into Yugoslavia." She brought a photograph for me to look at. "Here he is in Italy being presented with the British Military Medal for bravery by General Alexander." George had a thin black moustache then and looked very handsome. Soldier, playboy undoubtedly, as he was so handsome, and rancher—I wondered in which role he was happiest.

Time passed quickly while I was getting more information for my article; the fire was burning low. Rich still hadn't arrived; my article would need a different slant.

"Won't you stay and have dinner with us?" my hostess asked warmly. "George was returning to the ranch when you came, but I think he will stay. Maybe Rich still will come tonight."

I replied that I would like to stay, and while the meal was under way in the kitchen George and I sat on opposite ends of the settee and talked.

"You know I had intended to escape out of the back door a few minutes before you were expected, but you came early. I thought you'd be a snaggle-toothed woman. Instead I'm the one with snaggle teeth and you're blonde and beautiful," he said, grinning broadly, showing all the gaps quite unabashedly.

"The rest of my teeth all fell out in my hand after I hit them with a crowbar, changing a tire at forty below. I can't afford to do anything about them now, but my sister Lucia wants to treat me to a new pair." Pair? What a strange expression, I thought. "But what brought you to this neck of the woods?"

"Well, if you really want to know, I'm on my way back to England from Australia, via Canada," I replied, smiling. Encouraged by his obvious interest, I told him that with my doctor husband, I had left England for Australia in 1947—adding, "We had problems in Australia which we couldn't resolve and we parted. After four years there, three of them on my own, I sailed from Sydney to Vancouver on a cargo ship."

He asked me if I was divorced. I told him that I was not, as the British process took a long time. I had paused before answering, thinking how that bald statement concealed a whole world of living and an ache in my heart. A year previously I had left Sydney harbor in the brilliant summer sunshine knowing I might never return. I had come a long way since. I had worked through my marital disengagement painfully and my spirit had slowly rejuvenated.

"I'm divorced," George said in a matter-of-fact way, interrupting my thoughts. "But why did you come to this part of British Columbia?" he asked, looking at me quizzically.

I paused again before replying, wondering where to start in answering such a question; how much should I tell a man I had met only an hour or so ago? I was saved from answering immediately as George's mother called from the kitchen to tell us dinner was ready.

"I came to get a story, not to tell one," I responded, smiling. I put my notebook away as we got up from the settee. I washed my hands, and we entered the kitchen where the meal was set out ranch-style. The head of a timber wolf grinned from a wall. A poster was pinned there: "Frontier Jamboree Honoring Old Timers," it read. The jamboree had been begun that year as a tribute to Rich and his book, and was to be made an annual event.

"Aren't you going to wash too?" I queried, as George sat down without washing his hands. Whatever made me ask a man I had known only an hour such a question?

After dinner, Rich still had not come. I completed my notes, thanked my hostess, and George walked back to the hotel with me. We sat down at a side table in the hotel dining room and ordered coffee.

"Well, why did you come to Central British Columbia?" George reiterated the question I had not yet answered.

"After I arrived in Vancouver, I spent a few weeks visiting cousins. While I was with them I dreamed up the idea that I would make someone a good executive secretary if I learned the necessary skills. I was tired of teaching." I smiled ruefully. "I was by myself during the last three years in Australia and taught in school to support myself. I wanted to try something new after that and I enrolled in a business school in Victoria."

"To finance it I supervised homework in the evenings in a private girls' boarding school and lived there. Breakfast came with the deal—two slices of brown bread, butter and marmalade. I saved one slice for my lunch at the business school and budgeted a nickel for a cup of coffee to go with it."

"It doesn't seem to have done you much harm," George broke in, smiling. "What happened next?"

"Well, at the end of two months at the school, I could type indifferently, was top of the class in spelling, and failed shorthand, a rather spotty record. I had nightmares about the whole secretarial venture. I realized that I would never make anyone a good secretary. I needed to be doing something more exciting. I felt much better when I admitted this to myself. The time had come to make some kind of a move."

"Is that when you came up here?" George inquired, rolling a cigarette carefully.

"Yes," I replied. "A lunch companion suggested I shouldn't leave British Columbia without seeing the Central Interior and she knew someone who was looking for a driver for an Anglican Mission van belonging to the Diocese of Caledonia. The mission was to visit Indian and white children who lived in isolated areas too far away from an organized church to attend Sunday School and to arrange for them to receive Sunday School lessons by mail. The job was unpaid, except for expenses. I jumped at the opportunity. It appealed to my sense of adventure."

I told him of taking some hasty driving lessons to get my Canadian driving license, of getting the job, and of joining my sixty-year old companion from Port Credit, Ontario.

"You may have seen the van in Vanderhoof. It's like a rectangular box on wheels, painted gray, with the words Anglican Mission Van, Diocese of Caledonia on both sides. I believe New Caledonia was the name given to the whole of this area in the early days of the fur trade."

I smiled as I thought of the exciting three months we had spent driving round lonely lakes, into remote Indian villages, and getting stuck on narrow logging trails.

George broke in on my thoughts. "I've been up here six years and you've already been to so many more places than I have. Where did you go?"

I did not answer immediately. I looked at my watch. It was getting late.

"It's too long a story for now," I said. "I've got work to do."

"Yes and I've got to get back to the ranch and throw some hay to the cattle. They'll be bawling by now," George said, getting up. He took my arm as I got up from the table.

"I'll be seeing you soon," he added, as we said good night. I went wonderingly up to bed. The night air had filtered through the ventilation hole while I was away. It was invigorating. In bed, I turned over the happenings of the day. George had asked me why I was in that part of British Columbia. Why was I? Why had I stayed on after the summer driving job had ended? I disliked cold weather. One of the wonderful things about Australia was the warm weather. Why hadn't I continued with my plans to return to England? Had I gotten into the habit of drifting? Or had I found a country I didn't want to leave and was fumbling around for some kind of role to play?

These and other questions occupied me as I lay restless. For the second time that night my thoughts went back to the lovely harbor in Sydney on that hot summer day towards the end of 1951—a day that had ended a four-year interlude in that country and nearly two decades of married life in England and Australia.

At the time I was leaving Australia for Vancouver, the millionth displaced person from Europe was entering that sparsely populated country. As that person entered, I was leaving on a 100-passenger cargo ship for Vancouver, the first leg of my journey back to England.

The day of sailing was sunny and warm and the dockside colorful, with everyone in light summery clothes. I couldn't share the general air of gaiety. I had a sad good-bye to say.

My husband had traveled a long way to Sydney from Queensland to see me off. As if in a dream we said a final good-bye. He put an exquisite cut-glass miniature decanter into my hand. It had a silver top which covered a small glass stopper; a tiny silver cup which could hold about a finger of liquor fitted onto the bottom of the bottle. What did the little present symbolize? I wondered at the time. Was it to drink to dreams which had once been rainbow-colored? Or to a love which had been strong, but not strong enough to overcome problems? To pain, so that it could be eased? To time that was spent, or days that were to come?

We had met as students at Birmingham University in England when he was a first-year medical student and I was about to become a teacher. We were married in 1933. A few years later we had lost our only child, a premature son, who should have lived, but died because of human negligence. While the nurse was out of the room the oxygen tube had slipped out of his mouth. My husband tried to comfort me: "He is in heaven," he had said, "and will be waiting for you. I have baptized him." Heaven sounded not only a long way off but also a long time away; I was not to be comforted.

Then the war came, with many years of separation. My husband was both medical officer and commandant of a Gurkha regiment in the Middle East.

For me, during the war, home in England was a small schoolhouse adjoining a little country school in Cherington, Warwickshire, on the edge of the Cotswolds and just off the Stratford-Oxford road. I was the headmistress.

During the war, country schoolmarms were general factotums and I was no exception. I was a local air-raid warden, secretary of the church council, commandante of the Girls' Training Corps, president of the Women's Institute, a member of the Women's Volunteer Service, secretary of the local war savings effort and in charge of the emergency food supply for three villages in case of invasion. These and other war activities sufficed to keep me out of serious mischief for the duration.

At war's end my husband returned to England after several years' absence in the Middle East desert. He slept next to me with a kukri (a curved Gurkha knife) under his pillow. It made my life tremendously exciting and exclusive, knowing there couldn't be many women in England who had such a weapon handy in case the odd goat wandered into the bedroom during the night. There were even two tiny knives stuck in the sheath to skin it with. In my imagination I could see shadowy figures creeping up silently in the desert night—white-robed figures who were so skillful that they could turn a man over in bed without waking him.

Those times were restless, and so were we. We bought a thirty-foot converted Dutch fishing boat named *Zeehond*. We lived on her for six months, sailing in the English Channel and off the coast of Devon and Cornwall. When we finally decided to emigrate to Australia, we sold the boat. We drove our 1923 Rolls Royce, the Duchess, E 8449, down to Land's End to say good-bye to jolly old England, and sold her to a doctor friend. But we did not say good-bye to our restlessness, and it would not go away.

In the little bedroom of the Vanderhoof Hotel, the memory of this restlessness was vividly disconcerting. I got out of bed in the now chilly room, poured a drink of water, and putting a blanket around me, sat in the only comfortable chair. I put my feet up on the bed and continued to backtrack.

We had arrived in Australia from England early in 1947 aboard the ship *Asturias,* which had been converted to a troopship and had been hastily converted back for passenger use after the war. We had been lucky to get a cabin together. Most of the other passengers had to bunk down in separate men's and women's dormitories. I was elected by the passengers to be the games and social organizer on board.

While I organized, my husband studied medical books. We had bought a general medical practice in Western Australia, sight unseen. It was in a sheep and wheat-growing area a couple of hundred miles south of Perth. Since my husband had held mainly administrative positions during the war, he needed to bring his medical knowledge up-to-date.

At the end of the five-week voyage, we anchored off the port of Fremantle and awaited all the official things that had to be taken care of on board before we landed. I shall never forget that thrilling moment with the fragrance of burning bush fires wafting off the land. Ever afterwards this fragrance seemed to me the very essence of Australia.

We traveled south by car with the previous owner of the practice to our new home. The full moon shone on us—its face resembling a big tree by a village church, very different from the man-in-the-moon I was accustomed to in England. My hopes were high and the new life seemed promising.

I recalled my matter-of-fact statements made to George a few hours earlier. What heartache for long years of loving those words had hidden.

I had waved a final good-bye to the familiar figure on Sydney's receding dockside. When I could no longer distinguish my husband from the other people on the dock I had turned away and had symbolically drawn a line under that chapter of my life. Decades of living still stretched before me, if I was lucky. I had loved Australia, but there would be other countries to love. A relentless restlessness stayed with me.

The voyage to Vancouver was exciting. *S.S. Lakemba*, was registered in the Fiji Islands. The crew were Fijians, well educated in the British mission schools on the island. The ship's purser—not a Fijian—had put my name at the top of the list of women on board singled out for his particular attention. On comparing notes, the other women on the list, and I, concluded he was a fast and systematic womanizer.

The ship's doctor, a middle-aged Australian who had never sailed on a ship before, was taking a busman's holiday—his first vacation for years. He spent it under the weather, lying flat on his back on his bunk, until we all went ashore in the sweltering Fiji Islands, when he managed to struggle to his feet to accompany us.

Suddenly, the hot weather turned cold; the sea became rough. The mound of chili peppers drying on the deck just outside my cabin window to spice the crew's meals with had all been consumed and I had a firm friendship with a cockroach in my cabin I had named Archy.

Three weeks after leaving sunny Sydney, we reached cloudy Vancouver in a severe wintry storm. Clad in a black sealskin fur coat, I staggered up on deck. Beneath a stormy gray sky, I yelled "Hello!" to Canada and a new life. The blustery wind must have whisked away my Vancouver greeting far inland and here I was, a year later, in a little bedroom in a small hotel in the snowy central interior of British Columbia, a land which continued to say to me, "You've arrived; prepare to stay."

I got back into bed, and as I drifted off to sleep, I wondered about George Hobson. What had happened to him in the years before he came to live in British Columbia? I hoped that I would see him again before I left the hotel on my next trip "along the line."

In these past months I also had known loneliness, but like my wilderness acquaintances, somehow I had learned to make fruitful the aloneness and the solitude. Of late, the space I had occupied alone in my metaphorical home had become increasingly cramped, and I knew it was time to open doors into new rooms.

I felt I was fast rediscovering my identity after the painful and turbulent events of the last few years; I was forty years old, with everything such an age implies of past and future. I was feeling the most precious thing one can know at any age—a soaring joy in a clear sense of the rightness for me of that time and place—just where I happened to be. It was a feeling I had felt before, because for me, home was wherever I had happened to be with stars and sky, animals and birds, trees and plants, sun, wind and rain. I folded up the map and prepared for bed, looking forward happily to a meeting with George the next day.

TWO

The Jeep

A business-like knock rat-tatted on my bedroom door early the next morning as I was about to go down for breakfast. I opened the door. Framed in the doorway stood George Hobson. In outward appearance, however, he was not the George of yesterday. Instead of jeans and a logging shirt, he wore a long, dark-gray herringbone-tweed overcoat with a wide, otter collar and handsome black brogue shoes. A smart gray homburg perched dead-straight on his curly, gray hair. He held a small, worn, brown leather briefcase.

"Good morning," he said, removing his hat.

"Hello. Do come in."

George entered the room in a businesslike way and placed the briefcase, with his hat on top of it, on the floor next to the nearest chair. With a flourish, he removed the long, otter-collared coat, folded it neatly and placed it on the floor by the briefcase.

"You're looking quite chipper this morning," I said. "Do you always sleep so well at night?"

George smiled. "Only if I've been made very happy on the previous day."

We both laughed. "I'm quite curious as to what you have hidden in that little old bag. Could you have robbed a bank?" I asked.

"Hardly," he replied smiling. "But I do have one thing in common with a robber. My briefcase is loaded with paper, but as of now, the paper is far less valuable than currency."

Before I could reply, he had opened his briefcase and placed a tattered bundle of paper tied with binder twine

on the bed. "I'm writing an old-style Western of about
56,000 words. Like to hear some of it? It's called *Back
Tracks.*" He glanced up quickly, seeking my approval as
he undid the binder twine. "It's about an old-time gun-
man called Bill Quest," he continued eagerly, talking fast.
"He's 6 feet 4 in his high-heeled boots."

George read in a fast monotone, seeming to fear that
I would interrupt him before he had read enough. "I
take it everywhere with me," he said, stopping abruptly
and waving towards the manuscript. He grinned and
went on, "I creep into people's houses when they're not
looking, and before they know it, I've whipped out my
story and am halfway through it before they are able to
tell me that they are urgently needed elsewhere and have
to leave."

I took advantage of the digression from the reading
to glance at some of the manuscript. "Is this your
spelling?"

"Yes. I'm not a very good speller. I played hookey
a lot from school and spent my time in the woods or
went swimming. My father spent a fortune on my education, but I was kicked out of every school in California, both private and public," he said with some pride,
as he rolled a cigarette.

"Well, it's customary to have one *t* in writing and
hoping is usually spelled with one *p*. Anyway, how
about some breakfast before Quest's guns stop blazing?
I'm hungry," I said firmly.

We went downstairs to the small dining room, sat at
an isolated table, and ordered breakfast. Coarse woolen
winter underwear protruded incongruously several inches
below the cuffs of the elegant, immaculately clean
dickey-bosomed white shirt George was wearing. He
must have thought that my fixed gaze was on his
cufflinks, for he said, looking down at them, "They were
my father's. They're sapphires. Three stones are real
and one is an imitation replaced by a crooked jeweler."

Throughout breakfast George talked non-stop. He
was content for me to listen and not to respond except

at the intervals he chose to let me get in something like, "Yes," "No," "You don't mean it," and "Well, I never." He gave talking his undivided attention. He worked at it hard, looking intently off into the distance at his own private view of the subjects of his monologue.

Suddenly, he stopped talking, as if his distant view had changed abruptly, and looked straight at me. "I've got to go to the ranch now and throw the cattle some hay. They'll really be bawling since I stayed in town to see you today," he said, breakfast finished. "Come with me and see my spread. We can talk all the way there, too."

"I can't manage it today," I replied. "I have some work to do. I shall be in Vanderhoof again in two weeks' time to do an assignment at the Kenney Dam site. I'd like very much to see the ranch then."

"Then come back with me to Frontier House while I pack my grub up for the ranch and I'll drop you off at the hotel when I leave."

I agreed, and we returned to my room and packed up the manuscript. George put on his story-book coat and hat and we left for Frontier House.

We walked side by side down the middle of the snow-scraped main street. By now I felt that I also had a storybook role.

"Hi, George! Where are you going? What're you all dressed up for?" men shouted at us as we walked.

As we entered the house, George's mother was talking on the phone. "Well, I guess he's airing his New York clothes, Ronnie," she was saying and then hung up. "That was Ronnie Campbell, George. He saw you in the road a few minutes ago. He wanted to know where you were going all dressed up."

"Well, after I've changed," he rejoined, "I'm going back to the ranch, Mother. I'll probably not wear these clothes again for another six years. You can put them in mothballs. I'll put the grub on board, throw on the washing, and get moving. The cattle'll think I've forgotten them."

He picked up a large cardboard box containing his groceries, carried it outside and placed it onto the flat back of his jeep next to a big box of raw beef bones which I presumed were for his dogs. He then hurled on a canvas bag of clean laundry, which landed next to a large black drum of gasoline with a pump in it. Goodbyes said and a hug given to "sweet little Mommy," we advanced together towards the odd-looking vehicle.

"Six years ago she was new, shiny and red," George said, pointing to the jeep. "My son Teeney, then six years old, was with me when I picked it up in Edmonton the first time he came to stay at the ranch; he lives with his mother in New York. Now look at her after six years in this goddam swamp." He pointed to the jeep's top-heavy superstructure made of aluminum sheet over plywood. "That part's new of course." He yanked at the passenger door which stuck at the bottom right end. A couple of screws were missing in the top hinge, and the whole door sagged dejectedly. Finally, after more yanks, it flew open.

"Bit rough for you I'm afraid," George said as he held the door back with aplomb as if I were about to enter a Cadillac.

Peering inside I couldn't see anywhere to sit. There was no seat on my side, just a dirty, fat, hay-filled gunny sack with bits of hay sticking out all over it. The vehicle floor was covered with soil, straw and hay, and strewn with cigarette butts. Near the door a few blades of grass had sprouted and turned brown. Considering the welfare of my black suit, the only one I had with me, I stepped in apprehensively, sat down on the sack and gazed around me.

The superstructure looked as if it had been slapped on to the top of the windshield with no intention of making it fit. Behind me and level with my head was a small sliding wooden panel reminiscent of the speakeasy era; the panel was stuck in a half-open position, however, as the groove was filled with wedged-in bits of hay and straw.

The Jeep

I settled uncomfortably onto the gunny sack and thought nostalgically of the series of cars I had known intimately in England. All, like the jeep, were vehicles of some character, but each had an Achilles' heel. First, there was the natty blue Triumph sports car belonging to my fiancé. The gear lever had come off in his hand as he made a racing change entering Henley-in-Arden. He had waved the lever aloft as we coasted with abandon into a handy garage. When we were married we had a baby Austin Seven. Its hood blew off in a gale. We

retrieved it hastily from an adjacent field where it had
landed, folded it up like a gigantic fan, stuck it in the
back of the car, and continued the rest of the trip in
driving rain huddled under an army ground sheet tied to
the sides with binder twine.

Next came the Alvis saloon with polished walnut
dashboard rigged up inside like a stuffy Victorian boudoir
with its fabric-scented air. She swigged oil like a drunk-
ard from his bottle. When we went far afield, as
students do, all our spare cash was spent in maintaining
her excesses. In the pubs where we stayed we were
forced to live on bread and cheese and pickles.

The most palatial of all was the gray Rolls Royce
tourer of 1923 vintage which we bought from a friend.
She had front wheel brakes, a nickel radiator, and a
dashboard like an airplane. We called her the Duchess;
our friends called her the Hearse. But she took too
much gas to run and during the war she had to be put
up on bricks in a barn. I thought of the last car I had
driven along the dusty Australian roads—a red MG. She
had no faults, no grass growing on the floorboards and
seats of red leather . . .

A sound similar to an airplane taking off aroused me
from this reverie. The jeep leaped forward as if it had
been booted from behind by some heavy earth-moving
equipment; my head snapped back like the end of a
cracked bullwhip or a snake being shaken by a mongoose
and we lurched forward to an abrupt standstill. Where-
upon the whole performance was repeated again, with
more mechanical success. We took off, hitting a long
necklace of potholes. Instead of bounding upwards to the
roof as one would expect, the end of my spine ground
down like an auger into the hay of the gunny sack.

"Going along the level is the most dangerous,"
observed George dramatically. "You see, there are no
brakes. It's all right going downhill because you can use
the second gear and, of course, uphill there's nothing to
it at all."

I understood too well the whole situation when a red logging truck, laden with boards from a local planer mill, turned out from a side road and into our path. George stamped down on the completely useless brakes as we rolled on towards the towering truck. Grinning broadly, the driver accelerated out of our path with a backward glance and a "Hi, George!"

"You see what I mean," said George with a gesture just as if the jeep was alive and it was all her fault.

I sagged back, living from moment to dangerous moment until we arrived at the hotel. As we talked during the journey George asked me to promise to visit the ranch when I returned to Vanderhoof in about two weeks' time.

He got out of the jeep and dragged at the door on my side, and I tumbled out unceremoniously.

"You know, I really do need help with my book." He smiled as I turned to go, an eager, expectant smile.

I smiled also, thinking that wasn't the only help he needed.

THREE

Prospectors, Trappers & Loggers

In two weeks I returned to Vanderhoof to visit the Kenney Dam as planned. George was to be in town at that time to take me to the ranch before the visit to the dam. I looked forward eagerly to seeing him again.

In the quiet of the same hotel room I checked the notes of the last two weeks and recalled the places in the Central Interior that I had visited. I paused in flipping through my notes to open a map I had picked up along the line, *Sportsman's Guide and Corrected Road Map of Central B.C.* issued by the *Cariboo and the Northwest Digest*. It helped me establish the continuity of my experiences. I spread it out on the bed. A frame of photographs of mountains, lakes, roads, fish, fowl and game of the Central Interior surrounded the map. A composite photograph of a man-size mosquito attacking a man, with the caption "They're not THIS big," overlay it. "Are they not?" I said to myself, remembering the constant irritation of mosquitoes and black flies in the summer.

The map showed clearly that in many parts of the Central Interior, road, river and Canadian National Railway traveled together as though keeping company for safety. Only a few shacks at the turn of the century, Prince Rupert had become an important fishing port on the outside passage to Alaska. In Terrace it was mild enough for apples to grow. I had seen freight trains near there loaded with enormous trees which had been felled close by and were being carried to the pulp mills on the coast. Now Prince Rupert was a town of six thousand.

How well I recalled Burns Lake, the gateway to Tweedsmuir Park and railhead for Francois Lake. I had stayed there longer than I planned, fascinated with the hard reality of life and its bright confusion. Outside my bedroom window in the early dawn, hunters from Ketchikan discussed what to do with their quartered moose. Strangers in coats down to their ankles mopped up the melted snow on the floors of restaurants. Men in bright logging shirts, comfortable on their homeground, chatted in groups. And city slickers and salesmen of one kind or another all had business in Burns Lake.

While swapping yarns on the main street with Barney Mulvaney, magistrate for the district, I developed a rash on my legs which I later discovered to be frostbite. I drank Bloody Marys with a red-haired bush pilot whose job it was to drop poison on the frozen lakes to kill wolves. I picked glass splinters out of the eye of a traveler at my hotel—who had an accident because his tires were too slick for the icy roads; I occupied a room in the hotel between a wedding party on the left and a funeral gathering on the right. From the left, oddly enough, came the sound of uninterrupted weeping. From the right came incessant laughter—a celebration of death as a part of life.

I saw one of the smallest public parks in Canada in the waters of Burns Lake. Twenty years before, a young Ranger Band of boys and girls took possession of this one-acre island, beautified it and built a cabin-clubhouse there. It was dedicated by Lord Tweedsmuir in 1935 at the same time as Tweedsmuir Park, where the grizzlies range. The motto on the wall of the clubhouse reads, "Let no one say, and say it to your shame, that all was beauty here until you came."

I took away from Burns Lake an impression of life joyously celebrated every day. People there seemed to need to define themselves to themselves, to others around them and to things external to themselves in so many different ways.

One of these ways is the naming of new communities. For example, two places on the north shore of Francois Lake: Clemretta was named after a farmer's favorite cows, Clementine and Henrietta, and Noralee was a community christened by a man named Lee, in honor of his wife Nora.

And near Topley there is a mountain called China Nose. The story goes that a Chinese man, quizzed about abandoned placer workings in the hills had cryptically replied, "China knows." Glenannan, that part of the Stellako River where the fly fishing is incomparable, between the west end of Fraser Lake and Francois Lake, is named after Sandy Annan. Lovely in the moonlight it must have reminded him of the calm lakes cradled in the arms of the hills of his native Scotland.

The vignettes were clear and sparkling, so different from each other yet linked by common elements both abstract and real such as aloneness and their very real relationship with the environment, a struggling one sometimes—harmonious at other times.

Over the door of the little Anglican church of Endako, near Burns Lake, I saw a tablet inscribed "St. John's Lisnagarvey Memorial Church," dedicated June 18th, 1922. Nearby, I read "The congregation of the Cathedral and of Christ Church in Lisburn, Ireland, subscribed funds to build somewhere in Canada a worthy memorial to the men who gave their lives in the Great War. Endako was chosen. All the furnishings for the church were sent from Ireland, including a set of engraved communion vessels, a hand-embroidered linen frontal from the cathedral communion table and a brass christening bowl." A bell had been given also, but after it developed a crack, it had been removed from the belfry and placed at the side of the door. How eloquently this group of Irish people, distant and different, had demonstrated from afar, the underlying unity among men.

Government land was cheap to the early homesteaders, $2.00 to $4.00 an acre. A man could raise a family, if he could find a woman willing to lie down with him at

night in a tiny log cabin he had built on the land with
his own hands—a woman who thrilled to the howl of the
timber wolf or to the yip-yipping of a coyote on a distant ridge, and whose blood did not run cold when the
boom of pine trees expanding in sub-zero temperatures
rent the dark cloak of silent wintry nights.

Dutch farmers had homesteaded at Houston in the
rich Bulkley Valley, then a little village of 500 to 600
people. They now grew gigantic Danish Ballhead cabbages weighing fifteen pounds or more and sold them to
the families of workers in the many sawmills in the area
where burning sawdust piles turned night into glowing
day. I saw the cabbages packed away in enormous root
cellars built fourteen feet above ground and four below,
120 feet long and with cement floors. Pine slabs with
wood shavings packed between, made walls two feet thick
which kept the cellars frost-proof in the coldest sub-zero
weather. In their neat homes the Hollanders had shown
me their cherished wooden shoes, or "klompen," brought
from the old country. Undoubtedly, they must have
known their dreams would come true in this fertile valley
in their new country.

But whether they were early homesteaders or late-
comers, each man was individual and different. Some
seemed set apart from the times they were living in and
others clearly were part of the present world. But each
was a unique universe often obeying laws of his own
making, and all seemed to be a continuity of man's
eternal yearnings and dreams.

The lifeblood of the area was the sawmill, the dream
of the Swedes, Norwegians and Danes so skilled with
their relentless axes that the noble trees in the sleeping
forests must have trembled at their approach. New
roads were being made into tracts of timber for new
sawmills. Cabins on trailers were being moved in for the
winter operations which would maintain the heartbeat of
Prince George. Now, within a radius of forty miles,
smoke rose from 500 sawmills; rough lumber was stockpiled on River Road.

Sometimes the lumber "cut" was a summer one. I had seen signs of that earlier in the year when driving the van at Pendleton Bay on lovely Babine Lake. Enormous logging trucks had heated up the Burns Lake-Pendleton Bay road which staggered through Babine Provincial Forest. They left smoke screens in their wake. Babine Lake is 110 miles long, the longest natural lake in British Columbia and a fisherman's paradise. The water reflects the deep blue of the sky. Great jewelled pools of molten gold, the reflections of the yellowing poplars, lay cupped in its depth.

Travelers in cars, men looking for work, Indians looking for their pay, all gave the lake shore an air of extreme busyness. On the lake, tug boats were kept handy, should the bay water suddenly become rough, as lake water often does, and the booms holding the logs break sending hundreds of thousands of feet of logs "dusting about."

The great trees of the wilderness were not the only wealth men dreamed about. They also sought its mineral wealth. When Prince Rupert had only a few shacks and news travelled by "moccasin telegraph," prospectors were walking into the Central Interior with that optimism which is their birthright. Abandoned placer workings and trails that they had once worn, had since become inaccessible. Dreams were shattered in the then unconquerable wilderness and many men bequeathed their names to mark some lonely secret spot.

Tragedy and mystery seemed often to go hand in hand in the rhythm of their daily living, and when it is time to leave a place, a man draws a line under that chapter with an air of finality and starts another page of life's book. I had tracked down such a man, a prospector, who was leaving his one-room shack in Topley. He did not tell me why he was leaving. As we chatted, he took down the *British Columbia's Miners'* map from the wall and spread it on the bed.

"*Pinchi* means lake-creek," he said to me. "There are a lot of Indian names here. It's pronounced 'Binchay' by the Indians. The *Ta* in *Tachi* means 'three,'" he said, pointing to that place on the map.

He folded the map and placed it at the bottom of a small suitcase, which he proceeded to pack. He wrapped up what looked like a piece of dried meat in a piece of paper.

"That is the back muscle of a moose—sinew for sewing. I'm going to repair my moose-hide gun case with it," he said, matter-of-factly.

One suitcase for all these years, I had pondered as I had watched him packing. Then he took down a wreath of dried stag's horn moss from the wall.

"What is that for?" I asked.

"I'm going to put it on the grave of my Indian wife," he said simply, adding, "my children have been claimed by their Indian kinfolk."

His packing finished, we went outside. I watched him intently as he closed the door of the little shack. It was a silent good-bye as he headed south to the border. He intended never to come back, he said. We parted and each went his way.

Trapping still lured some men, although pelts did not fetch what they once did. Seven miles west of Houston in the Barrett district overlooking the rich Bulkley Valley and the Telkwa Range, I had climbed up to a ledge and the cabin of Bob Eichenberger, trapper, away from his native Switzerland for so long "a man forgets," as he put it. I stood facing his cabin, staring at a large, raw, reddish-purple carcass hanging from a tree on the right of the cabin. Silhouetted against a cloudless blue sky, it swung gently back and forth in the wind.

"What on earth is that?" I asked the genial trapper who was standing in the doorway. He had a goatee beard, and his eyes twinkled behind thick glasses. He smiled at my alarm.

"That's a timber wolf, a pup, born last spring. You can tell by its teeth," he explained, pointing to its bared fangs. "It's small in body, only about seventy-five pounds. It just hasn't filled out yet, although it's fully grown. The parents would probably be 125 pounds. I've shot two or three every year for four winters now."

We walked through the front porch into a dim two-room cabin. The skin of the wolf carcass hanging outside was nailed to the cabin wall. It stretched from the low ceiling to the floor.

"I'm waiting for the game warden to come and punch one ear and pay the bounty of $25.00," he explained. "The U. S. Army up north is buying wolf skins for parkas. I still trap for mink by the river, deep in the timber for marten, and for weasel, well, just about any place."

Bob Eichenberger was a man whose particular dream seemed to have come true. He could even grow corn on his ledge away from the frosts of the flat, and twenty years before he had spotted large-leaved wild strawberry plants on his land. He had cultivated them until he had two acres. People came long distances to pick the strawberries, and they called him "The Strawberry King."

But other trappers had broken dreams. They did not return at all from secret places in their private wildernesses with the pelts of a season's efforts. Occasional mention in the local newspaper that old Tom or Harry had not been seen recently was their only memorial.

About thirteen miles east of Terrace, not far from Usk, huddled beneath a mountain on the opposite side of the Skeena River, Gold Creek is a short distance from the road on a twenty-foot bank overlooking a tiny bay at the foot of a canyon. Here Joe Trulson from Norway had a log cabin and a private wilderness of his own. No sun penetrated his canyon home in the winter, but in the summer, deer could be seen silhouetted against the sun at the top of the canyon, a hundred feet above the frothing waters; and in the fall the tired cohoe salmon turned on their sides to spawn in the little bay.

He told me that he had worked on the railroad as a young man and after World War I had roamed the hills and creeks prospecting. When 133 acres of land along the creek was reserved for a park by the Provincial

Government, he had, over the last seven years, with pick, shovel and wheelbarrow, singlehandedly improved a pack trail to the head of the canyon, built a beach for the children, and cleared for a camping ground. This had been his dream. He seemed to need nothing other than simple things. He was a happy man.

I had long, intense thoughts about these men with whom I had had exchanges which revealed so much of how they thought and felt. I was fascinated with their lives, with their personal and often solitary daily affairs, their unending struggles, and their experiences in which they were forced to accept everything, including pain. Sometimes they were able to change these experiences into something rich, strange, and indefinable. Through these men I recognized the romantic in myself, and their view of life seemed to me eminently sensible. Nature nourished them; being in touch with nature, they were in touch with themselves.

I had occasionally met women also who lived alone. These frontier women talked most often of their men. I had met one of them in Francois Lake where the water was reputed to be so pure that car batteries could be filled with it. I was watching the first cut being put in the old iron ferry boat which had plied back and forth across the lake for twenty-five years until each winter, when the ice got too thick. The sparks flew as the cutting proceeded. She was to be cut up into six sections of about sixty tons each. These would be loaded onto low-bed trailers for Burns Lake and then onto flat cars to go by rail to Chase in Southern British Columbia. There she was to be welded together again to be used as a ferryboat on Shuswap Lake.

I visited Mrs. Jacob Henkel in her home nearby. "I hear that the new ferryboat is to be named after your husband," I said.

"So it is. My husband came into Ootsa from Bella Coola in 1904, the first white man to winter over. He built the first cabin in the area."

The kitchen in which we sat was the original cabin. The following year he had heard about the railway coming in, and he had cut the trail from Cheslatta to Francois Lake. He died in 1945.

"Look at the barn as you leave," she said, as I rose to go. "He built it in 1914, and the cache for flour and sugar still stands there on posts to keep the vermin out."

I saw the barn and the cache and noticed the old cedar shakes on the roof of the cabin still as good as they were when he had first split them. They had that beauty Willa Cather described as: " . . . the irregular and intimate quality of things made entirely by hand." How long I had wondered, would the *Jacob Henkel* cross Francois Lake in wind and storm before she would be replaced by another ferryboat.

The glimpses I had caught of the actual lives of these men and women, the realization of the fragility of their dreams, the understanding of the physical environment as partner or opponent inspired me to take a closer look at myself.

I had always felt a part of the natural environment and had known that nature was my greatest source of nourishment. When I was in direct touch with nature I seemed to be more in touch with myself. My relationship with these men and women confirmed what I already knew about myself and invested the natural environment with even greater meaning.

FOUR

Little Creek Ranch

George picked me up at the hotel as we had arranged, two weeks to the day. He wore blue jeans and a red logging shirt; his curly gray hair was still uncut, and he looked very handsome. I felt happy and excited to see him again.

We chugged out of town, crossed the bridge over the lovely Nechako River and turned left up a rise.

"That's our hospital! It's a fine one, run by Catholic sisters, and Mooney's a good doctor." George pointed out the building on the right. "Just after I came here I sliced part of the top of my thumb off with an axe and he fixed me up," he said, sticking his thumb up for my inspection. "He'd heard of Rich's vast number of cattle and didn't know then that there was another Hobson. 'I hear you have quite an extensive cattle ranch, Mr. Hobson,' he said, as he was fixing me up. I looked off into the distance, crossed my legs in my high cowboy boots, looked up at my cowboy hat hanging on his office wall and said, 'Well, at the last round-up, the boys and I tallied eleven head.'"

"Oh no!" I exclaimed, "Is that all you had?" thinking to myself that this must be the smallest ranch ever.

"Yes. You see, the first year I had the ranch, I went into clover seed. It fetched twenty-seven cents a pound then. The next year it dropped to four and five cents. So I started in the cattle business with three head. Now I have nearly a 100. That's a bird sanctuary on the left there by the river. It's a taking-off and grounding place for Canadian geese. No one's allowed to shoot them and they rest by the thousands in the fall on their way from the frozen north. When we see the first of them passing over again in March, we know that spring is on its way to release us from the ice and snow."

The dark-brown earth showed through where the snow plow had scraped the tops of the bumps in the road. The first snow of the winter had been piled to the sides of the narrow dirt road. Small, frame houses fronted on to the road, looking as if they had been casually dumped there and the rest of the household belongings thrown at them as an afterthought. An occasional house that stood farther back from the road was painted and had a cared-for look. For stretches at a time, spruce and jack pine bordered the road. "Small stuff" George called these trees.

"That's the way to Fort St. James on beautiful Stuart Lake," remarked George, pointing to a road turning off on the right. "Lots of Indians there. It is the oldest continually-inhabited white settlement in the province and a fine trading post years before the white settlers started coming in."

We had covered most of the nineteen miles to Little Creek Ranch by this time. It seemed to be getting colder—or maybe the perpetual draft was eating into the back of my neck from the partially open speakeasy window at the back of the jeep.

The late morning had become still and mysterious. Nothing moved. The trees seemed to close up even closer together conveying a secretive air that I had detected ever since I had been in British Columbia, and which seemed, at times, to be its very essence.

George broke the silence, and smiled. "Soon we'll see my dogs, the Big Bull Moose and The Ghost, coming to greet us along the home stretch. Ever since I left the ranch they've been dreaming of the bones I'll bring them."

We met the dogs sooner than he had thought. They bounded delightedly along the road to meet us. Moose was a large, handsome, tawny-red dog with a beautiful bushy tail, half St. Bernard and half German shepherd. The Ghost was a pure white German shepherd. They had evidently been ranging farther away than customary, as George had been gone longer than usual.

"They've been in the Prout," George explained. "That's a meadow which belongs to me two miles this side of the ranch. I put up the hay there. Lots of it is slew hay, and there's not much food value in it. I bale it and stack the bales in the meadow. I leave the cattle down there until it's all eaten; then sometime in January I bring them back to the Home Meadow. I had the first baler in the country," he said proudly, "wire tie, Minneapolis-Moline." To George, "country" meant his particular area.

"My tractor's the biggest, too," he added, "Massey-Harris." I had soon realized that big was a symbolic word to George. He seemed to draw emotional sustenance from the physical bigness of anything or any man.

The dogs bounded up to the jeep, tails wagging, delight expressed in every muscle. They kept a little ahead of the jeep, turning every so often to look backwards and then bound on again. We were now in second gear, that acted as a brake going downhill to the ranch.

"That's the back way to the house," he said, pointing to an opening on the left. "I can use it in the summer. Now the snow's too deep." We were coming to a little bridge at the bottom of the incline that was the road's end.

"That's the Little Creek," explained George, "comes right from the mountains, pure spring water which runs all through my ranch. I wouldn't buy a place without a creek."

"What's up there?" I asked, pointing ahead up a small incline where I saw a parting between the trees and an unplowed road.

"That's a section line. There's nothing up there, only jack pine and spruce, bears and moose, and one or two old cabins where an early pioneer fought a losing battle against the wilderness and maybe a baby's grave near one cabin. In the spring, little patches of rhubarb and a few currant bushes show that at one time a family lived there; a little of the bush has been cleared and there's a natural hay meadow."

We turned left at the bottom of the incline and drove through a wide gate with a big overhead bar above it and stopped a few hundred yards farther on at a small low log cabin on the right.

"This is where I used to live when I first came here six years ago. It's as old as I am. Hughie Goldie built it in the year I was born, 1910. He battled it out with his axe for forty years, grubbing a little land from the wilderness here and there." I could understand what that battle meant. I had talked with many men who had done this. I had learned from them that an axe was three feet long and that a man might clear two acres a year if the trees were not more than six inches through.

"He still lives in Vanderhoof," George continued, "crippled up with arthritis. He's a university graduate. Heidelberg—no, Edinburgh—that's in Scotland, isn't it? Can't go any farther in the jeep. Have to go on foot. When I built my new house I wanted it right away from the buildings and so I built it over there on a knoll."

He took an enormous bone that looked like that of a prehistoric monster, from the cardboard box at the back of the jeep, and pointed with it to the attractive log cabin in a clump of poplar trees. He threw the bone wide and scattered the contents of the box after it around the jeep. Fish heads, slices of salami, a hot dog or two, a moldy orange, and a smorgasbord of assorted garbage skidded along the ice-covered snow. The dogs inspected the manna from the jeep. Moose systematically cornered the most select mouthfuls and carried them to a place on the side. The Ghost, with a growl, had to be content with the leavings.

"Just bring yourself. I'll take the grub first and come back for the rest. That's the tool shed and garage," George said, pointing to a building ahead of the old cabin and on the same side.

We started walking along the little path that led to the cabin. "Over there is the hayshed I built. Biggest in the country," he said, pointing to the right. "There's the old barn over there, that log building by the corrals and the cattle chute. The cattle there are heifers which are going to calve next spring and the young stuff not bred yet. I keep them around during the winter."

A small group of Hereford cattle bunched near the barn. "Her-fords" George called them.

"The older ones are at the Prout Meadow," he added. "Careful how you go. Don't slip. I'll go first." I stood still to let him pass on the narrow icy trail that wound along the meadow towards the ranch house.

Dog trails crossed and re-crossed the meadow where Moose and The Ghost had gambolled together. George paused in the middle of the little bridge that crossed the creek to wait for me to catch up, steadying the cardboard box of groceries on his shoulder.

"That's where the Little Creek comes from," he said, pointing upstream to the south with his free hand, "and that's where it goes to the Nechako River." He swung around and pointed downstream.

With our backs to the little ranch house we looked past the corrals down a tiny valley. It opened out into a large meadow bordered with spruce trees away in the distance as far as the eye could see.

"That's where I grew my clover for seed. Makes wonderful hay now, mostly alsike clover. My horses rustle there all winter. They paw through the snow to get the dry grass."

George looked down at the creek which was about nine feet wide at that place, and remarked thoughtfully, "Soon the little creek will be covered over with ice and snow until spring break-up, but it'll be there flowing underneath, until in April and May it becomes swollen to overflowing with the melting snows from the mountains and then we'll see it again."

We walked fifty yards or so, until we came to a little picket fence of slender spruce poles an inch in diameter strung together with twisted wire. A small gate in the fence with a little archway over it had a horseshoe nailed on it. With a graceful movement, George stooped to make room for the box to pass underneath the archway.

The little log house stood in a grove of poplars at the top of the knoll overlooking the meadow and little creek we had crossed.

"Here we are," George said, smiling and putting the box down outside the front door. "Now look around you," he commanded, making a circular motion with his arms. "It's all mine, a whole square mile* of it, and I haven't a bean, except canned, and those aren't paid for. 'Don't put your money into gilt-edged securities; sink it in a cattle ranch, get your own spread,' my friends said to me after the war. Well, I did and it's sunk all right."

George hesitated a moment under the deer antlers over the front door, "Now don't forget that I have been a bachelor for ten years, six of them here at The Little Creek," he warned. "You won't find it very tidy." He opened the unlocked door, then stepped aside for me to go in. I wondered what I should find.

A large room about twenty by twelve feet ran the length of the house. On the left, in the end wall, a huge rock fireplace extended nearly the length of the wall and above it was an enormous moose head. The fireplace was filled with waste paper and eggshells.

"This is Bumpy," said George, introducing me to the moose head which just touched my hair when I stood under it. "He's kissed many heads, and some rather roughly," he added. "He didn't get the name Bumpy for nothing."

---

* Note: A square mile is called a section of land. Each township has thirty-six sections, and each section, four quarters. Each township has its sections numbered off from the bottom right to the left—one, two, three, four, five, six. Then above six is seven and so on to thirty-six.

"Bumpy"

At the other end of the living room a large bookshelf filled with books covered the whole wall except for a narrow window. On the wall to the left of the front door was a large picture window overlooking the meadow, and on the other side of the door, a small window.

Opposite the front door a large wood heater, made out of an oil barrel mounted on short, iron legs, stuck out almost halfway into the middle of the room. Doors on each side of the heater had animal heads mounted over them.

A roughly-made plank table, highly shellacked, with legs made from spruce trunks with the bark still on, took up a large part of the length of the outside wall. Numerous ashtrays placed here and there were overflowing with cigarette butts and out-sized matchsticks.

"We'll soon get a fire going, have some coffee, feed the cattle, and then toss on a can of beans for lunch," said George. "This is the kitchen." I followed him through the door to the left of the heater into a small room half the size of the living room and took in at a glance a make-shift sink with dirty dishes in a rough counter. The log wall was not boarded in. Cobwebs hung down from the beams in the ceiling. Open shelves were dotted with cans and bottles, and an old kitchen table was covered with empty milk and bean cans.

He opened the back door for me to see out. An enormous pile of additional milk and bean cans poked out from a snowy heap on the right of the kitchen door. We walked past them into the woodshed.

"This is where I stack slabs for starting the fires in the barrel heater and for heating the cook stove," George explained. Pieces of the outside "cut" of spruce and jack pine were neatly stacked to the roof of the woodshed. Everywhere I had been in Central British Columbia where a little sawmill had once been set up, I had seen these discarded outside cuts, like giant jack straws, lying crazily where they had been left. A little world had been there for a short time, then the little world had ended, and machinery, cabins, and men had moved on to another site, and so on throughout the year.

"That building over there is the warehouse where I keep my meat," George said, pointing to a building close by. "I often kill a moose for the winter. We'll look in it later." As he was talking, he stooped low on the woodshed floor and built up a pile of slabs on his left arm with the grace with which he did anything physical.

Back in the living room he stooped down, opened the door of the barrel heater, and placed the cut slabs in it.

"They're a bit green yet, so we'll put some kerosene on." He went into the kitchen, emptied a little kerosene from a can into an old cup and poured it on the slabs in the stove. Then half closing the heater door, he struck a large match with his thumb nail, threw it in, stepped back, and seeing that it had lighted, closed the heater door.

"Now for some logs and we'll soon be warm." He went through the still-open front door to a pile of logs. They were covered with snow and stuck together with ice, but with a kick or two here and there, a few were dislodged. He piled these up on his arm with the ease of long practice and dumped them onto the rock hearth in front of the fireplace.

"Now we'll put the coffee pot on, have a quick cup and then throw some hay to the cattle." A flat piece of metal was attached to the top of the barrel heater. George placed an old coffee pot filled with water from the bucket onto it. "Nearly out of water," he remarked. "While the coffee's brewing, I'll get a bucketful from the creek."

Through the window I watched him take the path to the bridge. Suddenly it had become silent and lonely in the room now that he had gone. I wandered into the neglected kitchen and gazed around. A stairway of rough lumber, with steps so far apart that they would be an uncomfortable stride even for a giant, led presumably to a small attic.

A door at the foot of these steps led into a very small bedroom. A double bed piled high with home-made comforters was turned back on the near side. The once-white sheets were a pale gray with use and there was a big depression on that side. George must creep in here each night and burrow down like a hibernating animal, and Moose and The Ghost probably sleep here too, I thought. I had met many bachelors in my recent travels, many of them Swedish, who could look after themselves so well that they would never need a wife. They were so neat and tidy in their habits that a woman would hesitate to take over. If a woman were to take over here she would hardly know where to begin.

"Hi Eve, where are you?" I heard the door bang. George didn't close doors. He banged them shut with unconscious aplomb. I entered the living room from the bedroom. A black cat had followed him in. The two of us were silent at the same time. For George, this was unusual; I had been silent throughout the whole tour. I was thinking of the remarkable enthusiasm of this man and of the sincere way he was trying to live all alone the life he had chosen.

"This is Jiggs," George said, lying down and stroking the black cat. "An old lady gave him to me when she went to the hospital. She never came back," he added.

He had set the pail down near the stove. I looked into it attracted by the tinkle of the chunks of ice that knocked against the side. Wee pieces of green weed rose to the top and sank leisurely down to the bottom of the bucket. There was something fascinating about this water that had tumbled down from the wild, lonely mountains; only moose and deer and the wild animals of the forest had drunk from it. It was ice-cold and uncontaminated. This pail of water had a special meaning for me then; it was so simple and so fundamental, almost a sacrament. It affected me deeply.

We were quiet over our coffee, our toes pointed to the cozy heater that had grown so hot with the addition of the logs from the hearth that the damper had to be closed.

"Let's burn that rubbish in the fireplace," I said, looking over towards the pile of eggshells and paper. Pools of water from the ice and frozen snow had melted off the logs and had settled into the irregularities of the rock hearth. Jiggs was lapping up the water thirstily. George put a match to the rubbish and the purifying flames spread, consuming the paper, eggshells, and as many of the cigarette butts and used matches I could recover from the ashtrays.

"I hauled every rock there," George said with the fine pride of man in his achievements. "Tommy Smithers built the fireplace and chimney. It's perfect, never smokes. He ruined a complete set of tools trying to shape up the rock, it's so hard."

The bawling of the hungry cattle pressed in on us as we talked over coffee. We rose, checked the fires, and put Jiggs out. Single-file we walked across the narrow icy path of the meadow to the barnyard. Moose and The Ghost had eaten the choicest pieces of their feast and had settled down comfortably on the blood-stained snow, gnawing at their bones. A chickadee flew up from one as we approached, settling a few feet away until we had passed by.

George unfastened the gate into the barnyard. It was secured with thick pliable wire.

"Useful stuff, this baling wire," he remarked, as if to hide the shortness of his temper because of the time it took him to undo it. "It keeps the ranch from falling apart." I thought how much easier it would have been to have a proper latch on the gate, especially as when we had gone through it, he had to start twisting and turning the wire all over again.

We crossed the barnyard, leaving the old log barn on the left, and entered the 100-foot-long hay and machine shed where the large rectangular bales were stacked right to the top of the shed except where bales, already fed out, had been used. Small poles, stripped of their bark to keep insects from attacking them, had been laid down to keep the bottom bales off the earth.

George hopped over the barbed wire fence, went around the shed, and took down a large metal hook hanging on the fence—the kind Captain Hook of Peter Pan possessed—and dragged a bale free from the rest. He pulled one wire loose from the bale and then the second one, throwing the wire aside. The dusty sweet-smelling hay fell apart into pieces like large sandwiches. George picked them up and flung them over the fence scattering the pieces widely apart.

"I distribute them wide," he said, "so that the cattle don't horn each other. One, two, three . . .," he counted, "one third of a bale for each cow. These bales weigh about 100 pounds each. I must keep track of them carefully so that I have enough hay to last the winter. Can't afford to buy any." He crumpled together the loose wire from the bales and tossed it in a little pile with a lot of other wire. Then he swung back over the fence.

Already one or two of the cattle were wandering towards the creek after getting a bellyful of feed. Their well-defined path to water showed up in the snow. For a few minutes we watched the cattle feeding contentedly. There was no bawling now.

"I was a big shot around here once," George volunteered. "I employed and fired men. I planted trees along the drive and the horses ate them all except one, and that's still got two leaves on. I bought paint by the can, by the pail, and finally by the barrel. Then Rich told everybody I was buying it by the carload. I painted all the buildings we put up, but it was rough lumber and the paint all sank in; it went the way of everything else. Then the Canadian Bank of Commerce got after me, and now there's only me, the cattle, Moose, and The Ghost, and of course, Bossy, Paint, and Jack."

"Who's Bossy?" I asked. "And who are Paint and Jack?"

"That's Bossy, dear old Bossy and her calf." George indicated an exceptionally large brown-and-white cow who was now ambling towards us. A big bell swung from her wide leather collar and rang slowly as she walked. "She's my milk cow. She came from Saskatchewan and went with the ranch. She's ageless. She gives me a calf every year and twice has had twins." I watched her as she walked. She kicked up her feet in front of her in a spastic manner and her toes were so long that it looked as if her feet were on short skis.

"What ever is the matter with her feet, George? I asked. "She looks as if she has difficulty walking."

"Yeah, I guess she needs her toes cut back. I'll get around to it sometime," he answered with a faraway look. "Paint and Jack are my saddle horses. They're down on the main meadow. We won't see them today."

We retraced our steps to the jeep, where George picked up the kerosene can. The dogs were ready to join us now. Moose walked behind his master, his head level with his master's hand. George caressed him gently. We all walked to the bridge and up to the knoll in the poplar grove and all filed into the log cabin, George, Moose, The Ghost and I. Jiggs raced in, bringing up the rear. What a contrast to the cold which had greeted us when we had first arrived that morning. The room seemed almost too hot now.

We "threw on" the can of beans. "Throwing on" consisted of opening the can and placing it on the flat part of the barrel heater. A couple of plates, some slices of bread, butter, and a knife and fork each and we were all set for what seemed like a real feast after having been out in the cold air.

"Have you read all those books in that bookcase, George? I queried, as I stabbed the last chili bean with my fork.

"Oh, no, of course not. Let me see, I've read all the Zane Grey, James Oliver Curwood, Robert Service, Jack London and one or two of the others. I like to see them all there. They've been given to me, or I've bought them at secondhand stores. The more there are, the better I like it. There's a large red book of famous paintings of the world on the top shelf and a priceless old book of western ballads. How do you like this cabin? It's built by one of the master cabin builders in this country. I did the bull work—cut, hauled, skidded, and skinned all the logs. It's the best in the country. Chinked with oakum, it is," he added with evident pride.

"What do you mean, 'chinked with oakum'?"

He rose from the table. "You see those small poles nailed between the big logs? Behind those are packed layers and layers of moss and oakum. You know, the stuff that boats are caulked with. The whole place is chinked with oakum, he said, expansively."

I found myself repeating in my head—"chinked with oakum, chinked with oakum, whole place chinked with oakum," as if I were working at self-hypnosis.

"It's like tarry rope, you know. I wrapped it around wedgelike pieces of wood, then hammered them in. From the outside of the cabin I hammered in moss. Makes a cabin nice and cozy in the winter and cool in the summer and keeps the bugs out—the tarry smell, you know." George sat down and rolled a cigarette thoughtfully to smoke with his coffee. We were quiet again, each thinking his own thoughts. The dogs lay sleeping by the hearth. Jiggs was lying on the day bed by the window.

"I'll really have to get back," I said, breaking the silence. "I'm way behind in my work."

We went into the kitchen and put the plates on top of the uninviting stack of dishes in the sink, closed the front of the barrel heater, called the dogs, and put the cat out. I had the strangest feeling that I was leaving my home as George closed the door behind us.

"Now all we have to do is to feed the cattle at the Prout and we'll have finished," George said.

We had just started off in the jeep when I was startled by George opening the door of the jeep and yelling, "Stay at home now. No goddam good. No goddam good." Dejectedly, the dogs turned back towards the ranch.

We passed a right turn about two miles from the ranch. "Those are my nearest neighbors, the Wiebe boys. They're Mennonites and have a little sawmill." A little farther on we turned right and on down a little road, stopping at a gate at the end. Two poles which slipped to the left opened up the way. We drove through. George pushed the poles back into place, and on we bounced over the rough meadow. The light was beginning to fail and it was getting colder as we clattered over a log bridge crossing a creek almost concealed by a high growth of coarse grasses.

"Most of the hay here is slew," George explained, pointing to the lush sedgelike growth. "Just a bit of red-top. But I have enough of that to feed them so there's no problem."

George employed the same method of feeding he had used at the Home Meadow, hopping over the pole fence where the bales were stacked, opening them up and scattering the broad-leaved slew hay as far as he could. I could see him inspecting it closely.

"Some of it is moldy," he said. "We had a wet summer, terrible time getting it in."

The feeding done, we recrossed the bridge. The sky was overcast and the light was fading. A water bird flew up with a wild cry. A slight wind was blowing. I thought I had never felt an atmosphere so desolate. I tried to imagine what this scene would be like in midwinter with the snow waist-deep and a cold wind out of the Arctic whipping across the meadow.

We made good time back to Vanderhoof. As we drove along, the day's happenings occupied my thoughts. I was learning to know a man who, like many others I had met in this part of Canada, was in direct and immediate contact with the things which made up his life, a man who had a dream, who relied on his own physical activities for many of his material needs. He cut the wood that fed the fire that warmed him. He had cut the logs that held the house together. "Chinked with oakum they are," he had said proudly. The phrase would not leave my mind.

When we reached the hotel we decided to have a cup of coffee. George took my arm and led me to the same little table we had sat at before.

"Did you like the ranch?" he asked.

"Of course I did. I loved it. It's just wonderful, so isolated and lonely."

George said suddenly, "Will you type my book? I'll give you a partnership in it. I can't pay you anything but we'll go halves when the book is published. Maybe you can get some writing done, too."

I did not reply at first. The thought that "the book" had not yet been born but was only gestating and of unpredictable length amused me. George was certainly optimistic. Maybe the book wouldn't be born at all, yet the bleak financial aspect of the proposition was of no concern to me.

I was thinking what a challenge life on an isolated cattle ranch would be for a short time, as I assumed I would have to live at Little Creek Ranch if I accepted George's offer. To have the same roof over my head even for a short time was a pleasant prospect.

"Let me think it over," I replied. "I'm going to the Kenney Dam site tomorrow for a couple of days and we can talk about it when I get back."

I got up from the table. He held my hand. His was firm, strong, and warm. He took my other hand and gently kissed me on the lips. I said nothing but held his hands tightly in response. We parted, and I went up to my room with a great joy in my heart.

I lay down on the bed and flung my arms wide as if in joyous welcome to a new turn of events . . . cabin chinked with oakum . . . oakum . . . cabin chinked with oakum . . . The words became a song in my heart.

FIVE
The Nechako Dam

VANDERHOOF—Passed away, on Wednesday, October 8, 1952, at 10:27 a.m., the ageless and mighty Nechako River.

The passing, which brings great sorrow to residents of the Nechako Valley, was slow and agonizing to the tens of thousands of minnows, trout and the few salmon trapped in pools along the gravel banks as the waters slowly receded.

The incident may well mark the first time in history such a large and majestic river has been so suddenly and completely stilled at its source in the name of progress.

The passing, due to the intervention of man, has destroyed forever a thing of beauty and of divine creation. Gone also, unless man again intervenes, is a haven to thousands of geese, ducks and swans at the Nechako Bird Sanctuary.

Add to this loss the treasured beauty of the broad expanse of water which has served as a jewel-like setting for the village of Vanderhoof, and as a landing place for seaplanes.

To Nechako Valley residents and to Vanderhoof in particular the loss is a tragedy.

Almost a year after my visit to the dam site, this "obituary" appeared on October 11, 1952, on the front page of the Vanderhoof newspaper, the *Nechako Chronicle*. (It must be noted that the river later returned through controlled gates when the reservoir level was reached.)

The Nechako Dam

🌲   🌲   🌲

On the day of my visit to the dam, almost a year before this appeared, the morning dawned sunny and cold. I had heard in the summer about the million dollar project of the Aluminum Company of Canada. The water system of the Nechako River was to be bottled up at its eastern outlet into the Fraser River by a 200-foot dam, creating a 358 square-mile reservoir. The total project included a ten-mile water tunnel through solid rock, a powerhouse inside a mountain, a transmission line over fifty-one miles of rugged country, and an aluminum smelter plant at Kitimat with access to the Pacific Ocean.

During our travels in the van in Ootsa Lake country we had heard of the negotiations already underway between Alcan and the homeowners on Ootsa Lake who would lose their homes when the lake was flooded. When I talked with some of them, they were asking: "Is Ootsa going to be logged off?" Veiling their anxiety about leaving, "You'll be able to catch whales there," they had said. I wanted to know more about this enormous private project and how drastically it would change the lives of these people.

As I packed my overnight bag an endless ticker tape flickered through my mind . . . chinked with oakum . . . help me with my book . . . oakum . . . book . . . it said continuously, reminding me of the decision I had to make soon on George's offer.

It was the end of November and had been seven months since I had left Australia, supposedly on the way back to England. For the first time in my life it seemed in this place as if time really belonged to me, as if it had taken on a human dimension I could control on my own terms.

The Alcan company car arrived for me promptly at the pre-arranged time and we set off on the sixty-mile trip to the dam site. I knew the road as far as the

Stoney Creek Indian Reservation, having driven there several times in the summer with Jack Sewell, an amateur archaeologist from Vanderhoof, to visit his Indian *tillicums*—meaning friends.

We passed two old buildings, the barn and the cabin headquarters for riders for the overland telegraph to Europe, which had been started more than fifty years before. The old cedar shakes on the roof were still in good condition. Nine miles south of Vanderhoof the new road to the dam began. I had heard that it went through Rich Hobson's ranch; and the road was the last thing he wanted near his ranch. A sign reading, "Warning—road to Nechako Dam—closed to public," told us we were on our way to the dam, key to the Alcan project. Now in the middle of the hunting season, there was a little snow lying on the ground.

"We had to stop for moose on the road before hunting season began, and now I seldom see any," the driver observed.

We had caught up with a heavy truck carrying culverts and passed another sign which read, "You are now entering Alcan Project 160, gate ahead 500 feet. Everyone stop." At the little gatehouse, Ross Starkey, company policeman, asked me what I wanted there. I showed my pass.

"Aren't you going to frisk me for liquor?" I asked, getting into the spirit of the whole adventure. "I've never been frisked before."

"No," he said, his face wrinkling in a smile. "That ban was lifted a few days ago. The men were discontented with a liquor ban and we had to allow it in. But are you carrying firearms?"

"Check me," I offered, jumping out of the car. He proceeded to pat me thoroughly down each side of my body.

"Still sixteen miles to Nechako," Starkey said, as we started off again, the frisking done.

A fleet of private cars was parked on the left as we descended into the new "mushroom" village of Nechako.

The Nechako Dam

It was larger than Vanderhoof and dominated by a water tower on which was written "Nechako, Safety First."

Technicalities completed for my overnight stay, Ellen Carter, secretary to J. R. Bremner, the project manager, showed me around the girls' dormitory and the bright quarters where each girl employee had a room. Complete living facilities were provided for them, and Mike looked after the housekeeping needs. Extra help was given when needed, by wives with business training whose husbands were employees.

What fun to have such a job I had thought—thousands of men and a handful of women. What more could one want? I had always got along with men. But if I were one of these women, I would be working in a world already ordered for me with little chance of creating a world for myself—such as working on a book about the Old West in a log cabin chinked with oakum and being directly involved in a love affair with the wilderness. This could be done in isolation, but not in the togetherness of community.

Chinked with oakum . . . help me with my book . . the endless ticker tape became an insistent signaling as I went to my separate room after an early dinner at five. Even the second sitting at six-thirty left a long evening with little to do. Breakfast was at seven and was a must, as the morning's work hours were long, starting at seven-thirty and ending at twelve-thirty.

My complimentary weekly meal ticket was punched for each meal entitling me to a place at any of the many tables and all the delicious food I could eat. The bountiful edible "staples" at one end of each table intrigued me. There were five kinds of cereals, preserves and fruit juices of many kinds, and assorted pickles and condiments to suit the most discriminating tastes of any nationality to supplement the varied and bountiful daily menus.

Construction workers are heavy eaters. It cost $5.50 a day to feed a man; he paid $2.50. Single women paid nothing. Keeping the men satisfied with their food paid off; there was little employee turnover due to complaints about food. This was vital to the operation of the company, because it cost between $200.00 to $500.00 to bring in each replacement.

Next morning after breakfast I toured the site with the camp manager, who looked after the sleeping, feeding, and entertainment of the Nechako residents. We visited a small hospital and then the kitchen. The chef told me that to feed this new community he needed: 120 gallons of milk, 150 dozen eggs, 125 pounds of bacon, 100 pounds of butter, 500 pounds of fresh fruit and 1500 pounds of meat a day. A germicide lamp reduced spoilage in the meat locker.

Turkey and fresh pineapples from Hawaii were on the menu for that night.

Nearby, an auditorium 28 by 102 feet, made from salvaged concrete forms was being built, together with a barber's shop, lounge, self-service counter, new post office, and store. The profits from the recreational facilities defrayed expenses for recreational equipment and paid staff salaries.

We walked over to Harmony House, a guest house for six people at the end of Harmony Lake, the quarters for married employees. A skating rink was ready to be flooded and ski slopes were being prepared by the ski enthusiasts.

After lunch I toured the dam site with Harry Jominy, resident engineer for Alcan. The area was so large that the construction vehicles, so enormous when close to us on the east side of the site, appeared from the west side to be crawling little moles on terraced earthworks. Pumps were draining water from the canyon where the coffer dam had been put in. We passed the screening plant, a quartz porphyry quarry, and the place where, before the road across had been completed, 100 tons of machinery had come across by ferry.

On the west side we drove up to 320 feet, the height the dam would be above the river. Sixteen hundred feet long and approximately 1600 feet wide at the bottom and thirty feet wide at the top, it was to become the biggest rock-filled dam in Canada. To fill it, an entire mountain close by was being removed.

The highlight of my visit was my ride on the big machinery. I was told I was the first woman to be allowed to do so, which made me feel pretty good. Pulled from above and pushed from below, I landed in the cab of an enormous Marion diesel electric three-and-a-half shovel which scooped up three-and-a-half cubic yards at a grab. Clutching a metal protrusion of some kind, there I hung, half deafened, and bouncing around involuntarily. The teeth of the Marion chawed greedily and rhythmically at the rocky soil. The juggernaut was only occasionally deterred when it shuddered for a second or two at an extraordinarily big rock.

One big Euclid dumptruck after another was filled with the grabbed earth and then driven away. Shaking noticeably from the vibration of the Marion by the time the second dumptruck had been filled, I jumped out of the Marion and scrambled into the truck and onto the seat next to the driver who was ready to dump the contents nearby.

The vehicle rode smoothly when full. We backed onto the edge of a precipice where the contents were spilled over the cliff. But now that it was empty, the return ride to the Marion reminded me of an old-fashioned cake walk machine at an English fair as I bounced about helplessly, teeth chattering. The driver had a steering wheel the size of a bicycle wheel to hold onto; I could find nothing to steady myself. I dismounted shakily, glad to find firm ground again as I walked to the single person footbridge to watch the pumps at work below. We then drove to the No. 1 mechanic shop where tired machinery was overhauled and even the biggest shovels could be taken inside for repair. The excellence of the new roads on the site kept repair bills down to a minimum. A warehouse nearby contained close to a million dollars worth of spare parts so arranged that the smallest part could be located fast when needed.

The tour was over, and Harry Jominy drove me to the airstrip. "Like to measure its length?" he asked, and we did—half a mile by the car's speedometer. From there I could see that a hangar was underway and the ski slope was taking shape. A deHavilland Beaver belonging to the Mannix Company, waiting to take off for Prince George with a company pilot, was all set to drop me off at the Vanderhoof airstrip.

We took off from Nechako village in the late afternoon sunlight. I sat behind the pilot and gazed down at the white ground. Smoke snaked straight up from the numerous sawmills. In timbered areas I spotted a dozen moose silhouetted against the snow. It seemed too short a time before I was on the ground again in Vanderhoof and in no time at all back in my hotel room.

Vanderhoof was already benefitting materially from the construction of the dam, but concern for its effect on the environment was already surfacing by the very community which was now benefitting.

I was greatly impressed by my visit to the dam site and the relationship of that project to what I had seen in that part of British Columbia. It seemed to me that three frontiers were coming together there. The first, the settlement of a rich but harsh environment by adventurous and hard-working men which had been going on for over fifty years and was still proceeding. The second, the manipulation of the environment by lumbering, mining and pre-industrial preparation as in the Alcan project. The third, man's realization that he is an integral part of his environment. This latest frontier was already upon us, as demonstrated in the *Chronicle* "Obituary" editorial. It implied the need for man to develop higher levels of his own self-awareness, to evaluate his place in the environment and to demonstrate the importance to all men of preserving and maintaining the natural environment.

The Nechako Dam

It was exciting and stimulating to meet so many new people, to see human knowledge and skills put into action in the Alcan project and to be, just for a short time, a part of it. I could have been happy working in the Nechako Village. And yet . . . a completely different side of me cried out for the solitude and aloneness of George's ranch. I felt ready to seek actively new directions, to explore again life's mystery and romance, to face anew its challenges and possible new hardships, and, above all, to simplify my own life after its recent complexity. I felt I had all the time in the world and that I could choose what to do with it.

My job with the newspaper was coming to an end. I had promised George we would discuss his offer after I returned from the dam site visit. That would be tomorrow. In the quiet of my hotel room I became involved in a silent triangular conversation in which I was sometimes speaker, at other times listener and observer. It went something like this: "What an adventure it will be!" "Oh, but what about your family in England?" "Do you want to be buried in isolation?" "He needs someone to type his story. Besides the cabin is chinked with oakum." "I think you like him. He's very handsome and quite an individual!" "Perhaps you'd better try it."

The finale of this mini-drama came early the next morning when George appeared at breakfast and before he had time to say anything, I greeted him royally with: "We will be delighted to help you with your book, George. When do we move in?"

SIX
The Western Novel

After making the necessary arrangements to end my job, I moved into the ranch with my one suitcase. The rest of my possessions had either been lost in a hurricane in Queensland, were with my husband in Australia awaiting my instructions for forwarding, or in storage in Victoria, British Columbia.

George wrote to his relatives that he had "a partner in his book." I wrote to my family that I had a new job typing a manuscript of 56,000 words. I made no mention of the remuneration: the roof of a cabin chinked with oakum over my head, food on the table, and good company.

My typing area was the large plank table with the pine-trunk legs. I sat at my portable Royal typewriter, my back to the cozy barrel heater. The light in the cabin during the day was like twilight, because the big picture window that George was so proud of was covered inside and outside with fly-wire frames to protect the glass, letting in little light. So the day after I arrived, I removed the frames and cleaned the glass of years' accumulation of thick, yellow film.

The light flooded in; the room was so bright that we stood speechless staring out squint-eyed onto the snow-dazzled scene. For several days afterwards I had to wear sun glasses in the cabin until I got used to the new brilliance. Now I could get on with my work during the day. It was difficult to type at night as we had only kerosene and pump-up gasoline lamps.

Preparations for the long, northern winter were nearly complete. The woodshed was stacked to the top with foot-long slabs for the cookstove. They were still wet, but as the weeks went by they would dry out and then burn so fast that one might wonder if there were enough to last the whole winter. George was still buzzing-up the last logs. A few yards from the front door, he had made a high pile of spruce and pine logs ready to feed the voracious barrel-heater. The pile represented weeks of work alone in the bush with his axe, falling, skidding, then buzzing-up and transporting the logs over the meadow by tractor and wagon before the snow came to stay.

The animals had been provided for with bales of hay stacked under the machine shed beside the machinery neatly lined up. It had been a wet summer and some of the hay was moldy. There was enough, however, to feed the cows, heifers and calves, and with luck, some left over to sell. The cows, as distinct from the heifers and calves that were kept at the home place, had been driven to the Prout Meadow and had already cleared up the stubble left there after haying.

As for the human family, shelter and warmth were assured. That year, instead of the customary moose, one of Bossy's calves would hang in the warehouse as soon as the consistently cold weather arrived. It would remain frozen for the rest of the winter until eaten.

George had no regular income for he had nothing to sell until the spring calf crop arrived, to be sold as baby beef later the same year or as yearlings the following year. He had nothing else to sell except possibly some hay towards spring. Dispensible assets already had been sold to keep the ranch going.

Everything that had to be bought, therefore, was charged. This method of accountability was new to me and I felt uncomfortable with it, although I, too, had been living on a shoestring for several months. Already I had to send to England and Australia for odd sums of money I had accumulated in various places in sundry small accounts.

Alone in the cabin during the daytime, I often raised my eyes from the typewriter to gaze through the window to a view which gave me second thoughts about the decision I had made to live, even for a short time, in such a cold country. After the war I had been glad to leave England for Australia because I was cold in the damp English winters and sick each year with bronchitis.

"Down Under" in Australia, and free from bronchitis, I had thought I would never want to leave that country with its heady fragrance of burning bushfires. I had loved the gum trees, the gardenias and the orchids. Now as I looked out onto the snowy wilderness, I saw, as if in a dream, the gaily-colored Australian parrots flying out of the bush in the early mornings only a few short months before, mornings more bright and untouched than any mornings I had seen elsewhere.

No exotic parrots, however, flew down to the bird-table in the snow to see if any food had been left there, only drab-colored Canada jays, sometimes called whisky jacks or camp robbers. A chickadee also flew down to make a casual inspection, and a woodpecker tap-tapped his way round a poplar tree in the little grove, arousing me from reverie to reality. I was no longer in a land of gum trees and orchids but in a cold, white world in a country where the snow flies in September and comes to stay in November, and where spring is captive in the anteroom of winter until May.

During the first few days when George, with the dogs, was busy on the ranch and I was alone in the house with Jiggs, in fantasy I often communed with the animal heads over the doors. Bumpy the moose was secured to the rock fireplace by a huge bolt. His magnificent pair of antlers supported two battered cowboy hats and a thirty-thirty rifle. He merely smelled my head as I passed underneath on the days when life beat at an even tenor. But if he was stepping high and had

the world by the tail and I was drawn up to my full five
feet seven-and-a-half inches, he bent down to nudge me
unceremoniously. Clouds of old-smelling dust puffed into
the room, and his singed, split neck showed the plaster of
Paris as he bent down for me to stroke him.

Bumpy's nearest neighbor was a mountain sheep
over the kitchen door. His right eye had an unhealthy
glazed look as if a cataract had formed. One day I got
up on a chair to investigate and found no eye at all, but
just a socket stuffed with a piece of green sock. Sock
Eye however, appeared to gaze admiringly with his one
good eye at the aristocrat of the outfit over the front
door, the Scottish stag. He and Sock Eye had a common
bond, each having lost a right eye. We restored the
stag's vision with a wonder plastic cement, keeping the
eye in place with a rubber band until the operation was
a success. Perhaps he was mildly resentful of such a
modern fixative but I believe he preferred its use to
blindness. The stag often used to tell the other animals
of his illustrious lineage as direct descendant of the union
of a Scottish stag and a Pacific deer.

In this goodly company I typed and retyped the
western story. I listened to the author's hints that I
knew little or nothing about the Old West, and learned
that cowboys' high-heeled boots were strictly functional,
that their language was picturesque in the extreme, that
a certain kind of large lizard was pronounced "hela" and
spelled *gila*, that the girls George admired wore natty
deerskin skirts which showed their pretty legs, and that
they swore and smoked like cowboys and yet were as
pure as a virgin stream, and that, above all, to George,
there was no place like the West.

It was a welcome break from typing, from rustlers
galloping and Bill's guns forever blazing red in a barroom
brawl, when George swung up the path from his work
with the cattle, walking in his customary relaxed manner
with Moose and The Ghost at his heels, as if he had all
the time in the world.

On his way back from the range he filled the two empty water buckets he had left by the bridge over the creek. As he entered the cabin with them he would invariably say, "Howdy, Wangs," (Wangs, a corruption of my name Evangeline), smile widely, and say, "Cup of tea, please. Bossy says howdy to you, too."

He would set the filled water buckets down on the kitchen floor, throw his old cowboy hat from the kitchen with considerable accuracy onto Bumpy's antlers. (What is it about certain hats and the angle at which they are worn that stirs the heart?), plunk himself down in the big armchair, stretch out his toes to the barrel heater, and wait for the tea. The cracked, brown earthenware teapot would be warming on the old black cookstove. I would throw on a few extra sliced-up slabs of wood, dip a little water out of the bucket, pour it into the kettle, and put it on the stove.

Dipping the water out of a newly filled bucket was fun, chasing the bits of ice around. I recalled clear trout streams in Devonshire and tinkling iced drinks in hot countries, and when some tiny living thing appeared in the bucket, there was the wonder of coming spring. George had drunk tea with the Englishmen stationed with him in Yugoslavia when he was a paratrooper, and when I appeared on the scene it didn't take him long to get into the habit again.

Apart from the progress made on the book, one might wonder what there could be to discuss each time George came in. There was no telephone, no daily paper, no mail each day, no tradespeople bringing snippets of news, and often no radio if the batteries of the little portable set were dead. But the inevitable minor crises, the personal predicaments, and the many little everyday things in our smaller world gave us a different perspective from time to time, of the ongoing battle in the outside world.

I found myself becoming involved in this new life; my creative potential was being challenged to make do with what we had available. I enjoyed to the full the simple, basic things of life—a cozy home, enough to eat, close contact with the land and the animals, and always the wonderful silence.

"We'll just have to stay out of town until our grub supply runs out, so that we don't spend any more than we absolutely have to," proclaimed George.

So we went into Vanderhoof as little as possible, seldom more than once in three weeks. Our base then was Mrs. Hobson's Frontier House, with the warmth of her hospitality together with some of the amenities of civilization, like hot baths and good things to eat.

We simply had to go in, however, when George ran out of Ogden's or Old Chum tobacco for rolling his own cigarettes, when there was no more of the mink food we bought for the dogs, or when the kerosene can for filling the lamps was nearly empty. Bringing up the rear in priority were coffee and cans of chili con carne for us, which, together with baked beans, seemed to have been George's staple diet. We would take in the letters we had written and collect the mail of three weeks' accumulation.

But things were not rosy all the time on these visits. I knew the time would come when George would say, nonchalantly: "I'm going round to see the boys." This meant, I soon found out, a visit to the beer hall which extended far into the night. At these sessions "the boys" got everything off their chests and far too much under their belts. Meantime, I was supposed to take the role of "the girls," to do the shopping, tend to any urgent business and deal with the correspondence. Not at all happily, I might add.

My spirits sank also with each visit to the grocery store; we could afford only the absolute basic necessities. Each time I became obsessed with the small slices of Danish blue cheese on display which I longed to buy. I also needed some clothes. I had few with me and they were not suitable for the severe northern winter.

Remembering the vest I had worn in my childhood in England, I suddenly thought that just such a garment could keep me warm again if I could find one. I entered the Vanderhoof clothing store and asked if they had any vests. The young clerk's laugh had an overtone of scorn: "We don't sell such garments these days. They went out with the ark." Feeling like a fuddy-duddy, thoroughly deflated, I returned to Frontier House. By the time George arrived back in the early morning, I was thoroughly annoyed with the situation I had got myself into. His airy crack o'dawn greeting to my despondent look was: "You look like a witch." I was so taken aback that for some days afterwards, I found myself glancing sideways in the mirror from time to time to see if he had reason for such a statement. No, there wasn't. My nose was not at all witch-like; it was rather a nice nose. Clearly the liquid refreshment he had found in the beer hall had made him boldly aggressive. Luckily, he never stocked any of it at the ranch.

As the little jeep left Vanderhoof, my spirits rose the nearer we got to the ranch, until by the time we met the dogs bounding along by our side, my joy was complete. For another three weeks we could forget our own economic crisis and I could forget the interplay of other personalities on George's sociable spirit which made his behavior quite different from when we were alone together. Cozy round the barrel-heater that evening George broke a long silence while we had both been reading:

"You know you must wonder sometimes why I came to this wilderness, and why my friends here mean so much to me. If Rich and I hadn't been raised in California but had remained in the East," he proceeded thoughtfully, "maybe my cameraderie with this country wouldn't have been possible. Rich always had a spiritual feeling about the wilderness and as a little boy he had back-packed into the high Sierras and woods in California learning to love them and enduring physical hardships. He also wrote stories about the woods and woodsmen when he was quite young."

George had told me of the sophisticated social life both brothers had led in New York. In his humorous way he described "getting smoother by the minute" as a young adult with a gardenia in his lapel. He related also his expectation of inevitable promotion and gaining wisdom as he ran round the streets for security houses on Wall Street during the Great Depression at $20.00 a week. He had thought that the faster he ran the more rapid the promotion.

Rich's surfeit of the social life and The Depression caused him to leave for the west and end up in British Columbia in 1933. I had seen Rich and his wife Gloria very little, only on the few occasions when we had all happened to be in from the respective ranches and at Frontier House at the same time. On these occasions I had become aware intuitively of the complexities of the relationship between the two brothers.

Again, George talked thoughtfully about Rich.

"When I became old enough, I went along with him and learned from him. I endured physical hardships—that became part of my personal code—and I dreamed of big deeds." He rolled a cigarette carefully, and continued.

"Even when I was in the mountains of Yugoslavia during the war I felt his presence with me. After the war, when I joined him here on his cattle ranch for a year, I learned from him about a very different kind of wilderness and he taught me many practical things about ranching."

"But when we parted company several years ago and I got my own ranch I still felt his presence around me here and I tried to live up to his expectations of me as a man. And as for my friends here," he continued, "they have little money, power or influence, but they speak my language. They tune in to the kind of things I do and share a similar view of life."

I made no comment. I was unaccustomed to certain aspects of frontier life such as the cameraderie of the beer halls which made me anxious. But in those few moments I felt I was beginning to understand who George was, both through my senses and my mind.

I thought then of the many men I had met in my travels in that part of the world and of the similarity of their dreams to his. I thought, too, of the men I had met in Australia. I wondered if George was the one for me.

There were few breaks in the daily routine other than the visit to Vanderhoof every three weeks. But one day we received a letter from George's sister, Lucia, suggesting that George (having knocked most of his front teeth out with a tire wrench) arrange to have all his teeth out and get what he always called a new "pair of teeth." She wrote that she would foot the bill for the necessary extractions and new teeth.

So we took the bus to Prince George, sixty miles east of Vanderhoof to visit the nearest dentist. It was the first time George and I had been anywhere together other than to Vanderhoof; it was a big adventure. I sat in a tiny waiting room adjoining the dentist's office. It took only half-an-hour for the superman Hocking, with only a local anesthetic, to extract George's twenty remaining teeth, which he had elected to have out.

A one-sided conversation was going on in the dentist's office and, as customary, George was doing all the talking—a strange reversal of the usual patient-dentist role. "That sure must be a strain for you, Doc." and "I hope you're not getting tired," and other similar comments wafted through the knotty-pine paneling to where I was waiting all screwed-up in a ball.

The operation completed, George emerged as jaunty as ever. His mouth was dripping with blood just as a vampire might look withdrawn unwillingly from a victim. We set out to walk the half-mile or so back to the hotel where we were staying for the night, George continuing to extoll, nonstop, the virtues of Dr. Hocking.

"My gums haven't struck bottom yet and I look like a bullfrog," announced George, standing in front of the mirror in the bedroom at the hotel. "When I close my gums together, my face looks like a dried-up raisin." He grimaced, first to one side and then to the other.

The anesthetic gradually wore off, but George continued to talk non-stop, outdoing his own previous records. I suggested we might go to a movie, but instead, I was entertained by a review of the more fascinating aspects of his past life. Maybe the continuous exercise helped the mutilated jaws. George, ever a child of nature, probably knew instinctively what he was doing. When the swelling eventually went down, he settled down happily to wait the six months until he got his new teeth.

🌲   🌲   🌲

Back Tracks was finally finished. The words were counted and noted on the front page. I packed the manuscript carefully between two strong pieces of cardboard cut from a box of Best Co., New York, in which gifts of clothing had arrived for both of us from George's sister and brother-in-law. The manuscript was dispatched with due ceremony, high hopes, and injudicious judgment to one of the most conservative publishing houses in the United States.

The typing finished, the pattern in the kaleidoscope of my life shifted. My divorce had become final. What next? Over the months of sharing happiness and hardship, George and I had developed a close relationship which we seldom discussed but always felt. One of the most appealing things about this man who had sunk his all into an isolated piece of land and some buildings, was his propensity for doing with all his might what he considered to be the "right thing", even if, pragmatically speaking, the odds were against him. In dramatic and potentially dangerous physical situations he had an immense reservoir of courage, endurance, and self-reliance. However, in small mundane matters his threshold of frustration was extremely low, and he ignored the less dramatic.

It did not take me long to realize that as far as material success in his present situation was concerned, the odds were greatly against him, so much so, that on occasions I felt he was taking himself "for a ride." But I also believed that success can be defined in more than one way and on the ranch I had come to experience in the adventure of living with George, a feeling tender and exhilarating, completely disassociated from success in material affairs, an intense, exalted joy in the simple things of life. I realized I was happy living here.

One bright sunny morning a few days after I had finished the typing, George, as usual, returned to the cabin after feeding the cattle. Instead of the customary greeting of "Hi, Wangs," he announced:

"There's only me, Moose, The Ghost, Jiggs, Bossy, the cattle and horses, and the cabin chinked with oakum, but we'd all be glad if you would join us and become a Little Creekman, too."

His dark eyes were shining. He took me in his arms and held me tight. Tears of joy crept down my cheeks and ran off onto the roughness of his heavy wool shirt. I opened my eyes and looked over his shoulder to where the dogs were stretched out by the barrel-heater. I looked past them through the little window and beyond to the far meadow and the jack pine and spruce fading into the misty distance beyond.

How strange fate was! If I had not been ten minutes early for an appointment and a man had started out for his ranch as soon as he intended to, we would never have met.

I was home again! The wilderness surrounding the cabin embraced us closely. We became as one.

Hand in hand we walked over to the big window and gazed out over the ranch buildings to the meadow beyond. A new life had begun.

SEVEN

Wedding in the Poplar Grove

We were married in late September, on a brilliant fall afternoon, in front of the ranch house. We stood together in an aisle of golden-leaved poplars under a ceiling of blue sky. Steve Holmes, English-born and the local magistrate in Vanderhoof, read the necessary words. His wife, Lil, was there. Sam Cocker, Scottish pioneer and orator, Pat Patterson, blacksmith, and his pregnant wife, Pat, were there. George's elegant mother, Grizelda, represented the Hobson family. Moose and The Ghost lay close by, heads between paws, their bodies pointing towards Steve, and Bossy's bell rang softly in the distance for our wedding march. George slipped a ring onto the finger indented indelibly with the mark of another wedding ring. A few more words were spoken. George smiled a toothless grin—we were still waiting for his new teeth. He kissed me, and I became a Little Creekman.

We stepped into the ranch house aflame with large containers of fireweed and cranberry branches which I had picked close by. Lil had made a big white cake covered with coconut, George's favorite.

We all sat down at the table set with hors d'oeuvres and canapés which, guided by a fancy cook book, I had labored at for hours previously. It was evident, however, that the men's real interest centered on a bottle of Scotch at the far end of the table where they had gathered.

"Do you like your ring, darling?" George inquired, after everyone had gone. "Pat made it in his workshop

Fireweed

out of a stainless steel horseshoe nail. No one else could possibly have one like it."

I examined the skilled workmanship. It was a perfect fit. "A really rugged ring, eh?" George pronounced. I nodded. Secretly I decided I would always wear it with the join at the back of the finger where it wouldn't be seen. Certainly, no one else had one like it and it did look like platinum.

The Indian summer days which followed were filled with a golden glow. The yellowing poplars absorbed the glow, and it lingered in the evenings after the sun had gone down. It was the season of frosts at night, mists in the morning and burning hot days. Each successive frost loosened the dying leaves. The faintest breath of wind sent a light shower of gold drifting to the ground. The vivid crimson cranberry leaves curled with the cold. One had only to pass by to dislodge them and send them rustling down to earth, leaving a scarlet cranberry showing up more clearly on the bare stem.

The fireweed, kissed coldly by the frost, dropped its lance-like leaves. Its seed-dispersal mechanism was half completed; delicate wirelike patterns at the lower half of the pod showed that the plumed seeds had already floated away to their new homes and had probably lodged firmly enough in the ground to form a new plant in the spring. So effective is the system of seed dispersal of this plant that the bombed sites in England were often completely covered with fireweed a few months after the war had ended.

The upper parts of the pods were opened ready for the faintest breath of wind to carry away the little parachute seeds. They still seemed reluctant to leave when the breeze blew and clung to their parent with tiny, outstretched hands until they felt their little parachute launch them into the soft air. They then sailed confidently away, shining silkily in the sunshine.

The misty mornings revealed innumerable spiders' webs glistening in the morning sun and dandelion clocks sparkled with a myriad of diamonds. Mushrooms poked up everywhere. All living things seemed to realize the urgency of the time. Young grouse, frequent visitors to the cabin back door, hastened away at our approach like little old ladies clutching umbrellas at their sides, their little bonneted heads leading the way to affairs of extreme import, probably the nearest red berry patch.

The trusting "fool hen", however, a grouse protected by law, did not move at our approach. She continued soberly on her way, her darker plumage lending her a quiet dignity which one respected by instinct, tiptoeing away and leaving her to her own concerns.

The Indian summer fooled some of the birds. They thought it was a second spring. While looking for mushrooms a few days after our wedding, I saw a grouse in a small arena of grass between the poplars. Two yards up on a poplar tree another grouse sat up straight, elongated, and drawn up to its full height. The vain one in the arena raised his dark neck feathers like an Elizabethan ruff, and his tail spread fanlike to its fullest extent. With controlled and fascinating movements like a Javanese temple dancer, he stepped stiffly away from the watcher on the tree. The witness on the tree suddenly saw me. With an agitated cry she flew off. The exhibitionist showed by an increase in his paces that he understood that she was no longer there and that it was time to go, but he was unable to quit his posturing immediately. Suddenly, I felt that I should not be there

Wedding in the Poplar Grove

to see his sense of loss. So I crept away, leaving him to finish his speeded-up show alone.

Thanks to the bonus of the Indian summer, George had two-thirds of the hay crop baled and under cover in the barn and sheds, or in stacks on the field. Since the construction of the Kenney Dam and higher wages, ranch labor was harder to come by. This labor situation was a serious problem to ranchers, as the season was short, and the hay had to be got in. George had been successful in previous years in meeting this challenge.

On hot summer nights when the beer halls of Vanderhoof were teeming with loggers, miners, prospectors, dam workers, and cowboys, George was on the prowl for a hard-working ranch-type man to help him put up his hay. He would drift into the bar and usually by the early hours of the morning would be on the road back to the ranch with a hired man. On the following morning when hangovers had replaced the jubilation of the previous evening, and fortified with George's sincere and persuasive cameraderie, the boss and worker relationship seemed to vanish and George had not only a helper but a buddy.

However, this particular year the labor shortage had become more acute and George's powers of persuasion and low ranch wages could not compete with the inflated wages of the Kenney Dam workers. He had had to tackle getting in the hay crop virtually single-handed. We would arise early, and after breakfast, George, the dogs and I would head for the meadow with our lunch. After the morning's work, in the shade of the willows by the Little Creek, we would munch our sandwiches and sip hot coffee. Spreading out before us and into the golden distance were stacks of baled hay to load onto the wagon and hay-rack and haul to the machine shed or to the corrals to be made into hay stacks. Nearby was "Big Red," the tractor, the wire-tie baler, two wagons complete with hay racks, the mowing machine, and the rake.

It was at this time in the season that Stuey appeared on the scene. He arrived with a friend of George's who had helped George build his cabin and who now lived in Prince Rupert. Bob, Bob's wife and child, and Stuey, whom George did not know, all arrived out of the blue packed tightly in an old jalopy.

Stuey was a teenager of Swedish descent, blond, slim, and good-looking. He had spent most of his young life in the woods along with more seasoned men. His ambition was to make money and plenty of it by logging or working the waterfront during the season. He would then hit town and spend it all by "living it up big." He loved nice clothes, taxicabs, and the radio songstress, Kay Starr.

But his activities after he had left the Queen Charlotte Islands loaded with months of pay from hard work in the backwoods, had been rudely curtailed. Overnight, he had been "rolled" and fleeced of all his money except enough to pay his hotel bill. Bob had given him ten dollars and in return Stuey had given him his pack.

Bob's idea in bringing Stuey along was that George might be able to use him for the tail-end of haying so that Stuey could eventually earn enough money to make his way back to Vancouver and the rough dockside life to which he was more accustomed.

Since George no longer hired and fired men as in the early days, he welcomed him with open arms if not an open purse. Stuey proved to be pleasant to have around the house and he liked my nutmeg-topped rice puddings.

At the time of his arrival, the weather was too wet to bale hay, so without hesitation George started him forking out the manure from the barn. Although George had removed tons of manure from the barn over the years, of late he had let it go, and it was built up so high that he could not enter it standing erect. I had asked him whether he was considering training the cows to bend also in order to enter, and George always san-

Wedding in the Poplar Grove

guinely chanted: "Someone will come along some day," and indeed he was right. There was Stuey.

Stuey brought out the manure, barrow load by barrow load, building a stack that promised to be in time as high as a hay stack. My admiration for Stuey grew with the growth of the stack.

Back at the house after the first half day's work, Stuey observed, "If I ever have a ranch, I'll have a horse ranch. I think cows are dirty animals. I won't eat beef either. I'll stick to horse meat."

His inherent Swedish cleanliness caused him to change his clothes outside in the woodshed before coming into the house to wash from the waist up. Stuey seemed to accept the filthy job stoically, but, putting ourselves, figuratively speaking, into Stuey's manure-covered boots, we decided that half a day off should be offered, if we wanted to keep him. George and he disappeared into Vanderhoof one afternoon, returning only in the early dawn with every sign of their having been with "the boys." The next day little work of any kind was done.

George's mother had been staying with us for a few days. She had a sore throat, and we had all retired early. She had our bed. I was sleeping on the day-bed in the living room, and George and Stuey were bunked up in the attic.

I was awakened at three in the morning by Moose barking on the bridge and the sound of a car. I sat up in bed and looked through the picture window. Two sets of headlights were following each other closely.

"George," I called up to the attic, "there are two cars coming and they're stopping by the little cabin."

"Go in with Mother," George commanded.

George had dressed quickly and was looking for matches with a flashlight as I left my warm bed for our room where his mother was sleeping. He lit the gasoline lamp and put it up on its customary hook. The cars had stopped by the little cabin across the meadow and the lights were turned off.

All was silent for a moment. Then wild voices rent the silence in a blood-curdling crescendo ending in the shrill whoops of an Indian war cry. Numbers of people seemed to be advancing gradually nearer to the ranch house to the steady beat of a drum, tum-tum-tum-tum, pause, tum-tum-tum-tum, accompanied by wild coyote yells. Could it be the war dance of Indians? Do they still go on the warpath even though they drive in cars? Why would they be coming here? I thought of the Indians I had met. It didn't seem likely. I was puzzled.

I stood in the bedroom doorway and saw George suddenly move fast. He reached up to Bumpy's antlers and took down the thirty-thirty calling out, "Stuey—warpath!"

In obedience to another peremptory command to me to go inside the bedroom, I lay down beside George's mother and we whispered together.

The rest of the action I only heard through the door or had recounted to me when morning came. George had flung open the front door and pointed his gun out into the early dawn as the "Indians" arrived.

"George!" rent the air. "Hello, George!" Girls' voices mingled with men's. "We've come out to see you as you asked us to, and we've been stuck in your lousy mud-hole for two hours."

A few seconds passed before one of the men realized that he had been looking right down the barrel of a gun.

"That's a gun," he said in wonderment, "I was sure looking right down the goddam barrel a few minutes ago."

"What a reception," chimed in one of the girls, "aren't you going to ask us in?"

"Yeah, come on in. Mother and Eve are asleep in the bedroom. I thought you were Indians on the warpath. What the hell did you want to come out at this hour for?"

"Have a beer?" chipped in a male voice to break the awkwardness of the less than perfect welcome.

In true frontier style, after several beers and boisterous laughing and kidding, our guests finally departed as dawn became morning and time for the Saturday night party to break up before the Sabbath.

"I thought they'd come after my hide," said Stuey over the breakfast eggs, and then the whole murky story came out.

The night before in Vanderhoof, George and Stuey had been drinking beer at a corner table in the beer hall when Stuey's eye was caught by a flirtatious Indian girl at a nearby table. When Stuey responded with more enthusiasm than tact, the Indian girl's boyfriend challenged him to a fight. Stuey had learned to defend himself in Vancouver, not only with his fists, but with his feet too and had given the Indian a good working-over.

When George shouted, "Warpath!" Stuey had been certain that all the Stoney Creek Indians led by the chief must be on his tail. Clad only in a shirt (he could not explain later why he had chosen a shirt and not pants when there was time to throw on only one garment) and clutching a shoe for his weapon, he had stood in the kitchen doorway to fight it out to the last. Only when a pretty girl appeared in the front doorway did he suddenly become aware of his state of dishabille.

We had no more shivarees—the popular noisy mock serenade to newly married couples who are supposed to provide refreshments to silence the visitors. The unusual reception at Little Creek Ranch must have led to many shakings of the head and comments that George Hobson's sure changed since he married that Englishwoman.

The next morning as I watched the barrow loads rumbling out of the barn I could sense from as far away as the house that all was not well. Stuey started to dance around on the manure pile like a dervish. Imprecations of extreme volubility and full-bodied flavor wafted over to the house. I began to fear for Stuey's reason. The big black cowboy hat which George had given him was flung with superhuman strength into the bull pen. I watched with grim fascination. Stuey then strode over the meadow towards the house, covering the ground briskly as if he really knew where he was going. He entered the back door. George was out working far away from the house and wouldn't be back for an hour or more.

"I'm quitting, Eve," he said. "Thanks for the rice puddings. I've got to go. I don't like ranching. I'm going to pack. Don't bother to get anything for me to eat. I'll walk to the road and get a lift. I don't want any pay."

He ground out the staccato sentences like a machine and then immediately went up into the attic where I could hear him shifting about as he packed. He came down dressed to wait for George to come in. When George arrived he told him the same story. We had recently sold the anvil out of the tool shed and with a few dollars in the bank, George was able to make out a check for Stuey. He told him to cash it in Vanderhoof on his way through.

"I'll take you as far as the Braeside Road and you can pick up a lift there," George said.

George told me that he had given Stuey some advice before they had parted. I gathered it was about a real man not quitting on a job when things got difficult.

"It may come in useful later in his life," George observed.

It must have, for months later we heard from Stuey. A girl had written the letter for him. The gist of it was that he had often thought of George's words about quitting and wanted him to know how useful the advice had been now that he had joined the army. At least half the manure had been cleaned out of the barn but there was no one now to help with the rest of the haying, except me. We missed the fair-haired boy who fought with his feet, loved my rice puddings, and could have listened to Kay Starr on the radio all day.

Wedding in the Poplar Grove

🌲   🌲   🌲

When George had moved from Hughie Goldie's little cabin to his new home across the meadow, he had managed with the barest necessities. He reminded me: "I was a big operator around here once. I employed and fired men. I had a bunkhouse filled with beds and men to put in them. The men left, and I had to sell the bunkhouse. I even had a woman to look after us once. Now there's nothing. I've sold everything I could do without."

I could never quite make out how much exactly George did owe, and he and the bank manager never saw eye to eye on the exact amount. It did boil down to the fact that there was never any money in our pockets except what came in driblets for me from a few sources in the Commonwealth or when we sold some mysterious bit of machinery lying about idle in the toolshed, or when we sold the calf crop. It was obviously up to me to practice the strictest economy in every way and to show that two could live more cheaply than one.

But why did we always buy cans of milk when there was a milk cow? I had questioned: What on earth was Bossy doing? Didn't milk cows give milk? Bossy had a calf—she got milk from Bossy. Why couldn't we? That would save us some money.

"Don't you think we should be drinking Bossy's milk instead of buying canned milk?" I suggested one day when we were looking at Bossy eating. George enjoyed watching animals eat. He was never happier than when any animal was tucking away whatever is its custom to tuck away.

"Well, I guess I could wean Bossy's calf," he replied reluctantly, gazing admiringly at the calf, which by now was nearly as big as Bossy. "After all she's been sucking for nearly a year." After three days of frustrated bellowing and jumping of corral fences, Bossy's calf was weaned, and George came back in the middle of the morning with a pail of milk, demanding a cup of tea as a reward.

"It's not as if the calf were puny," I contended, to console George.

"We must see that not a drop of her milk goes to waste," he admonished. George did his part. Every time he came from the barn he drank a long draft straight from the bucket. He started drinking at the bridge while the milk was still foamy and warm. It invariably spilled on his shirt, as he kept moving while he drank; he finished drinking when he reached the front door.

Slowly and insidiously life around the house became more complicated. Every large vessel became full of milk, with a jug and mug handy to draw attention to Bossy's product. The kitchen began to smell like a dairy. This filled me with nostalgia and sent me back to childhood days and holidays spent on farms. I spent noticeably more time in the kitchen. George had to bring more water from the creek to wash the extra vessels.

"How much milk have you drunk today?" George would ask every time he came in. I liked milk and drank my share, but my capacity had limits. I began to feel guilty thinking of the calf nearly as big as Bossy deprived of all that milk sitting around in the house. The nostalgic feelings quickly faded. I didn't like the smell of milk anymore. I began to be afraid that, like many farmers, I would never drink milk again.

Imperceptibly at first, but more obviously later, I noticed an embonpoint, a subtle rounding of the hitherto lean and muscular contours of George's beautifully proportioned figure. I dared, however, make no direct allusion to this development.

Bossy produced even more milk. The quantity was becoming a problem.

"I wish we could sell some," remarked George thoughtfully one day. "But there's no one near enough to sell it to and there's not enough to take into Vanderhoof. We could give more to the dogs and save on their food bill." The dogs loved the extra ration of milk but it seemed to act as an appetizer. They ate more food, not less, and one day we noticed that Moose had broken out in sore spots all over his body. So we cut out the milk completely.

George's jeans began to split at the crotch and the whole household was acquiring what came to be known as the "Bossy Layer". Bossy was now rearing George instead of her calf.

"Bossy's making a little fat man out of me," he admitted, "but," he added, drinking another glass of milk, "this is what I should have been like all these years, don't you think? I was too skinny before. Next time we go into town we'll see what I weigh on the hoof."

Bossy's milk by this time had become an all-consuming problem we decided to solve by making butter. How many skills must have been learned and how many gadgets made to work by the visual aid of Eaton's mail order catalogue! From this valuable tome isolated mothers could dress their pretty daughters in the latest styles, and greenhorns at the game could find out how to harness a horse. Then with each new issue, the old catalogue could be relegated to the outhouse to be read through all over again, as one page after another vanished into the deep earth. From the catalogue I learned how to use a separator.

George had a table separator left over from the days when he employed a woman to cope with the household. He had often seen it used but had no idea how it worked. He wanted to get "someone"—that vague mysterious somebody often referred to in the best-organized households, to show us how to use it, but I was all for figuring it out for ourselves.

The catalogue showed a similar separator all set up ready for working, not a bit like the mess of seemingly unrelated parts I had found in the cupboard. By trial and error, however, the handle was finally made to turn, and a powerful sound emerged, suggesting that all was ready for the final tryout.

Two vessels were put under the two outlets of the separator. Neither of us knew out of which outlet the cream would flow. We poured the milk into the container, got the handle going, turned the tap and the milk trickled steadily down into the works. We gazed steadfastly at both outlets but no white liquid emerged from either. Where was it all going? We soon knew.

George was turning the handle, his gaze as fixed as mine. Suddenly he leaped to one side. It's going into my boot," he said accusingly as if it were all my fault. He was wearing high rubber boots with plenty of space between his leg and the boot. A steady white stream was spurting out from an unnoticed outlet at the right-hand side of the machine and cascading into the top of his boot.

An ever-widening white pool covered the floor. We stopped the operation with George laughing and cursing and me lamenting the state of the floor, George's boots, and his milk-soaked jeans. We took the contraption apart and changed a mysterious rubber ring to another place and found this time that one outlet did indeed spout cream, and the other, milk.

After I had cleaned the 101 parts that made up the separator, I decided that there must be something more in life than operating and washing a separator every day. I now understood why George used canned milk. However, in order to see the whole "Operation Bossy" to the end, I decided to save the cream by skimming the cream off so that we could still make butter.

We bartered the separator a few days later for a large sack of potatoes, which we kept in the tiny cellar under the kitchen. They lasted us for the whole winter except for an odd one or two which became frostbitten when the temperature plummeted to sixty below zero.

The only time I had ever made butter previously was when I was an eight-year-old. My mother had given me a small bottle of milk to take to a picnic. When the time came to drink it, it had produced a minute lump of yellow butter from being bounced about.

We had a butter churn in the kitchen cupboard—rather a big one I thought, wondering how George had acquired such a large one. It was metal and over a foot in height and had wooden beaters with holes in them. They looked like big slabs of gruyère cheese. It would take us an age to salvage enough cream for those beaters to work on, but after all, I had been a successful little dairy maid at eight and at forty I should be able to produce butter on a grand and efficient scale fit to put into a county fair and carry off first prize.

While I saved the cream, I gleaned scraps of information from my butter-making neighbors. Most important was that the mixture had to be at a temperature of sixty-eight degrees. I had a thermometer which I had previously used for testing photographic solutions. It had traveled so far with me from one end of the world to the other that it had become disoriented. It took patience and a strong arm to shake its life blood into one continuous line.

I saved the cream for two weeks, poured it into the bottom of the churn and tested the temperature. It was under fifty degrees so I set it on the cook stove in not too warm a place. I had set aside the whole afternoon for this process of butter-making, realizing from past experience that anything to do with milk is a fundamentally slow process.

At first I tested the temperature every few moments, losing a blob of cream each time. An hour later I was still testing the temperature. The afternoon was already well under way and the amount of cream was growing less. It was nearing supper time when I finally started churning.

By this time, there was little cream in the bottom of the churn and the paddles didn't really enter much into its thickness. However, when the lid was on and I turned the handle, a satisfying smacking noise resulted and little splashes of cream were thrown up through the hole in the lid.

After the first fifteen minutes, I peeped in. It smelled hot inside but the contents looked exactly the same as when I had started, except that, if anything, they were more fluid.

Two hours later when George came in with two friends who had arrived unexpectedly for supper, I was still churning. Both men had witnessed butter-making at home but didn't know the fundamentals. Before supper each man took a turn and a slight thickening could be detected, but the contents did not look like grains of wheat as I had been led to expect they would.

But the mess inside had thickened visibly, and it was suggested that the time had come to add water. The water didn't improve matters; the mixture became more dilute than at any previous stage. The chemistry of the whole operation was out of kilter.

Our guests, not unexpectedly in the circumstances, began to depart earlier than anticipated. No butter was ever made, but with the punished liquid which remained, batches of delicious fluffy biscuits popped out of the oven. We bartered the enormous churn for a quarter of lamb and bought a tiny glass churn from the catalogue which made butter equal to the butter I had first made as a child of eight. But if I only had one day to live I'd spend it churning butter. Time passes slowly when you churn!

EIGHT
Pack Rats

The significance of the late fall days was felt by humans and animals alike, and the pack rats were no exception. Every building except the cabin received their attention. A favorite place was the warehouse where the winter's supply of meat would hang once it became cold enough for it to remain frozen all winter.

The warehouse contained a conglomeration of old clothes, discarded boxes, ancient stoves, bottling jars, paint cans, and gunny sacks. This was the pack rats' man-made obstacle course. The winners won nibbles at gunny sacks. Each sack cost us a dollar. My formal declaration of war on them was provoked for aesthetic, and not economic, reasons. The autumn-colored leaves were dropping rapidly; only a few green ones were left. I had read in *The Prairie Free Press* that if suitable sprays were gathered before the leaves began to turn and their stems were put first in salt water and then in a solution of glycerine and water for three weeks, they would turn a lovely color and remain that way for the winter.

I had gathered the sprays somewhat late and had searched carefully for green sprays of fireweed and other plants with leaves not yet parted from the stems. As directed, I set these sprays in a salt solution in the warehouse for one day. The next day I planned to inspect them preparatory to putting them into the glycerine solution, which had been outrageously costly for our budget. But what a world of pleasure it would give us gazing at the brilliance of fall leaves when the world around us was cold and white!

I entered the warehouse with a warm feeling of accomplishment, anticipating my dream bouquet, but there was no bouquet. All that remained of the beautiful sprays were a few inches of the stems, and the wild hops I had gathered with such care from under the eaves of the cabin where the frost had not yet touched them had completely vanished.

I hadn't far to look for the explanation. An expanse of pack rat nest under construction covered a box containing heavily-patched long winter underwear. Fireweed lined the bottom and sides of the nest and the twining hops held it all together. A raw bone the size of a big pack rat crowned it all in bloody splendor.

Up until that moment I had been half entranced with these pretty silvery-gray bush rats with the bright beady eyes, not at all unattractive like the European rat of ill repute. I had been prepared to like these rats, for I had once known a pet white rat of exceptional intelligence which had accompanied my sister to France in extreme secrecy one year when she was a student there.

But it was war on all rodents now. I had double ammunition, traps, which we already had, and poison, which I bought the last time we were in Vanderhoof. I felt out of character in this drama, for after all, the rats were doing what pack rats do. I was ill at ease in this murderous role of making the order of my existence affect that of other creatures. Deciding to try the traps first, I gathered all the spare traps from every other building in order to concentrate on the warehouse. Then I planned to move to all the buildings in turn.

I set the traps in the daytime. Within an hour of setting them in the warehouse I heard a thrashing-about of trapped pack rats that made my blood run cold. George wouldn't be back for at least an hour. I thought of their intense suffering. Armed with a hammer and a cloth, I rushed from the kitchen into the warehouse, covered each trapped rat in turn with the cloth, and closing my eyes tightly, banged with all my might with the hammer.

Sickened by the whole proceedings, I returned to the house to watch for George. When I saw him coming, I ran out to the bridge to meet him and told him the whole story. I had once been told: "Don't start anything you can't finish," and with a stern resolve to see this job finished—I could hardly believe it of myself—I urged George to re-set the traps immediately. On his return from the warehouse he observed quietly, "I'll start when we've got some new traps. You smashed all those."

The next day I declared war for the second time. I tore off the corner of the packet of poison, "Non-poisonous to humans, poultry and pets," it read. "Spread in small heaps near the runs. Do not handle with hands."

I gazed around for the most strategic places to put the stuff. The chain of a rat-trap hung from the wall and a small sack of sheep's wool was leaning against the wall immediately underneath the trap. The sack was obviously part of the run. I started to pour some of the vile stuff onto the top of the sack. Something moved, and in an instant I was staring into a pair of bright eyes above quivering whiskers. I was transfixed. Those almond-shaped eyes belonging to the head and shoulders popping out of the sack, for all the world like a toy out of Santa Claus' sack, were not those of a pack rat. They were a squirrel's. He just gazed at me, then lowered his gaze and buried his face into the wool bursting out of the top of the sack. This was unusual behavior. Perhaps, I thought, the trap belonging to the chain on the wall was buried in the top of the sack and the squirrel was caught.

I ran out of the building as fast as I could several hundred yards to where George was, on the other side of the granary. We hurried back and George released the squirrel.

Pack Rat

"Probably one of the young ones born in the spring," George said. Maybe he had intended to build himself a nest in the high spruce tree just outside the warehouse and line it with the sheep's wool he had discovered in the warehouse.

He was weak and his right front paw was injured. We put him in a little box with some food and water, but the ordeal had been too much for him. In a few hours he tucked his tiny face down trying to get into the secure small shape in which he had been warm inside his mother only a few months before. Soon he became too weak to sit up, and lying down on his side, he gave a few twitches of his tail and died.

Such disasters of interfering with the natural way of life of the pack rats, and my sincere love of animals might have deterred me from further interventions. But we had mouse trouble too, and this was inside the house.

Sleep was often impossible because of the nightly carillon of crockery and cutlery. I set traps with bits of the Danish blue cheese which I had eventually succumbed to buying as a special treat for us, but it was left untouched. Sudden death by drowning in an open bucket under the counter accounted for a few. With the ever-increasing cold, still more mice moved in, and one night, after a lengthy excited rustling in a box in our bedroom, I appealed for help from the sleeping head of the household.

"I'll get Jiggs," a sleepy voice observed nonchalantly, and a sleepier black tomcat was pushed into the bedroom a few seconds later. "He'll deal with the mouse. You just watch. He's a wonderful mouser."

I lay in bed imagining Jiggs shaped up tensely ready to pounce on the intruder. The night was dark, the cat was black, and the room had no lights, so I couldn't do much of the watching George had recommended. George himself had lingered by the warm barrel heater smoking a cigarette, undoubtedly thinking cattle thoughts while waiting for action in the bedroom. But the rustling still went on, and a few seconds after, a loud purring started up near my ear followed by the movement of a soft body snuggling down by my side.

"How's he getting on?" called George in a voice whose lazy tones betrayed his almost total unconcern.

"He's in bed with me—Jiggs I mean—not the mouse," I answered with a sigh of resignation. "You'd better get him and carry out the box with the mouse in it too, and let's get some sleep."

The next day when I reached a box down from a high cupboard to get some mending material and found the top spread with bits of macaroni, prune stones, and miscellaneous trifles, I had to declare war on the mice too. I opened the small packet of seed marked with a skull and crossbones. It looked like linseed, shiny and clean. What a quantity of this lethal seed could be packed into one small packet! I thought of all the places I knew mice ran, and distributed the seed there, in small heaps.

We were cozy around the barrel heater that evening after supper, our pressing economic problems forgotten for a while. Moose was lying on a calf skin. The Ghost was under the little iron bunkhouse bed rigged up as a day bed by the big window. We were discussing how to make the bed look opulent without having to buy anything.

My trunks and suitcases had recently arrrived from Victoria. We were having fun unpacking my clothes which I had brought with me from Australia and the few "lares et penates" needed to set up a bachelor-girl existence for settling down again. We were planning what to do with the gold-bordered gossamer sari given to me for my birthday by the daughter of the Nepalese Minister to England, whom I had met on the ship to Australia, and deciding what use we could make of this or that, and where we could put a certain cherished heirloom.

In the midst of this deliberation, the floor scattered with torn pieces of the *Sydney Morning Herald*, grape scissors, and fish knives which one never used any more, The Ghost suddenly tumbled out from underneath the iron cot with a low cry and retched.

"Wonder what ever's the matter with The Ghost?" George questioned, springing from his chair. He picked up the desperately sick dog in his arms and went out through the back door. I followed closely. "What ever can we do for him, Wangs?" George asked, supporting him in his arms. The Ghost looked up at George beseechingly between the tearing convulsions, each one more racking than the one before. In a few seconds Ghost lay stiff and dead.

Without a word, George carried the white dog to the woodshed and covered him with a blanket and we returned to the house.

"Poison," he pronounced, "but where could he have picked it up?"

The sudden realization came to me. This was retribution indeed for my onslaught on the pack rats and mice. "George," I said in a low voice. "It's my fault. I put a small heap of mouse seed under the cot and it's not there now. He must have eaten it. I never thought about a dog eating it. Please forgive me. I'm so terribly sorry."

Tears that would not stop trickled down my face. I knew what George's dogs meant to him. They had been his constant companions for six lonely years. I loved The Ghost, too. I remembered the days the previous winter when he had crossed the snowy meadow like a wild thing, traveling fast in a dead straight line in the direction he wanted to go, crouching low and using his back legs from the joint down to support him like snowshoes.

The passing of that wild unbroken spirit left us mourning. George buried his body deep in a knoll overlooking the Little Creek Ranch. He covered the grave with heavy branches so that no marauding alien animals could reach him. He spent the next day at his blacksmith's forge in the toolshed making a heavy iron cross to mark the place. On the nearest tree to his grave he nailed a carved wooden tablet: "So Long, Pal," it read. He hoped to see him in the hereafter and roam with him again in Elysian fields.

Soon quiet snows would cover the grave of the white dog of the North. The coyote's call from a neighboring hill would now remain unanswered in the lonely night. Only in the memory of those who loved him would he hunt again in the fields of the Little Creek, ever alert, fast as the wind, senses keen as a coyote, instincts undimmed by the love of humans. He died as he lived, blameless, leaving us behind to mourn.

The weather was getting steadily colder, and when accompanied by whistling winds the subzero weather found cracks in between the logs. We stuffed the holes with cut-up old winter underwear. Jiggs knew it was colder; he ate all the time as if he intended to hibernate like the bears. He had to be put out of doors forcibly.

He didn't go far and was back in seconds meowing at the door. The creek already was frozen over in places. The ground was covered with a foot of snow and we were expecting the first really heavy snowfall.

It came silently, like a stranger in the night, and when we woke in the morning the sky was gray and all was more silent than ever. Large flakes floated down softly to top the snow already there. No wind stirred. All was silent. A strange lightness from the all-white world outside lit up the cabin.

Inside, we got the barrel heater going, and George stepped outside to get some large logs for the open fire. He brushed off the surface snow before he brought them inside and stamped his feet to free his boots of snow. There was something indescribably cosy about the sound of his stamping feet. He set the logs up on end on the rough stone hearth. Pools of snow water soon settled in the rock depressions and Moose and Jiggs lapped them up appreciatively.

I brushed off the snow from the bird table in front of the big window. Immediately, the Canada jays circled around and as soon as I got back indoors, they dropped noiselessly down to eat what I had put out for them. George had named them the Crumb Boys.

The trails around the house and barns were completely covered with fresh snow. We often slipped off them into deep snow that came over the tops of our high boots. We were completely snowed in, cut off from the rest of the world. It was unlikely that the snow plow would be out that day as the roads round Vanderhoof would be opened up first. Our narrow, remote road would be last, for it was a dead end swallowed up in the wilderness.

Unexpectedly, the snowplow came out the next morning. The big shiny blade threw the snow up on either side of our lonely road. The plow then turned at the toolshed and went back. A few minutes after the sound of the snowplow had faded, we heard a car coming and watched it from the window until it came to a stall outside the toolshed. We didn't recognize the two men who approached the house. George opened the door to greet them. One was a handsome game warden and the other a friend of his.

"Hi George! Howdy. I've got a cablegram for Eve, and the postmaster asked me if I could bring it out to you. Hope it's not bad news."

"Come in," George invited. They stamped the snow from their high-laced rubber boots, removed their hats, which had ear flaps, opened up their parkas, and stepped inside. I opened my cablegram anxiously. It was from my sister. "Daddy very sick," it read, nothing more. I felt helpless.

My father had been ill for some time. The message was obviously urgent. I had a one-way ticket to England by train and boat, but it would take too long to get back that way. Neither of us had any spare money, and the United Kingdom was several hundreds of dollars away by air. The men stayed only a few moments, realizing that we had matters to discuss. The decision was no problem for George. I had to go home immediately to see my father.

"I'll sell some of the baby beef to buy you an air ticket," he announced unhesitatingly. "We'll get Bob Creasey to come out and give them the once-over and ask him for the best price and you'll be with your family for Christmas." I knew what this decision must have meant for him. He had built up his little herd after his first venture in clover seed had failed because the price had dropped. He had started his herd with three head and now had a hundred, counting calves. He had wanted to keep all of them over until they were yearlings before selling them.

"We'll go into Vanderhoof today and arrange it all—get Bob Creasey to come out—ring the airport at Prince George to arrange your flight, and if we're lucky we'll be in Prince George the day after tomorrow. You'd better not wait any longer."

We did all this and collected the mail. The manuscript *Back Tracks* reappeared as new and neat as the day it was dispatched. Accompanying it was a short note regretting that the material was not quite what the publishing house had been looking for. This discouraging message did not have the impact that it might have had at any other time.

Bob Creasey came out with his trucks later that afternoon, looked the cattle over, priced them, and drove away with sixteen of our baby beef priced at an average of sixty dollars apiece. In a daze I watched them being loaded into trucks from the chute.

We planned to return to Vanderhoof the next day, go on to Prince George the same day, and stay overnight there; I would catch the morning plane to Vancouver. That night I threw some things into two bags, planning to sort out at the hotel what I really needed to take with me and send the rest back with George.

The next morning George threw some extra hay to the cattle to hold them until he got back from Prince George. We didn't say much on the way. Suddenly there didn't seem much to say. It was one of those important moments that couldn't be put into words.

While George was in the lobby of the Prince George hotel talking to some old acquaintances, I scattered the contents of the two suitcases over the bed. In the middle of this display of feminine garments there was a knock on the door, and George, beaming broadly, waved into the room an old friend of his, Rusty Campbell, accompanied by two of his friends. I'd heard that what Rusty Campbell didn't know about that part of British Columbia wasn't worth knowing. He had traveled over much of the province with the earliest surveying parties.

I was going to miss Rusty, Red, and Cy and the Buds and Busters, for if I remembered correctly—and it seemed so long ago—males in England were all called

Mister. One could claim long acquaintance with a
Canadian and not even know his last name. On the
other hand, in England one could know a man for years
and not know his first name. But I was going home to
see my family who meant so much to me; to my father
and mother, who had initially enabled me to develop
self-confidence and the capacity to learn and to love, and
to my only sister, Dorothy, a little younger than I, whom
I loved dearly.

Prince George airport was left behind, and George
returned to the ranch alone. By the small gestures and
significant exchanges which tell so much about the way
people feel about each other, I knew I was leaving my
heart in safe keeping while I was away.

Like cool veinings in marble, snow lay on the dark
peaks. The plane pushed south following the opaque,
olive-green Fraser River to Vancouver. Frothy drifts of
meringue-like clouds spilled over into the black chasms
bounded by peaks that looked as if they were dredged
with icing sugar.

Dawn was breaking the next day as we reached
Winnipeg. A train puffed away far below, leaving a
lighter-wick trail in the still air. Flat, and like an
architect's model, the prairies lay below. There was little
snow. Patches of trees stood out like outcrops of black
mold, and the waterways were barnacled tracks on a
ship's hull. Day dawned and glowed blood-red on the
farthest engine paling the flame dancing within it.

The plane nudged its way forward, nosing a little to
one side and then to the other. Bridges looked like
matchsticks. As I looked back over my shoulder, I saw a
scene uncannily like a motion-picture "still" of the sea
with the sun setting below the horizon. The clouds
curled like toppling sea horses to complete the fantasy.

Towards the end of the trip the Prestwick landing
was made in a sixty-mile-an-hour gale. Bumping
violently, we circled over a rough gray sea, green fields,

and gray stone houses, through a Scottish mist, over a towered stone church and a large old-fashioned rectory.

From Prestwick to London the visibility was poor until we were almost ready to land. The stalwart old elms and oaks looked friendly, and the familiar ploughed fields looked from the air like patches of sand marked with a comb in an infant's sand box.

Elegant Englishmen were draped around pillars in the coming and going at London airport. When they spoke, I suddenly realized for the first time what Canadians meant when they said that English people speak with an accent.

There was a new variation of the unmistakable English flat-topped cap, a corduroy cap, looking pukka-sahib, and speaking subtly of class distinction. I was indeed back in the land of my birth.

NINE

Frontier Living

My father was very ill, but we were all together again after the five years I had been away from England. I shared my new life with them and talked about George.

George had been writing regularly to my father during his illness. Throughout this time, he had extolled the virtues of physical exercise, in which he himself placed so much faith as a cure-all for all ills. It was too late in the day for exercise but George's sincere concern for my father had established a close bond between the two men who would never meet.

After a few weeks with my family, I returned by ship using the ticket I had bought in Australia for my return to England from Canada. The ship docked in New York. I was met by George's sister, Lucia Stokes, and her husband, Bill. I felt as if I already knew them. I must have seemed rather odd, however, when, in addition to an unconscionable number of suitcases filled with treasures from home, I carrried in my hand, unwrapped, my own four-ten double-barrelled shotgun and a large copper lantern given to me by a friend. Both were too precious to let out of my sight. The lantern had once hung fom the mast of *H.M.S. Ganges*. A plaque on it said that the ship had been built in Bombay in 1921 and was broken up in Plymouth in 1930 and that *H.M.S. Ganges* was the last sailing ship to serve as a sea-going flagship. I had in mind a place deserving of it in the cabin chinked with oakum.

At lunch at the Colony Club in New York I met other members of George's family, including his uncle, George Hull, and an aunt, Lucia Lindeberg. I spent several happy days at Lenox, Massachusetts, with Lucia and Bill and their children, Houston and Sylvia.

A highlight of my visit in the East was a stay with George's uncle, Lytle Hull and his wife, Helen, at their estate in Staatsburg-on-Hudson. At afternoon tea I met Vincent Astor, Helen's former husband. At dinner, where guests included Prince Serge Obolensky, Lytle asked me if we had water laid on in the cabin. Surrounded by the luxury of the elegant mansion, our darling little cabin chinked with oakum appeared in my mind as if in a "bubble" in a cartoon and I replied proudly, "No it doesn't . . . and we don't have an indoor toilet either." Sudden silence fell on the animated conversation. Lytle smiled, Serge winked at me, and the irreproachable English butler and maid went about their unobtrusive duties more unobtrusively. I dipped my fingers elegantly in the crystal finger bowl with a rose geranium leaf floating in it and turned my horseshoe-nail wedding ring to where the join in the metal wouldn't show. I knew that at that moment I had made my place in my husband's family.

I returned to British Columbia by train, visiting on the way cousins who lived in the prairies. The Red Cap porter in New York who handled my baggage, hung the copper lantern on the handle of his barrow and called me Florence Nightingale.

When I arrived back in Vanderhoof, I was still carrying the large lantern and the unwrapped shotgun. I did not relinquish them until I had presented the fourten to George. He placed it on Bumpy's antlers, side by side with his thirty-thirty. I hung the lantern in the window to be a light overlooking the distant meadow and the wilderness beyond—the scene engraved on my mind when George had asked me to marry him. At that moment, a strong bond was forged forever between the old country and the new; between my past, the present, and the future.

While I was away, George's sister-in-law, Gloria, had given him a young female puppy because she couldn't housebreak it. The puppy was like a little fox, light brown, with pointed ears. She was supposed to have some wolf blood in her. George named her Wampus, and made her a kennel near the back door. She flourished as an outdoor dog. Moose loved her at first sight and she got along well with Jiggs.

Abe Wiebe, our Mennonite neighbor, had helped George butcher Bossy's calf while I was away; I was glad I hadn't been around. They took her hide off and nailed it up stretched on the outside wall of the toolshed. They cut her up in quarters and hung them up on strong butcher's meat hooks in the warehouse. Her inside organs had been given to Abe's wife, who could make use of them in her recipes.

Preparing meat from Bossy's calf was a laborious business, especially when the weather was well below zero and the quarters were frozen solid. George would say to me after breakfast, "Do you want any of Bossy's calf for dinner, Wangs?" If the answer was yes, George would go into the warehouse, bring out the quarter we were eating and hang it up in the kitchen to thaw.

We would poke at it at intervals during the day to see when it was soft enough for George to take the sharpest knife we had, an old one with hardly any handle, and proceed to carve slices off any part which took his fancy, all the while extolling the wonderful job Bossy had done in rearing her calf.

The slices looked like no cut of meat I had ever seen. "Do you always cut it off like that?" I asked George. "Haven't you noticed that when it's cooking in the pan it curls up and never stays flat? I've never seen any meat do that before. It isn't cut properly."

George was unimpressed with my objections. Anyway, his slice was always minced because he had no teeth. It was Bossy's calf, and anything that had to do with Bossy was O.K. by him. This method of carving the thawed quarter continued until all we had left were enormous bones, pounds and pounds of them hanging together by shreds of meat. I diligently made soup with these bones. After we had been eating soup for days, I observed to George, "Haven't you noticed that we eat all the meat first and then we have all bones? We can't just eat soup made from bones for months. We'll get tired of it. You should have cut up Bossy's calf into small joints when she was first butchered, the way they do in butchers' shops."

But George was satisfied with the status quo. He continued to saw up all the bones; I made quantities of soup. Day after day we ate it; thin soups, strained, transparent, and sparkling; thick soups laced with Bossy's cream; consommé, broth, and bouillon. "Who for such dainties would not stoop, Soup of the Evening, beautiful soup!" as the Mock Turtle sang to Alice in Wonderland. We had it for lunch, too. And besides, because George still had no teeth, soup was an easy dish for him to eat. His habitual observation was: "This must pack a lot of nourishment, Wangs, don't you think? Soup is one of your strong points." We ate bravely on.

None of Bossy's calf could be wasted. When we had finished with the bones, I felt I should degrease and deglue them and make them into steamed bone flour for the garden or to be fed back to the cattle.

Fortunately, our diet was varied from time to time. When a hen stopped laying, George brought it, decapitated and ready to be plucked, and hung it in the warehouse. Several years before, when he had lived alone, he had tried to keep his little flock through the winter in an unheated chicken house. Predators had made off with most of them, and in one particularly severe spell of below-zero weather, the rest had frozen their combs and wattles, so he had brought them all in the kitchen to thaw out, where they had perched more comfortably on the kitchen chairs. Because he didn't want our hens to freeze, he didn't keep them through the winter.

A few weeks after my return, the biggest snow of the winter fell. The Crumb Boys squatted ruffled up in the poplar tree above the bird table waiting for us to brush the new snow off and put food there for them. Lately, I had been more confined to the house with the colder weather, and I sensed that I needed to walk into all that whiteness to dispel the shut-in feeling.

It was not as cold as I had thought as I started out, but a vagrant wind was becoming more organized as I crossed the bridge. The creek was completely concealed, the snow piled up on its frozen surface. We would not see the water flowing again until spring except where we chopped a hole in the creek by the barn each day for the cattle to drink and at the bridge for our own water.

I walked on across the meadow and out through the gate opposite the little cabin where Hughie Goldie the pioneer had lived for forty years. Desolate now, its front door was ajar, as it would no longer close because the frost boils of many previous hard winters had heaved the foundation. When George had lived there, he had sawed off the bottom of the door a little more each spring to make it fit. Peeping in, I saw the ceiling, loose and sagging, resting on my big wardrobe trunk. It was stored there as it was too unwieldy to take into the house.

It had traveled with my previous husband from India to England, then from England to the Australian continent from west to east and then with me in the hold of a cargo ship from Sydney to the Pacific Coast of the North American continent. It was full of acquired material possessions with weblike memories in which I got caught from time to time, and it was still unpacked.

Turning out into the road, I walked toward the first gate. Mine were the only footsteps in the new snow. The silence was brooding, and the wind was gathering. Strange how little wind we usually had here, I thought, and even more strange that the occasional winds were big blizzards.

I stood by the front gate and looked up the tree-cleared section line into the spruce and jack pines moving gently in the breeze, shedding their powdery covering of snow. Soon I would not be able to walk there unless the Wiebe boys decided to cut some lumber and keep the trail free of snow.

Turning back, I retraced my steps. The wind had whipped off some of the loose top layer of snow on the Home Meadow. The cleared surface looked like hard sand after the tide has receded. I closed my eyes and stood still. The biting wind seemed to change to a balmy breeze; the smell of the sea was in my nostrils; its taste on my lips; the boom of the breakers in my ears; and in my imagination I saw the pools left by the tide.

The visions changed from the lonely windy Cornish coast to the unsurpassed beaches of Australia. I smelled that exciting fragrance which to me was Australia—bushfires, gum trees, tropical flowers and fruit—the scents I could never forget.

It was too cold to tarry longer. The wind was blowing with increasing intensity from the north. The visions were gone. I opened my eyes. In those few moments my tracks had been filled in and I could not see the trail to the house.

Back in the warm cabin I looked out onto the snow which might so easily have been sand and watched a white cloud of snow like a gossamer sheet being whipped off the old barn roof. I closed my eyes again; a sand cloud swirled into nothingness blown from a dune way back in my youth.

Frontier Living

Those long winter days gave us time to create our little indoor world out of what material things we had between us. Experience in England during the war when materials were in short supply came in handy to supplement these. I had learned to make baskets from pliable hedgerow twigs of different kinds, for willow was scarce. The army had commandeered it to make messenger-pigeon baskets and for other war uses, and no willow baskets could be obtained.

One Christmas Day during the war, a basket was left on the door-step of my rural home in Warwickshire, England, where I was teaching. It had a little note inside on a small piece of cardboard. "This my work, Franco." Franco was an Italian prisoner of war billeted on a farm nearby. I learned from him how to make stronger baskets from hedgerow materials. He taught me how to make a specially firm edge and handles that would not pull loose.

The creek was lined with willow trees. If I were to use the twigs that winter, I knew that I had to cut a supply before the snow got too deep to walk on without snowshoes. With knife and string I ventured out in my big, wool-lined rubber boots to the bank of the creek in the big meadow. The willow leaves had fallen, revealing the different colors of the year's long, slender growth of willow, some bright green and smooth, others rough and a deep rust color with a strange, mysterious fragrance when cut. Other willow was a shiny bright yellow.

Buckbrush grew nearby. It would add a different texture and another shade of red to weave in with the rest. I tied the various bundles with string and left them on the snow in a place where I would remember to pick them up on the way back. I knew that when the moose got hungry in late winter, they would come down close to the house to feed on willow tips. But there was plenty for all; the moose would not go hungry.

In places where the ground was uneven and the snow had drifted deeper I stumbled and sank in over the tops of my boots. When the trapped snow touched my legs, it felt like a knife thrust. I stood stork-like on one leg at a time and emptied each boot before going a step farther.

Baskets large and small filled the house when all the willow was woven. As a special present for George I mounted some cowboy prints by the Western painter Charles Russell, on plywood, and framed them in woven willow. We hung them on the walls. They fitted in well with the rustic surroundings.

Adding to our interior decorations, I used materials old and new to turn into cushions stuffed with the wool from George's sheep of previous years. The sewing had to be done by hand for we had no sewing machine. I also put empty cans of Ogden's or Old Chum tobacco into circular cloth linings. Then stuffed all around them with hay, sewed a cloth top on and they became footstools. Tanned calf and bear skins already covered part of the floor. We had two timber wolf skins also which could be used on the floor, but they looked better on the wall.

My heavy thirty-six inch jarrah-wood loom had recently arrived from Australia, where I had improved my weaving skills. The loom had left Sydney in three large parcels, but only two of them had arrived at the ranch. The third had been lost. Harry Goodland, an old-time craftsman in Vanderhoof, reconstructed the missing parts of the loom from my sketch, and with a little chisel work here and there, I set it up in the living room with a certain amount of resistance from George. Being a person of the moment, at times he was suspicious when he couldn't see at once how something worked; a large loom takes forever to set up. I spent days threading up the warp, and all he could see during this time was a mess of threads, and an enormous, meaningless structure taking up much space, with no results.

Before we could relegate the loom to the attic a few busy weeks later, I had cut up every pair of old jeans and all the worn-out wool socks and torn up all the bright logging shirts I could find to weave them into floor mats to brighten and warm the bare wooden floors.

I had looked forward to the softness of the mats, as there was nothing but bare boards for my feet when I got out of bed. I had been promised a calf skin for my side of the bed, but somehow it had not materialized. One day, with great despatch and obvious enthusiasm, George had gone into the attic where I shortly heard a great commotion. Moments later he had come down the steps pursued by a crackling, bouncing sound. He was dragging a large, rigid, untanned calf skin.

"It'll do for your side of the bed," he announced. "Let's see if there's room to put it there. This is the skin of one of Bossy's twins. It isn't cured," he added as if that was quite immaterial—and not obvious.

It wouldn't go through the bedroom door sideways as it was too rigid to bend, but he maneuvered it on edge to where he could gaze at it admiringly.

"You try that tonight, darling. I'm sure it's the very thing," he said, with much sincere enthusiasm.

The new floor covering caused great excitement among the animals. Shortly after it was installed I heard a flapping noise in the bedroom and rushed in to find Moose tearing off the meatiest part of the hide where the head had been. I turned him out and left the skin there. I had promised George I would try it out that night, feeling that this was another opportunity for me to acquire some of the toughness of the West, which George thought so desirable.

Of course the hide refused to lie flat and proved a distinct hazard in a room where we had no light and had to get into bed in the dark after turning out the gasoline

lamp in the living room. Getting up in the night was in
any case a nippy operation as sometimes the fire in the
barrel-heater in the living room would die out during the
night, and since there were no storm windows, the bedroom temperature could get to below zero before morning. I had forgotten about Bossy's calf's skin when I got
up that night and stepped out unsuspectingly onto the
floor. A loud crunching, booming noise startled me as
my feet hit the hardened skin reminding me of the
shaking of a piece of metal off-stage to simulate thunder
in amateur dramatics.

"What the hell is that?" mumbled George, half
asleep.

"I think we'll take Thundercalf back to the attic
tomorrow, darling," I said soothingly. "He's not exactly
a success as a rug." And we did.

Later, while I was still full of enthusiasm for beautifying the house, I remembered Thundercalf again. I
dragged him down and put him on the floor of the living
room for inspection. For $5, Harry Goodland had made
us a wooden chair, the kind people have on their lawns.
It was bare-looking and we were trying to think of ways
to make it look more like an indoor chair.

"Maybe we could cut Thundercalf up and put strips
of it on the back of the chair," I suggested. But no
knife we had would make any impression on the tough
skin. It lay around for a day or two constantly in the
way until Jiggs discovered that what was left of the part
that had interested Moose, also was attractive to him—
not to eat, but as a toilet. So after being cleaned,
Thundercalf was relegated to the attic for the last time
and made no other appearance.

"What do you know?" exclaimed George one morning a few days later. "Moose has torn down the skin of
Bossy's calf off the toolshed wall, and there's a big hole
in it. We can't let it go to waste. It's not dried hard

yet. I'm going to fetch it over, and we can use it on the chair instead of Thundercalf.

The skin was supple, but meaty. I expressed a doubt that it was ready to serve as the back of a chair in the living room. George did not agree.

"That'll soon lose its smell," he affirmed. "I used to bring all kinds of skins into the house when I was a boy; rat skins, mink skins, cat skins . . . " he chanted, "and none of them smelled."

When an idea that fires him up hits George, it gets his undivided attention. We immediately sat down on the floor with ruler, knife, and tacks and measured for the strips needed to cover the back of the chair. Moose was taking an inordinate interest in the skin. George noticed it and remarked dryly: "When the moose push a long way north and we get low on meat, we can always slice off a few slabs from the chair and throw them in the pan." Putting more hide on the chair was our nightly occupation until the calf skin was all used up. We made the strips fast with innumerable tacks.

George stretched out in the finished chair with smug satisfaction. "No one else in the world has a chair like this," he boasted contentedly.

We had used many tacks, and as the hide shrank, the odd tack tore away, leaving the detached hide, as sharp as a knife, digging into one's body. It was so uncomfortable that no one sat in it after the novelty wore off.

I had hinted from time to time how good it would be if we could have linoleum for the kitchen as other women did in other kitchens. After all, a few years before I had a Rolls Royce and a yacht—a little linoleum seemed not too much to ask. George had stock replies for suggestions that he didn't want to act upon, either because he wasn't interested or because he just didn't wish to entertain the idea or he thought the whole thing outrageous.

Another idea that I had secretly entertained for realization in a problematical rosy financial future was that one day we might have a bathtub in the house and maybe even a bathroom, and pipe the water from the creek.

"Think how far down you'd have to dig to lay the pipes," George exclaimed in an even louder voice than usual when I broached the subject. "At least six or seven feet to get below the frost line, and it would cost a fortune!" His voice was still raised. "And as for a bath, you can get one at mother's when we go into Vanderhoof."

My ablutions at the ranch invariably reminded me of a talk I once had with a sprightly eighty-year-old woman pioneer I had met in Kalgoorlie, West Australia. Ever since exciting geography lessons about the gold mining towns of Kalgoorlie and Coolgardie, these towns had always fascinated me. I had stopped off at Kalgoorlie when crossing Australia from west to east, for the sole purpose of going down a gold mine to see some gold. She told me: "Before the pipeline from Perth to Kalgoorlie came in, water was very scarce and we only had a little for washing ourselves in. We used a small basinful when we had it. We washed up one day and down the next."

George found the present water arrangements quite satisfactory as he wasn't particularly interested in baths other than swimming in the creek. One day a little later, however, I did find him poring over Eaton's catalogue at the linoleum page.

"How do you measure for lino?" he asked abruptly. This question did not surprise me as George was an out-of-doors man and an exercise in domesticity such as measuring linoleum did not inspire him. He often used an expression which until analyzed did not strike me with the full force of its implication. It was: "I'll let you do it." Just as simple as that. When I was young my father had presented me with several sayings for me to base my life on. "Beware of flattery," was one of them. He was probably thinking of something like George's "I'll let you do it."

Recalling my father's words, I replied, "I'll let you do it this time, George. You multiply the length of the room in feet by the breadth to find out the number of square feet. You do it this time, George."

"There're some lino squares at sale price," he said, pointing to the page, "and there's lino that they sell by what they call a running foot. What the hell's that?"

He got pencil and paper and put some roughly calculated figures down, did some laborious working, and in a few minutes exclaimed, "Why, we'd have to sell three cows to get enough for our tiny kitchen." The mathematics must have been wrong even at the low price of cattle, but the whole affair was essentially an academic exercise. We couldn't afford lino on the kitchen floor at any price. It was just a pleasant pipe dream.

🌲   🌲   🌲

Extremely cold weather persisted. Each day, George rode Paint two miles down the little dirt road to our wild hay meadow to feed and water the cattle. After feeding, he axed-out a long narrow waterhole in the creek because each night it froze over to a depth of over six inches to a foot. By keeping it narrow and long, the cattle would not crowd up and injure themselves by horning or risking being pushed into the water from behind.

George's footwear always gave him trouble. Both summer and winter footwear took a beating. He had a pair of Air Force lined boots which he had worn successfully the previous year, but they were too big and not intended for rough work. They were war surplus bought cheaply, and warm. They had kept the snow out for the latter part of the previous winter.

But this year cracks had started to appear in them because they were too big. The deep snow at the Prout Meadow had sifted in through the cracks, and when he returned to the ranch house, pieces of frozen snow were stuck to his socks and to the sheep's wool lining of the boots. The big red rubber "hot patches" we had put on the surface of both boots, gave them a harlequin appearance. But the cracks persisted and extended beyond the patches until finally it was impossible to patch them effectively any more. We were in a real predicament. They just had to last the rest of the winter months. We didn't have the money to buy any more and the snow had to be kept out somehow. We thought of the small cotton sacks in which we bought mink meal to feed the dogs. One of us hit upon the bright idea of tying George's boots into the sacks. We used binder twine to hold the bags to the tops of his boots. He made an incongruous picture tramping off down the trail, Moose following close behind evincing an intense interest in the new footgear and the inviting smell it left behind. However, the sacks were thin and wore out quickly and soon all the sacks had been used. The boots were too large to pull any kind of overshoe over them. They were so large that in the winter George's feet reminded me of the little "insect men" in cartoons with feet shaped like big black music notes.

I remembered seeing a pair of rubber overshoes knocking around in the attic. They were too small to go on the outside of the boots, but I thought perhaps they would go on the inside. We crammed the overshoes into the boots and pushed them way down into the foot, the soft sheepskin accommodating them easily. They fit! Although he was slowed-up considerably with those two weights attached to the ends of his legs, the snow and cold were kept out successfully.

When we had solved the problem of George's boots, it was time to go into town again for our every-three-weeks' trip. Although George didn't say anything, I could tell he hadn't been feeling too well. This was quite unusual for him, so we intended to stop at the drugstore on the corner of the main street in Vanderhoof to see if we could get some medicine for him.

It was the store with the step sticking out, the one I had nearly tripped over on my way to visit George's mother when I had first met George. The little white-clad man I had seen on that occasion was Bob Steen who dispensed prescriptions. He was an independent Irishman whose mother had a baker's shop near his drugstore. She had been known to withhold selling her bread to certain people because, as she declared simply, "You should make your own." From time to time we had to visit Bob to get certain things like toothpaste for me or veterinary supplies for the animals; he stocked everything we needed.

"What's good for gas, Bob?" George asked as we stood at the counter of the drugstore where we had stopped first. Without batting an eyelid and looking steadfastly down at the floor while his customer finished speaking, Bob reached up to a shelf of Rexall products, took down a package, wrapped it in white paper, slapped it down on the counter without a word, and snapped out the price.

"Charge it, Bob," George said airily. "Oh, and Bob," he added as an afterthought, "What's good for sore tits?" Bob looked up quickly, somewhat taken aback. "Oh, it's for Bossy, Bob," George hurried to explain. "I guess Bag Balm is as good as anything."

Bob wrapped up the familiar green square box of Bag Balm, wrote out the bill, and secured it to the already fat stack of our bills to await the day of reckoning. George hastily seized two parcels from the counter and we were on our way.

By the time we got back to the ranch he was feeling really ill. We surmised that he probably had a dose of stomach flu. We opened the drugstore packages. The one for Bossy contained an assortment of lipsticks which George had picked up in error! Poor Bossy! How incongruous she would look if we had applied them, but then, maybe there would have been enough lanolin in them to take care of those cracks caused by the cold winds after she was milked.

"Let's try the stuff Bob gave me," suggested George from the depths of his big chair.

I made no comment when I saw what Bob had given us. It was bismuth. I had taken it once for a sick stomach and it caused disastrous vomiting.

"Perhaps this will do the trick," I remarked hopefully, put on my most reassuring smile and handed a dose to the patient. He raised the glass to his lips with a movement strangely reminiscent of a ventriloquist's dummy. An empty chair, an open door, a blast of cold air, and a prone heaving figure in the snow; it did the trick all right!

"What's the green stuff?" asked George when he re-entered more slowly than he had gone out and walked hesitantly back to his comfy chair by the barrel heater.

"I think it's bile," I replied.

"What's bile?"

"Bilious-the bile duct, you know," I volunteered.

"Well, it sure is a lousy thing."

He got better after a few days. But I felt that this insidious germ had struck at his very manhood. All his previous adult bodily hurts left visible scars of which he could be proud.

On the rare occasions when we were sick, it seemed a long way to our can, John, outhouse, or what have you. It was hidden away in the trees through the most impressive gate on the ranch. Inquiring guests were directed to bear south. When the cattle were ranging, the gate had to be closed so that they could not get to the cabin, but when they were around the barn or in the meadow it could be left open.

Except in winters, when the temperature dropped to forty or more below, this trip through the trees could be a delight. At times it could even be packed with excitement due to its not being close to the house. It was only a little farther than the woodshed or the warehouse, but just far enough away to feel that you had been somewhere.

In the spring you could report on the opening of the first wild rose, on the growth of the range, or, how tall the pea vine was. Maybe you returned to the house fuming because you had stubbed your toe on a tree root while looking up through the trees at the haloed moon.

In the deep winter night as you returned to the cabin, creeping along the path like an Indian, you could be so absorbed in wonder at the profound silence and the inky blackness, that you did not realize, until you were inside the warm kitchen again, that instead of grasping the flashlight you had started out with, you were clutching a nearly finished roll of toilet paper and had left the flashlight on the seat.

It was not a trip to be undertaken lightly; anything might happen on the way there or back. In the winter at forty or more below zero, if you missed your footing and slipped from the hard-beaten trail into several feet of snow, the visit was curtailed considerably by freezing feet in snow-filled boots. But if the sun was shining, the deep imprints of former travelers who had slipped along the way were lit up with an ethereal turquoise-blue so beautiful that you could gaze upon the miniature caves in rapt attention for unnoticed minutes. So traveling to the outhouse was an event, and so much could happen that we always announced our intentions to the one left behind.

The author of a little Australian classic entitled *The Specialist* would have approved of its solid structure.

(The Specialist made privies and was an expert in that craft widely practiced in the Australian bush.) When I had first arrived in Australia fresh from England, my husband and I traveled overnight some 200 miles south of Perth to the little sheep and wheat-growing town in Western Australia where we had bought a medical practice. I had gazed out of the window of the small hotel where we first stayed to see what looked like numerous sentry boxes like the ones at the gates to Buckingham Palace. They stood out, starkly realistic, at the bottom of each little strip of garden. I had naively asked my husband what they were. Comings and goings were public knowledge there.

Not so with our outhouse in Canada. Ours was private. The slabs it was made of gave it a rustic appearance which blended into the bush and was a part of the lush growth which surrounded it. It was also on wooden skids. A lot of things were on skids in that part of the world, including some houses, one-room schools, and sometimes people. When one hole was filled up, the outhouse could be skidded over another hole.

The only fault with our outhouse in the Canadian wilds was that there was an enormous space between the super-structure and the pit, which exposed the whole sordid contents; definitely a fault in structure of which the Specialist would not have approved. I tried to throw earth and bits of wood I found lying about to close the gap, but it was no good. They either dropped in the pit, filling it up, or they wouldn't fit around the space.

George didn't approve of putting anything alien like bits of wood and earth into the hole because that would fill it up too quickly and he was thinking of the time he would have to dig another one. From time to time I scattered the top of the contents of the hole with a white powder from a cardboard container. Eventually the powder got all caked together so I had to shake it out on the expansive wooden seat, squash the lumps up and shoot the powder down into the depths through the hole in the seat, thus serving two purposes in one—the aesthetic and the sanitary.

However, the really aesthetic aspect of our outhouse was "The Light." At certain times during the summer if we visited it around mid-morning, we asked each other on returning, "Have you seen The Light?" The Light was a resinous knot in the wood on the right-hand side of the edifice which gave off a bright red glow when the sun filtered through the undergrowth and hit it at this certain time—an unexpected and much appreciated bonus in our simple life.

TEN

Frozen Nose

We were eating dinner one cold day—soup aux fines herbes containing a soupçon of boeuf à la Bossy's calf. The dessert course—snappy milk à la Bossy—had been elegantly served by the French maid (me), when George suddenly broke the spell. "I don't know how anybody can chew with his gums only, although I've been managing it for months and my top gums haven't even been formally introduced to the bottom gums yet."

He had been getting along well on the soft diet we had been eating since he had his teeth pulled. Such fantasies and an endless variety of milk products had been sustaining him. But after long months in a totally toothless state, he was looking forward with eager anticipation to the arrival of his "pair of teeth" and a more varied diet.

"I mustn't forget to remind Hocking to put at least one sweet tooth among them," he remarked as we polished off slices of "economy cake" and a generous serving of "cream ice" as ice cream was called when a French chef first served it to Charles I.

Our cream ice was made from Bossy's cream with eggs added—an old French recipe. We had taken turns churning it in an old-fashioned ice cream maker, using snow from outside the front door.

"Whatever would we do without Bossy?" the French maid asked, as she wiggled her fanny pretending to bring

Frozen Nose

in exquisite finger bowls with a perfumed rose geranium leaf floating on the water.

"Serve coffee in the library," commanded George airily, the repast ended. He rose from the table and pretended to be taking a fistful of wafer-thin chocolate mints before he settled down in the big armchair by the barrel-heater.

The weather had been consistently cold for some time; ominous crackings in the logs of the house and loud explosions like contractions, in the trees outside, informed us regularly each night that the temperature was plummeting.

At 4:30 one especially cold morning, I awoke to find George over the bed putting the cover in place.

"My nose is frozen," I wailed.

"Why don't you stick a piece of this on it," George suggested flippantly, passing me a piece of sheep's wool that was escaping from the seam of one of the handmade comforters piled high on the bed.

"No, I'll use cotton wool. It'll be cleaner. Bring me a lump of it and some sticky tape."

George returned with the cotton and two small lengths of tape, not long enough, however, to fasten it to my face.

"One long piece is the only thing," I said, after unsuccessfully trying to get the tape to stick. "Get me a long piece."

Amidst shrieks of laughter from me and oaths from George, who was getting impatient, I attached the cotton to the middle of the tape, put it on my nose and strapped the ends across my face. The numb feeling gradually eased and I fell asleep. My frost-bitten nose took several days to heal.

The following morning was the day after the first official day of spring. George got up at 3:00 in the morning to attend to calving heifers and had not returned when I rose at 7:30. The bull's unfortunate escape from his pen the previous year meant that the cattle were bred too early. Now calves were being born in the severely cold weather.

I dressed in the living room where it was warm, threw a few extra slabs of wood into the barrel-heater, and looked through the window at the outside thermometer—twenty below zero. It seemed to have been stuck there for several days.

As I was slipping on an extra sweater, I saw George coming across the meadow, hatless, and without his heavy coat.

"Where's your coat?" I asked reproachfully before he had time to close the door behind him.

"It's keeping a calf warm," he replied, and in the same fast breath added, "I've got something complicated and I want you to help me. Put your "longees" on, an extra pair of socks, and warm hat and gloves, because you don't know how long you'll be out there."

He rolled his inevitable cigarette, and put on another coat before we strode out across the meadow in the early morning sunshine. The snow was like salt and squeaked as we walked.

"Come behind me quietly." George spoke in a low voice as we crossed the barnyard.

The heifer was lying on her side in the snow, neck stretched out, her contour moundlike. Every few moments she heaved. One hoof of the calf trying to be born, the color of old ivory, was barely emerging.

George took off his coat and laid it on the snow just behind the animal. Then he tied a short rope onto the protruding foot. It was a rope originally taken from the stepladder in an earlier emergency of the same kind. He now used it on all heifers when necessary; he felt it brought good luck. He twisted a six-inch spike used for fencing, into the rope to make a grip. Then he knelt beside the heifer, pulling on the calf's foot each time she heaved.

After ten minutes, George said, "Fetch the old comforter out of the toolshed, Wangy." I thought he wanted it to put over the heifer. When I returned, a calf's slimy little head was resting on his coat.

"Arrange the comforter so that when the calf comes all the way out it doesn't wind up on the snow," George instructed.

I pushed the comforter under the head and far back under the cow and the little fellow plonked down onto it followed by a mysterious array of tubes, slime, and blood.

"That was a hard pull," observed George, "Now we'll cover the little guy over and let his mother rest for a few minutes."

The calf was all covered up except for his head, which was raised inquiringly. He shuddered. How cold the below-freezing white world must seem to him compared with his mother's warm inside.

George went to look at the other little calf that he had delivered earlier in the night telling me to keep any curious cows away from mother and baby. He was back in a few minutes. He lifted the calf in the comforter, brought it around to the front, and placed it by the heifer's nose. She immediately became alert and got to her feet.

"Now we've got to get her to the barn as quickly as possible." George carried the calf the 100 or so yards to the barn, and the cow followed.

She was now safely inside the warm barn with the other new mother and her little calf. Her own calf rested on the dry sweet-smelling hay she now found more appealing than her calf. She began to eat the hay hungrily while the other heifer came over and started licking the newcomer until she was diverted by faint noises from her own calf a few feet away.

The new calf's mother took little interest in it while she was eating the hay. The other mother lay down by her sleeping calf. George put his coat over the first-born calf and returned to the newborn, rubbing it down with a clover sack to prevent its freezing while we were at breakfast. We let the other mothers and babies out of the adjoining shed, where they had been all night keeping warm.

The next night George was up with another calving cow and heifer. When he came in at 4:30 in the morning, it was thirty-three degrees below zero and we had eleven new calves.

He returned for lunch later in the morning carrying the milk pail in one hand and a water pail of solid ice in the other. As he came through the door I could tell that he was beginning to feel the strain of the last few days. He said testily that he wanted to thaw out a water pail full of solid ice. He needed it to take water to the cows and heifers in the old barn.

The watering operation went something like this: Each animal drank about two buckets of water a day. With eleven animals in the barn excluding calves, that was a lot of buckets of water. If all the water had not been drunk from the previous watering, there would be solid ice in the bottom of the bucket. This could not be removed except by thawing it out before the fresh water was added. That meant less water in each bucket each trip. When George put the buckets down, snow stuck on the bottom which froze to the buckets.

In addition, snow was piled so high on either side of the barn trail that the buckets dragged on the snowy surface and gathered even more snow. To add to his miseries, frozen clods of manure hidden under the snow lay in wait for him to trip on when he returned to the barn. When he set the buckets down on arrival at the barn they would frequently tip over because of the uneven frozen bottoms and have to be refilled. If he attempted to clean off the clumped snow from the bottoms, his gloves froze. Yes, I could understand why he wasn't throwing his hat up in the air and cheering.

All I could find to say in an effort at communicating in this trying time was to ask about the little calf at whose birth I had assisted.

"How're Creepy and Crawly?" I inquired.

"Well, Creepy has learned to find his mother's bag. He used to look under lumps of manure for it before. Now he makes a bee-line for the right place, creeping on all fours with his hoofs bent under him. He follows me around everywhere—thinks I'm his second mother. By the way he said hello to you."

"I turned the big brute of a cow out today. You know, the one with the horns more than a foot long. She goes around waking the calves, prodding them and throwing them against the walls of the barn. I got so mad with her that I turned her and her calf out with the older ones."

After lunch, when he was ready to return to the barn, I helped him fasten the buttons of his parka. His fingers were all split from the cold and done up in tape. Watching him walk across the snowy meadow I wished the spring would come. The Crumb Boys, undaunted by the cold weather, pecked around the bird table. One of them flew up into a poplar tree with what looked like a crust of bread. I looked again. It was a piece of Moose's hair. Was the Crumb Boy thinking of building a nest? Did he know spring was on its way?

The long awaited time had come for George's teeth to arrive by mail from Prince George, and we arranged our regular visit to Vanderhoof to coincide with their probable arrival. We made the post office the first port of call. Among the three weeks' accumulation of mail was the little package from Dr. Hocking.

We scampered to Frontier House as fast as the jeep could scamper. In the living room where his mother, his sister-in-law, Gloria, and I were sitting, George unwrapped the little parcel containing the teeth. If they had been my teeth, I would have wanted a dress rehearsal in private, but not George. He had no vanity. He wanted everyone present at the very outset to take part in the great occasion.

He tore through the tissue paper with his usual force. The top denture flew out of the paper and across the room like a small pink bird. It hit the wall on the other side.

Feminine squeals on different notes were emitted in chorus from George's mother, Gloria, me, and the daily helper, who was peering though the kitchen doorway all agog, smiling broadly with her two lone eye teeth.

He scrambled for the pink bird, adjourned to the bathroom, and emerged seconds later, smiling broadly to reveal a mouthful of teeth. His dramatic entrance was greeted with peals of laughter from me as a privileged wife aware that her husband was the best sport she had ever encountered, a quieter titter from Gloria, and a wondering silence from his mother to whom this occasion probably meant more than to anyone, even than to George.

Six months of looking at him toothless, following a period when his teeth had been indiscriminately scattered around his gums, had not prepared us adequately for the total stranger who now seated himself comfortably in George's favorite chair. He smiled continually, all the time keeping up a running commentary in a voice which had new body in it with an occasional coy sibilant which sometimes reached the proportions of a resonant whistle.

"I've never found it so easy to entertain before," George announced. "All I have to do is sit here and do nothing but smile, and everyone goes into peals of laughter."

But the stranger didn't turn into George. When the hilarity had died down and we had examined him and reexamined him from every angle, we couldn't see

George. His profile wasn't that of the erstwhile handsome man to whom we had been accustomed. His lips protruded like an ape's. But we had all waited so long for this occasion that nobody was about to give up only a few minutes after the new "pair of teeth" had arrived.

To test their chewing capability, George and I went out to the smaller of the two restaurants in town and ordered a chicken-salad sandwich. The occasion was a total failure. The teeth rocked visibly from side to side each time he took a bite. He declared that he couldn't taste a thing; it was like eating flannel. I could not eat my sandwich out of sympathy for him.

He shouted to the waitress to bring him an extra glass of water. Without the slightest trace of embarrassment, and in an extremely businesslike way, he dumped each denture separately into the water before returning them to his mouth. We left the uneaten sandwiches on our plates, paid the bill, and called it a day. We returned to the ranch hopefully surmising that all that was needed was perseverance until George could eat comfortably again and began to look like his handsome self.

I had the curious impression that two men were living with me. George the First, with puffed-out lips, appeared at meal times only. George the Second, was usually out and abroad most of the time, his teeth carefully wrapped in tissue paper and placed on my dressing table. The handsome man of my dreams had gone "walkabout", as the Australian aborigines do, and I didn't know when I would see him again.

One morning a few days after we had returned from Vanderhoof, George the First passed the kitchen window where I was working, still a complete stranger!

"Darling," I said, when he came home after an hour or so, "those teeth aren't right for you at all. However hard you try you are never going to look like George Hobson again unless we have something done to them.

They want filing down or some such thing. We'll have to go to Prince George again to get it done."

We prepared to go after attending to the animals, in case we were delayed overnight. We opened the small trap door in the kitchen floor that went down into the cellar and stowed away the perishable vegetables and liquids in bottles on the top shelf to keep them from freezing. Then we made a quick trip to Prince George.

Back at the ranch after the teeth were fixed, George sat at the table in utter rapture, arranging and rearranging his teeth in endless combinations.

"Wangs, come here!" he commanded. "Look at their delicate structure. I'm crazy about my teeth. Dr. Hocking is one of my heroes."

I watched with amusement as the teeth popped between his lips and vanished as completely as a sword swallowed by a sword swallower. George Hobson had returned from his walkabout.

He grinned affably, rose and studied his handsome profile in our one and only mirror in the bedroom. "They're a wonderful pair of teeth," he concluded, his dark eyes shining like an excited child's. "Now I can do packrat and elephant faces," he said, giving me an expert demonstration.

"But let's not forget our old friends, Beaver Face and Pop Eye," I said. He took out his teeth again to show me they would indeed not be forgotten.

ELEVEN

"Bossy is Bald!"

Spring was so long in arriving that I yearned for the taste and smell of something green, so I decided to plant some cress seeds. I spread two yellow wash cloths on two dinner plates, sprinkled the seeds around the outer rim of the plates, stood them on larger plates full of water with the edges of the cloths dipping in the water, and put them in the sunny kitchen window.

"I see you've made some pies," observed George on arriving for lunch. "They look good."

"Pies!" I exclaimed, wondering where he had seen any pies.

"What are those, then?" he asked, leading me to the door of the kitchen and pointing to the platefuls of cress seed. Suddenly, through his eyes, I saw the strange-looking yellow "pies" sprinkled round the edges with an interesting seed-speckled decoration.

Over lunch of shepherd's pie George had a particularly long spell of what I had come to recognize as his "cattle look," characterized by a faraway gazing into space. I wondered if he were preoccupied with Creepy and Crawly.

"Have you a little brush and a pair of scissors I could use? Bossy's got lice," George said in a matter-of-fact manner.

I had no idea that cattle could have lice. All I could think about at that moment was that Bossy's pride would be hurt; she was a most dignified cow. I put a pair of scissors and a little brush in a small dog-food sack, and George left for the barn.

A week or so later, after another spell of the cattle look George remarked in a singularly colorless voice, "Bossy's bald—there's not a hair left on her. She's running round in the bull pen naked, and Ferdinand is delighted."

I uttered some kind of noncommittal monosyllable signifying only surprise at the startling revelation. I had learned to make allowances for the extremes of George's imagination.

"Well, what hair she still has left is coming out in handfuls," he explained, rolling a cigarette as he spoke, as if it were quite common to have a bald cow.

He had recently been reading some management-theory literature advocating the elimination of unnecessary motions on the job. Bossy had been the job. She was a large cow, and finding that spraying her with a small mosquito spray-gun containing the lice lotion was too tedious and time-consuming a task, he had poured the contents of the whole can over her trusting and aged body, rubbing it in well with disastrous results.

It was still very cold and I had visions of George commanding me to make an enormous coat to keep Bossy warm. Even if I did, I wondered, would her own new coat grow long enough to protect her from the ravages of the first mosquitoes in early May?

Bossy became the cause célèbre for the next few weeks. Each time George returned from the barn, regular bulletins were issued on her progress. A few new hairs were reported each day; she was weathering the cold spell. George fed her the best clover hay to restore her faith in man and to give her something to brag about when there were uncharitable sniggers from the well-clad cattle.

I had long suspected a form of class distinction and pecking order among the cattle. On a day that was warmer than usual, I was watching the patient herd waiting to be fed and thinking how good it was, now that it was warmer, that they no longer had to go around with a layer of solid ice on their backs for months at a time. Suddenly, I caught a glimpse of something bright glimmering off the front foot of one of the two-year-olds.

Strolling over to her I saw that her hoof was completely encased in a half-pound tobacco can. It fitted perfectly around the hoof as if specially designed for her. All the rough edges had been smoothed down and it conformed exactly to the shape of her hoof. A blacksmith couldn't have done a better job.

Looking closer to see if there were any likelihood of her new footgear injuring her I was amused to see the word "Vogue" (the name of that particular tobacco) written on her new shoe. It was perfectly centered in the front of her foot, and she looked quite stylish, but she was a cull, a poor specimen, and it was evident that her status in the herd was not established sufficiently for her to become a leader of fashion. The new Vogue did not catch on, and a few days later she had discarded her new shoe.

One morning in late March we were reading quietly while Moose slept on the floor beside us. Suddenly, we looked up simultaneously, startled by sounds like a throng of boys and girls coming up the path to the house, laughing and talking excitedly. Why on earth would such a thing be happening on this cold day, when the snow was still deep on the ground? We thought of the radio, and checked to see if it had been turned off.

"Sh . . . ush," said George, his face suddenly lighting up. "Geese! The geese have arrived!"

It was the most thrilling sound I have ever heard. For the next few days the Canadian geese wheeled and turned in ever-changing, pulsating formations, conversing excitedly as they winged their way north. Spring was on its way at last. But as is usual in the cold north, even when we saw signs of spring, the temperature was usually so low the jeep had to be thawed by building a fire in the barrel-heater next to her nose at her parking place in the tool shed.

Not until early April did the snow really start to go. Tiny rivulets of water began to creep down the sunny southern slopes. The little creek awakened slowly from its winter sleep making a zigzag pattern across the meadow where the ice had melted and fallen in. Our old footprints grew to a foot long and filled with water as the snow melted, and in the still-white expanse of meadow, olive-green patches appeared where the water was rising under the snow and melting the surface crust.

Once the snow began to go, it went rapidly. George placed a stick in the snow, and we saw that it was melting at the rate of an inch a day. Snow also disappeared from the woodpile, revealing that we had more logs left than we had thought. A flock of juncos descended to peck trifles from the new patches of bare ground surrounding the pile. They were not interested in the bird-table-offerings I had placed there for the Crumb Boys. By now I had to stretch up to the table to put out the feed because the two feet of snow that had piled up on the ground during the winter had almost gone. Yet immediately outside the front door, which faced northeast, a solid mass of ice still remained.

From time to time wading birds screamed their melancholy cries as they circled the barn against the background of gauzy mist that veiled the trees across the meadow. In the cabin the first big housefly buzzed distractedly in a sunny window, and a refugee mosquito from the previous year crawled out slowly from a dusty corner. Though it was still cold at night, these warmer days jeopardized the remaining quarter of beef hanging in the warehouse. One particularly warm day, I went out to inspect it. Beads of blood like small rubies, oozed through the dried-out cut surfaces of the meat. Something must be done with it or it would go bad.

Suddenly, a slight movement in the slabs stacked at the back of the warehouse caught my attention. Two bright beady eyes gazed out from a pointed white face. The little animal had not yet realized that I was there. He ventured forward a few feet and there he was, all of his lithe body, a brilliant white down to the black tip at the end of his tail, a royal ermine—a weasel in his winter-white coat. I stood still and watched him run in and out of the pile of slabs. I felt guilty that I was contemplating the removal of what was his permanent table d'hôte.

We loaded up the remaining quarter of Bossy's calf wrapped in our best mattress-cover, and drove into town to put it in a rented freezer before the roads became impassable from spring break-up.

The remaining snow was pockmarked and dirty, as if smoke from chimneys had settled on it. Logs on each side of the bridge poked out through the remaining snow, and tufts of Moose's hair stuck in patches on his favorite resting place near the bridge.

Fortunately the night had been frosty enough to give the road a harder fudge-like consistency so that we would not tear the guts out of the jeep. But in places, it was still soft, and large gobs of mud spattered up on the jeep as we ascended the hill from the ranch, making a tom-tom thump on the sides of the vehicle like the sound of a beaten drum.

A couple of miles from the ranch we slipped into the ruts made by a logging truck and swayed from side to side like a train on a narrow-gauge railway. It was as much as the gallant little jeep could do to make it through. In a few days the road would become impassable, even for the jeep.

While we were in Vanderhoof we bought the pair of unlined rubber boots which George had promised himself

for spring breakup. The old weighty horrors he had
worn all winter were packed up at the store in a colossal
box. Revivified, George marched out in his new boots
glancing proudly down at his feet every few steps.

He was still gazing at his new footwear when we
stopped to speak to a small group of people. I could
hardly restrain myself from saying to them, "Don't you
see that he wants you to admire his new boots!"

I could not take my eyes off him. He had been
transformed into a graceful dancer. At first he had
difficulty walking normally; he lifted his feet too high
after months of winter shuffles on weighty feet.

But in a few weeks' time the marvelous new boots
were kaput, split in several places at the back. During
the winter months he had become so accustomed to
thrusting his heels down first and digging them in for a
better grip that he had created another heel in the new
rubber boots part way up the back of the leg.

Fortunately they lasted him for the worst of the
muddy weather, and again I found a pair of discarded
rubber overshoes in the attic, which, with a little stretch-
ing, he was able to wear over thick socks. He worked in
these for another few weeks until the bush tore them to
bits. But at least they lasted until haying-time, when he
always allowed himself one pair of tennis shoes for the
summer.

A few days after our visit to Vanderhoof, Creepy
died. The tiny roan calf looked somewhat like a Nean-
derthal man. With head bent low, peering from under
lowered eyelids as if he were nearly blind, tail between
bowed legs, he had followed George around at a slow
dogtrot ever since he was born and right up to the time
he could no longer make it.

George was saddened by Creepy's death but it had
another effect on him also. It made him angry. The
hostile environment and the futility of his efforts to make
a reasonable living discouraged him. Perhaps things

would be better now that spring was on its way and new life was burgeoning all around us.

A few days later, the first grouse of the spring walked slowly past the kitchen window. As he slowly advanced, placing one foot carefully in front of another, he reminded me of an errant husband, creeping back at night, shoes in hand, cautiously transferring his weight so that the floor boards would not creak. The sun shone on the grouse's compact plumage, making it look like polished marble.

Buoyed up by such signs of the time, each of us made his spring plans. George had fence work to do as soon as it was practical. Moose and bears played havoc with the fences each winter. The bears would go in between the strands of wire and break them; when jumping over the wire, moose caught their hind feet in the top strands. Where there were rails at the top of the fence, and not wire, damage was less great, as it was easier for the moose to see a rail than a strand of wire.

One week I planned a big washing day. It happened to coincide with Easter Sunday. I did not like washing days, but I looked forward to this one because I thought I would be able to hang the clothes outside for the first time since the beginning of winter, instead of in the attic.

I put on an old pair of dungarees and became completely absorbed in my wash day preparations. It wasn't until George remarked that I looked like a little dwarf that I realized the straps were too short and that I was unconsciously stooping to prevent them from cutting into my shoulders. I proceeded, heedless of my odd appearance. We expected no visitors, as the dirt roads were too bad for anyone to venture forth except in case of emergency.

We had a washing machine run by a gasoline motor. I had never had to do my own laundry before, so it was a big operation for me. We kept the machine in the bedroom, as we were short of space. First it had to be maneuvered into the kitchen over the little step which separated these two rooms. If it were lifted a few inches off the ground in the maneuvering process, the legs dropped out of their sockets, immobilizing the machine completely. Although we put a piece of plywood between the rooms so that we could slide the machine into the kitchen, at least one leg usually fell out. The collapse of a leg of the washing machine during "Operation Wash" was highly irritating to George, in the same frustration category as his occasional one-man struggle with bed mattresses.

Whenever such inanimate household objects did not perform as they should, temporary transference of ownership of the objects took place rapidly from George to me. They always belonged to me when anything went wrong! In the same way projection of blame was transferred. The problem was mine. Fortunately I understood how George felt about such things. But these unappealing domestic events always generated a certain amount of anxiety in me.

This time, however, I was prepared to enjoy this washing day to the full. I took the radio into the kitchen to listen to an Easter Day address above the noise of the gasoline motor. Canon Raven was the speaker. His voice brought back memories. As a student I had heard him at 1929 Student Christian Movement Quadrennial Conference in Liverpool, England. I had returned from the conference with a book he had written, *A Wanderer's Way*. It had greatly influenced me at that time.

When the basket was full of clean clothes, I prepared to hang them out on the line at the back of the cabin. Filled with the joy of spring I skidded across the slippery ice which led to the clothes line. Little snow had melted there as the back of the house had a westerly exposure.

I stood on the firm top of the two feet of snow which had only just started to melt. Towering over the clothes line, I leaned forward to hang out the first clothes. As I stepped unsuspectingly farther on the snow, the top crust suddenly gave way. I went through. The long winter underwear sank into a dejected heap on the snow. Large pieces of granulated snow sank down into my wool-lined boots. I dragged my feet out of the holes and moved to firmer snow. From this secure position I emptied my boots and proceeded to gather up the pairs of long johns spread-eagled on the snow. I threw them with disgust on top of the rest of the clothes in the basket and staggered back to the cabin with the heavy load.

I hoisted the heavy basket one step at a time to the attic and sank to the floor to rest. I had never before encountered piles of wet laundry at such close quarters. In England, my used linen had been whisked away miraculously by an unobtrusive laundress. In Australia, the laundry was a family affair, ready the same day. A group of aborigines from the nearby reservation encamped all day under the pepper trees in my sunny backyard. They drank gallons of hot, sweet tea and gossiped. Large, blue-tongued goanna lizards basked in the sun watching the relaxed proceedings. With no effort on my part, the clothes emerged at the end of the day in clean, neat piles.

But I wasn't in sunny Australia where wet clothes dried in a few minutes. I was sitting on a splintery, rough board floor of a cold little attic in a log cabin chinked with oakum, in the middle of a jack-pine and spruce forest in Central British Columbia. I stared dismally at the chilled pile of wet laundry which probably wouldn't dry for a week.

I was getting cold. I thought of the cozy barrel-heater downstairs and the little black cookstove. I recalled all the things I had made and all the things I had learned to do for myself. I had made Little Creek Ranch my home. I suddenly felt good about all of it.

I got up from the floor with recovered vigor, and pegged the clothes on the lines strung across the attic. I'm part of the tough west now, I thought as I descended the steps with the empty basket. I threw a few pieces of kindling into the cookstove, put the kettle on and soon had a comforting cup of tea made. I sank down into George's big chair by the barrel-heater to drink it. The wet laundry was forgotten . . . this evening, I reflected happily, I may see, as well as hear, the clanging chains of geese as they cross the moon in their flight north.

TWELVE

Moose and the Porcupine

George was looking forward to the time when he could turn the cattle onto the open range and not have to feed hay any more. One perfect early spring day we saddled up the horses, Jack and Paint, called to the dogs, and rode to the Dugan Place to inspect the new growth. Since I hadn't done much riding, such occasions were very special to me.

The clearing was always a sad and lonely sight; the remains of a little cabin sat on a knoll, with the root cellar next to it. Clumps of rhubarb, already a few inches high, and a row of currant bushes showed where the garden had been. One gatepost still stood, and a sawhorse was falling apart where wood had once been sawn. A broken fence enclosed the few square yards where someone had been buried, probably a child, a reminder of the transience of life. The vetch was five and six inches high, and snowberry and twinberry leaves were fully developed.

"There's plenty of feed here," George observed, pointing to the great variety of new growth which the cattle would be able to pick up.

We reined-in at a tree. Fragments of cream-colored wood were scattered around the bottom of the trunk and a flicker, flashing his white patch, flew away from the far side of the tree. Four feet from the ground was a large hole, but we could not see if there was a nest at the bottom.

A few yards farther on, just above eye level in a
blue spruce tree, we saw a squirrel's drey, an untidy
nest. The bole was surrounded by piles of broken cones
and the remains of the winged seeds thrown down by the
squirrels after feeding. There were two more nests above
it, a whole high-rise of squirrel apartments. We dismounted, tethered the horses, and explored the new
growth on foot. The dogs bounded ahead delightedly. A
leaf of Oregon grape, a brilliant pink, stood out amid the
tender spring growth, and when I touched it, its leaflets,
long since visited by death, fell to the ground. But
nearby I found two "pinkies"—the first orchids of the
year. Lush, tender green feed was becoming abundant;
the cattle would be out on the range by the middle of
May.

The dandelions made a show on the southern slopes
by May 21st. Previously I had always associated the
blooming of dandelions with May 1st, May Day. This
was the date when dandelion gatherers in Warwickshire,
picked the golden heads to make dandelion wine. It had
been a popular beverage in Southern Warwickshire
around haying time, when a large barrel would be tapped
for the helpers. Two strengths were made in the spring
—the less potent kind was drunk by the helpers, the
stronger by the family.

Remembering the earlier springs back in England, I
considered three weeks later here a good effort for our
dandelions. The flowers had no stalks yet, of course;
their heads were still buttoned tightly to the ground. At
the beginning of July I picked a dandelion thirty-one
inches long from the top of its gray-beard head to where
it joined its rosette of leaves—a credit to the rich
bottom-land of the ranch.

As the young poplar leaves matured, they lost their
early, shiny, varnished appearance. The young growth in
the bush matured rapidly, for after the cattle had been
out on the range only a day or two, they stopped coming

back to the barn at their former feeding time to see if any more hay would be forthcoming. They were evidently well satisfied with the new green growth. We missed their comforting presence around the buildings.

One morning a few days after the cattle had been turned out, I was watching for George's return. I saw him coming slowly towards the house, limping badly. He had sprained his ankle jumping over the fence to water the bull—one of the few chores left to do around the buildings now that the cattle were ranging. We were grateful that the accident had happened at a slack time.

But Bossy had to be milked. I could not milk a cow. In my youth, my farmer friends had advised me never to learn as that was the best way to avoid being called on to do it. So Bossy had to be brought to George, instead of George going to the barn to milk Bossy.

"Bossy loves oats," George said, instructing me as to the best way to lure her as near as possible to the house so he could milk her.

"Quarter fill the bucket with oats. Let her smell them and take a mouthful, then start walking fast, calling, 'Come on Bossy' and she'll follow. Then tie her up to the nearest tree, leaving enough rope so that she won't strangle herself but not enough so she can kick the bucket over."

All went according to plan, except that Bossy was rather unenthusiastic about the oats. The new green feed was now her love, and a mere whiff of the oats wouldn't do the trick. I had to let her bury her head in the bucket. I discovered that a cow's head in a bucket is extraordinarily heavy and extremely difficult to get out.

I tied Bossy to the nearest tree and reported her presence to George in the house. In slippers and dressing gown and with the aid of a stick and my shoulder, he limped down the pathway to the place where Bossy was peering over the fence with oats stuck all over her moist spotted nose. Mosquitoes decorated her still sparsely-haired pink patches after her ordeal with the lice lotion. As she saw me approaching with pail and stool, the expression on her intelligent face seemed to say, "What's going on around here?"

At the exact moment that George began to milk her we were inundated by the first real downpour for days. We had been expecting rain; the clouds had gathered, but the wind had arisen and blown them away each day until today. Before George had finished milking, he was soaked through. The milk in the pail was rapidly becoming more diluted as we hurried to the house as fast as George could go.

I now had to feed the bull. The instructions were: "Get over the fence, but be careful not to break it down. Reach up and grab a bale. You'd better not use a baling hook—it can be dangerous. Just pull it down and be careful it doesn't fall on you. Take the axe and chop through the wires. Don't undo the bale too near the fence because if the cattle return they'll be able to get to it and push through the fence after it. Ferdinand will need a quarter-bale now, and another this evening. Dump the quarter-bale over the fence and then get yourself over. That is, get both yourself and the hay in the same place at the same time."

The instructions were precise like those of a military command. My instructor, a pound of butter in his hand to represent the bale, was going through every step of the maneuver thoroughly, barking out the orders like a master sergeant clearly enjoying his role hugely. He proceeded on: "Put the hay over the top of the corral and then go round to the gate, where you'll find two buckets. He'll need two buckets full of water. Only carry one at a time and you needn't fill it to the top. You'll have to lift the gate to open it. Then while he is eating, you can fill his trough. Be careful to close the gate properly because if he once gets out we'll have a helluva time keeping him in at all."

Oddly enough, I had no difficulty carrying out the instructions and I reported back proudly, "Mission accomplished." The plan was successfully implemented each day until the ankle was better.

At the time the cabin had been built near the house, a fenced plot had been set aside for a garden. For some time we had planned to have a vegetable garden, not only because we thought it would be fun but to help with the exchequer.

"I don't know whether I can plough it," said George doubtfully, surveying the small enclosed plot near the kitchen window. "The tractor is so big, and there are no brakes on it."

I could quite see the problem. It was a good thing the plot was almost level. But the alternative, digging it all by hand, appeared an even bigger problem. So, after much skillful maneuvering, a circular level patch with a diameter of nine yards duly appeared. The ploughshares shone. Little birds, seeing the turned earth, pecked enthusiastically away at the new sweet-smelling surface. Moose laid the foundation stone by burying a big slab of wood in the centre of the plot to herald the new activity and a contingent of mosquitoes buzzed excitedly up and down.

To cut up the sods, we borrowed a disk from our neighbors, the Wiebes. The ground had not been summer fallowed, and we knew that later on we would have a battle on our hands with spontaneous growth of timothy, clover, and dandelions.

After the plot had been disked, George set off to return the borrowed equipment. He was back in an unusually short time, and burst into the kitchen.

"Do you want to see something fantastic?" I envisioned some wonder of nature, "A little thing of the wild" as George often put it. But this was no wonder of nature.

"The bridge on the road has collapsed!" Luckily, George had made it safely over, and fortunately there was a back road to the house. During the winter, a tree had fallen over this road which we seldom used, but a little axe-work soon cleared the way so that we could use it until the bridge was repaired.

Our diet had already become more varied with gifts from the spring—dandelion salad, nettle greens which tasted even better than spinach, and Mr. Dugan's rhubarb. We were looking forward to even better days with offerings from our new garden.

In anticipation of the summer months, all the good things I would be picking from the garden and the increase in the fly population, I asked George if he would make me a cache to keep the flies out of the food. I remembered Jacob Henkel's food cache at Francois Lake. George had no formal carpentry training, but he became completely absorbed in making the cache from plywood and aluminum sheeting.

"I don't think flies will ever get in there, do you?" he asked, opening and closing the little doors of the cache with evident pride in his workmanship. "Isn't it beautiful?" He stood as far back as he could to admire it.

"Yes, it certainly will be when it's finished," I said, hugging him. "But where is the wire?" In his complete absorption in constructing the frame he had forgotten to put in the wire. When it was completed, our Little Creek Ranch food cache worked remarkably well. We stuffed Kleenex in any little space where we thought an especially small fly might creep in.

As it was still a little early to plant seeds in the garden, I put some in a shallow box in the kitchen.

"Have you watered your seeds yet?" George asked at supper one day.

"I don't have a watering can, and I can't think what to use for one," I replied.

He got up from the table and took a big spoon-like object with holes in it out of the cupboard.

"I've never been able to figure out what this is," he said. "It's too big to go in any of the saucepans. Maybe you can use it." He took a jug of water and poured water through it onto the kitchen floor.

"A bit laborious," he remarked. "I know!" he said with considerable enthusiasm, producing a colander and proceeding to re-sprinkle the floor. But the stream which emerged was a far cry from the gentle watering-can spray to which I was accustomed.

Not satisfied with the results, he said, "I'll make you something with some wire like the fly wire I put in the doors of the food cache, or maybe I could put a few more holes in that leaking pail that froze up," he added, laughingly. He strode over to a cupboard, grabbed some old rags, and started to mop up the floods on the floor that had resulted from each helpful suggestion.

One day we felt that the time had come to check up on the cattle on the open range. Some of them had come in on the previous day for their salt blocks, but a number of them had not returned at all since they had been turned out. We located them by the sound of their bells. They were in bear country. George usually rode Jack or Paint to inspect them, but on this occasion we walked, the dogs bounding along in front of us. We crossed to the north of the meadow and scrambled through the wire fence to the bunch of cows, calves, and yearlings. What a change the spring feed had made in them in the short time they had been out on the range! They were sleek and glossy, with only a few patches left of their rough, winter coats. This was the bunch which had not been in for their salt. When we started back, at first they followed us for a few yards, then branched off and took a shorter cut to the ranch.

On our way back, we spotted a porcupine feeding contentedly in the middle of the meadow. The westering sun was behind him, giving his quills a soft and yellowy-green appearance, as if he, too, were clad in new spring growth. At first he ignored our approach, then as if he had suddenly remembered a previous engagement, he ambled off, bearlike, toes turned in, tail moving slowly up and down, until he disappeared completely in the tall, thick slew grass.

A few days before, Moose had an encounter with a porcupine, one of several recently. He never seemed to learn from experience. On that occasion he had been out all day. When he returned, he nuzzled up unusually close to my side. I glanced down and saw saliva dripping from his mouth. He was looking up at me beseechingly, his face crinkled up just as if he had eaten a slice of lemon. His muzzle and nose were covered with what looked like stubby, white whiskers.

George hog-tied him while I got the eyebrow tweezers and a pair of scissors. Wherever possible the scissors were used first to clip the quill tops to release the vacuum inside and make them easier to remove. An hour later, George had removed over seventy quills from his nose, mouth, tongue, and throat. George had had a number of opportunities to learn about porcupines. He told me that wolves often attack a porcupine without harm to themselves by harrying the animal until there is an opening where they can attack the vulnerable underside and rip it open.

British Columbian law now forbids the killing of porcupines. When the law was framed, and since porcupines are tame, it was thought more fair to both animals and men that they be left for hungry people who could kill them easily and who might otherwise starve. However, porcupines can cause havoc in unoccupied cabins by gnawing the perspiration-soaked handles of tools to get the salt they crave.

Porcupine

When we got back to the ranch, the group of cattle we had seen was licking the blue, salt blocks, several cows to a block, except for the cow we called the Killer Cow. She was alone at one block, except for one other cow that kept well out of range of the Killer's long horns.

Before returning to the house, we paused to watch the swallows building their nests on the toolshed wall. The dogs lay down and waited. We counted twenty-five nests in various stages of completion. Two were finished, and their occupants peered out triumphantly to watch the others still feverishly building. The birds constantly swooped down to the banks of the creek to pick up mud, hovered for a second or two, then turned, and as regularly and as orderly as an aerial display, flashed their white undersides as if to signal to the next in turn.

With drill-like precision, each bird laid its little piece of
mud in the right place, and then instantly changed places
with its mate. Although it was a sunny day, much of
the mud in each nest was not yet dry. From time to
time, the birds bickered, and at intervals, an unusual
noise or movement disturbed them and they all flew
away.

In their continuous activity the birds vied with the
myriads of mosquitoes dancing up and down in a monotonous two-step, humming like the sound of telephone
wires when one puts one's ear to the telephone pole.
Innumerable clouds of them concentrated their attention
on the few heifers left around the buildings waiting to
calve. George led Bossy off to the barn which he had
been spraying regularly to keep down the mosquitoes.
He gave her an extra spraying as protection from their
constant attacks.

The mosquitoes were hard on the cattle. They kept
them on the run on the range and when they were particularly bad, they hardly had time to graze as they spent
so much time in the willows in the bottomland, brushing
themselves against the branches to rid themselves of the
blood-filled pests.

The cattle were not the only ones plagued by the
insects. I did not go out unless all my exposed parts
were covered with insect repellant, or I would have been
eaten alive. The dogs too were attacked and brought
mosquitoes into the house on their noses and backs.
When they pushed past me as I opened the door I tried
to brush as many of them off as possible as they entered,
but some always escaped and ended up buzzing in the
windows where I caught them.

As soon as the wet ground dried, George had planned to sow part of the Prout Meadow with clover and
timothy seed. The seed had been stored in the granary
in the big meadow after the abandonment of his clover
seed operation of a few years before. The timothy grass

had gradually invaded and taken over the clover. The granary was in the big meadow. It seemed as if it were in the middle of nowhere and it had an air of mystery about it.

I held a 100 pound sack open while George shoveled the seed from the floor of the granary into it. As we worked, we were enveloped by a blizzard of dust so thick that we could not see each other, though we were only a few feet apart.

When the sack was filled, we cleaned the seed in a yellow and red old-fashioned seed cleaner that looked like a small hurdy-gurdy. It had a handle at the side and lots of trays with different sized wire bottoms. This time I did the shoveling into the cleaner and George turned the handle.

A worse blizzard of chaff and dried weeds whirled around us. It settled on our clothes and fell down our necks as the machine racketed round like an old-fashioned "cakewalk" at an English fair. The heavy cleaned seed streamed through the little door underneath the handle. As it passed through, the dust danced merrily in the rays of sunshine glancing through the granary window, as if rejoicing after so many years of inactivity in the granary.

With the sowing of the seed, spring slipped almost imperceptibly into summer. Humming birds flashed scarlet and iridescent green as they gathered nectar from the wild flowers, sometimes mistaking for real flowers the primroses and violets painted on a glass cup and saucer in the kitchen window. Small and delicate and not as long as one's thumb, with beaks hardly bigger than a thick sewing needle, they did not seem to belong to the cold north but to some distant tropical paradise. Their sudden and more frequent visits and the rapidity of their movements were a poignant reminder of the fleeting nature of the northern summer.

THIRTEEN
Bears, Pigs, and Pullets

A dry spell followed the sowing of the seed. When rain came the appearance of the meadow was completely changed. The Prout Meadow was partly under water, and the rest was alive with young grasshoppers. The Home Meadow was white with dandelion clocks as far as we could see. We called to the dogs and went on an inspection tour.

"I wish we could bale this," George remarked as we came to a particularly dense patch of dandelions in the Home Meadow, "though I've never heard of anyone doing it."

The hollow stems of the knee-high dandelions popped like little balloons as we trod them underfoot. Small clumps of timothy grass showed between the dandelions; when the dandelions died, the grass would grow more freely.

We came to the part of the meadow where George had sown the clover and timothy seed we had cleaned. The familiar three little leaflets of young clover showed just above the bare earth, and in between the clover, minute green spears of timothy sprouted. The recent rain had washed in the seed and it had germinated, showing a good "catch" and promising a good crop the following year.

The clover that had been turning brown and dying before the rain came, was now a spread of rich green, while in some parts of the meadow the delicate blades of redtop were strong and healthy and already "heading out", George's term for the flowering of the grasses. An irregularly shaped patch of particularly green grass showed up ahead of us. Both dogs ran on in front, and Moose picked up something in his mouth. When we reached the patch, George kicked at what appeared to be a scattering of bleached bones.

"What on earth died here?" I asked, noticing a variety of huge bones.

In answer, George leaned over and picked up two large specimens. "Notice any difference between these two?" he asked, holding them out for my inspection.

"Yes, of course, but what are they from?"

"This one is the back leg of a black bear and the other is part of a horse's front leg." Noticing my puzzled expression, George continued, "This bone and some of the others here are from an old work horse of mine named Darky. He died of old age during a very severe winter several years ago in the days when I still used horses. At the end of the winter the wolves had cleaned up most of him but not all."

George continued, "One day in early spring, when there was still about a foot of snow on the ground, I came across a big "Black" finishing him up. Bears rarely come out of hibernation until the snow has gone, as the snow hurts their feet, meaning this bear was very hungry. This worried me because I had just left one of my cows with a newborn calf under a spruce tree right over there." He pointed to the woods at the edge of the meadow.

"I think I know what's coming," I interrupted.

"I rarely shoot black bears because they're not like wolves and don't mess around much with livestock. But this time I didn't want to take any chances, so I shot him with my thirty-thirty."

George called Moose over, took the bone from his mouth, and after examining it, dropped it on the ground.

"What happened after that?" I asked.

"A band of black wolves cleaned up the carcass, hair and all. Of course, I got the cow and her calf back to the barn." He reached for "the makings" and rolled a cigarette.

I was silent. George knew I was thinking about bears. He knew I liked them. I had seen several black bears when traveling in the summer. I had picked berries only some hundred yards from bears who were also berry picking. What is it about a bear that makes him lovable? His big archaic feet? His rolling gait?

I met a family when I was driving the van who had a pet black bear at one time. He had been the only surviving cub when his mother was shot one early spring morning. At two-and-a-half pounds, they kept Teddy in an apple box and fed him milk from a bottle. He rapidly outgrew a series of other boxes made especially for him. Then he was chained to a tree, from which he would escape from time to time, climb onto the house roof, tear off the cedar shingles, shake the stove pipe, descend from the house, and then get up on the bunkhouse roof. There he would dance a jig and terrify the men sleeping there. When he was two-and-a-half years old, he had become a big problem; so he was shot and the family ate him.

I never could understand how they could have eaten their pet. Was there no tenderness for an individual they had known since infancy? It seemed to me that to eat him was carrying practicality too far. I had eaten part of a bear but then I had never been on intimate terms with him. When I was driving the van, a forest ranger had brought some young bear meat to me at the children's camp we held on Fraser Lake where I was the camp cook. The raw meat which had a strange translucent color was delicious when I fried it. The rest I had stewed with vegetables and it did not taste like gourmet food.

Grizzly bears are quite another story. I had never seen a grizzly bear but I had talked to Joe Murray in Vanderhoof who had lived to tell the tale about his fight with a grizzly bear in 1914. He had been inspecting his trapline when he came upon an angry grizzly which charged him. Although he wounded the bear with his 303 Ross rifle, Joe went down when his rifle jammed. Only the intervention of his three dogs distracted and finally drove away the fierce animal which had attacked his face and injured one eye with his terrible claws.

A movie I had seen about a grizzly was filmed by a hunter from Seattle and shown by him in Burns Lake. I could never remember later whether that particular animal was ten feet tall and eleven feet wide or the other way round, but I did remember that his feet were fourteen inches long which led me to decide I'd rather stroke a stuffed one.

"And thinking about tame animals instead," George said, interrupting my bear thoughts, "tomorrow is the day we collect our new Little Creek additions. We'd better get back now to prepare for them." We returned, walking slowly, delighting in the lush, green meadow.

We already had two roosters and for some time we had been planning to buy eight Hampshire pullets and two little pigs to help with our food budget. They were to be delivered to us the next time we were in Vanderhoof.

The pigs duly arrived in gunny sacks and the chickens in a crate. We transferred the pigs to a box into which they fitted tightly, head to tail, like sardines in a can. The day was unusually hot, and holding their mouths in an "O" shape they panted continuously, reminding me of the way I looked when I was learning French phonetics and had to gaze into a little hand mirror to check the shapes of the various sounds I made in imitation of my French teacher.

We had hoped to leave Vanderhoof immediately after the pigs and pullets were delivered but were delayed, and George grew increasingly concerned about the pigs' tight quarters. He decided they had to have room to run around and that no better play space could be found than the woodshed attached to his mother's house. That swine should be accommodated there, even for a short while, was not an idea that appealed to his mother, and she protested strongly to George. However, there was no debate where the well-being of animals was concerned.

They were released in the woodshed and soon were guzzling the last of the milk in the house and all the tidbits we could find to accompany it. They were so comfortable in their new quarters that their stay was extended for the night.

After breakfast the next day the pigs were squeezed into their box, and George, armed with a broom, hose, and disinfectant, advanced woodshed-wards to make good the cross-my-heart word-of-honor oath he had sworn that the shed would be left cleaner than it had ever been before.

We arrived back at the ranch with the livestock and a sack of pig-starter. From the moment that George gave the pigs their first meal he was won over by their charm. He loved to see all animals eat. I had assumed that I was to be the feeder-in-chief but I soon found myself in the minor role of second-in-command.

The pigs approved of their spacious wired-in run and cozy house. The two little sisters, like Peter Pan and his shadow, ran around together, little tails twitching and loose skin wrinkling. Only the appearance of food broke the harmony between them, and between gulps of food, the slightly more buxom sister nosed off the smaller one.

Pigs were a familiar part of my life. As a young child, I had been fascinated by biblical stories of swineherds and swine and the illustrations in old engravings. When visiting farms I had loved to feed them with little boiled potatoes and to give them cinders to crunch up. In story books, pigs dressed up as human beings had always intrigued me. They had such dainty feet, and I always felt that they could wear the smallest size shoes, the ones displayed as models in shop windows, which were always too small to fit my feet. And there were more recent memories of pigs. Just before World War II a German friend driving with me in England in the Cotswold countryside, seeing a herd of saddle-back pigs had remarked cryptically: "Even your pigs are camouflaged."

The New Piglets

Chickens, too, had played a part in my life. I used to spend many happy childhood summers with an aunt who kept a few hens, and I struck up close chicken friendships each summer I visited her. I was particularly devoted to the cozy Rhode Island Reds and the white Wyandottes with the vivid red combs. I didn't like the Plymouth Rocks; they became the villains of the fantasies I wove around them. When I found nests piled high with eggs laid far away from the hen house, I reported my findings to my aunt. Filled with a sense of importance as I led her to the wonderful cache, I felt like Columbus, relating his explorations to Queen Isabella. Clearly, pigs and chickens had added a dimension to my life.

When released, the new chickens seemed well pleased with their home. They jumped up on the roosting perches and inspected them leisurely, taking everything in their stride. The two resident chanticleers we already owned had taken complete charge of the newcomers and were marvelling, like Chaucer's Partelot, about their good fortune in the arrival of such attractive fowl. The general calm was disturbed only once as a great fluttering brouhaha greeted the production of the first wobbly egg, resembling a small crookneck squash.

The new residents of the Little Creek were the temporary center of interest not only for us, but also for the cattle who had just come in from the range for their salt. With their moist noses pressed against the wire of the pen, they stood watching the pigs intently, and the pigs, apparently aware that they were the center of interest, put on a command performance.

As a prelude, they scuttled into the shed sticking as close to each other as a form and its shadow, then stood side by side in the doorway gazing out together. Then suddenly, in an erratic burst of emotion they charged at the wire where the cows stood. The larger of the two then soloed in the center of the pen, stood on her head, and balancing miraculously, scratched herself with her back leg.

The smaller one then took over the spotlight and started to dig a hole in the ground. Dandelion roots and grass sods flew in all directions as she bulldozed on, apparently realizing that the presence of such an admiring audience was not an everyday occurrence.

The bull had joined the cows for the finale. The little pigs entered the house together and side by side, waved goodbye with their tails, slowly at first, then working up to a crescendo, their tails moving faster and faster like two batons in the hands of a frenzied conductor. As if realizing that the show was over for the day, the bull lumbered off, his magnificent dewlap shining. He followed the first of the departing heifers, who led him coyly up the barn path.

The hens and pigs added new interest to Little Creek Ranch. This was good, for this was to be the beginning of a very special summer for us. In a few days I was to meet my stepson for the first time. He would be spending two months of his vacation with us. Teeney, as George called him, was thirteen and was at St. Pauls, a boarding school in New Hampshire. I knew him from his photographs. He was a handsome boy, tall, with dark, curly hair. I also knew him from what George and George's mother had told me about him.

I was looking forward to his stay with us with great anticipation, and as I went about my daily chores I planned for the additional member of the family. There would be many activities to occupy his days, horses to ride, learning to drive the jeep, target practice, fish to catch, bales to handle . . . What could I add that would be typically English? I put a dart board in the attic and secretly practiced in order that I would stand an occasional chance of winning at something now that there would be two men around.

Teeney had seen Vanderhoof last when he was six, half his lifetime ago. He and Vanderhoof had grown considerably. He had not seen the new ranch house; when he had visited George before, he had stayed in Hughie Goldie's tiny cabin which he had built for himself fifty years before. I wondered how he would like the new cabin, the cozy cabin chinked with oakum.

FOURTEEN
Teeney and Friends

We met Teeney at Prince George airport after his flight from New York. We saw him advancing toward us with long determined strides. He was just as I had imagined him to be—tall, dark, and handsome. A big smile lit up his thoughtful face, and his voice when he greeted us was low and musical. I loved my stepson at first sight. After a night in Prince George and an overnight stay at Frontier House in Vanderhoof, we piled into the jeep and were on our way to the ranch.

I need not have been concerned about Teeney's liking the new ranch house. He loved it. Burying his hands in Moose's thick coat, he told us so with great seriousness. After lunch and a preliminary settling-in, Teeney went with his father to inspect the big meadow and the new ranch buildings. I watched them walk away, father and son, as it should be. The dogs bounded round them both. I couldn't have been happier.

The rain persisted for three weeks. It hindered the outside work that had to be done, causing Teeney to engage in more solitary pursuits than he might have had if the weather had been better. I was glad for the dart board in the attic.

He wrote letters; to his mother, his grandmother, his friends and to "Pet" who had been his beloved French nurse and governess. He kept a detailed diary, and he painted. He wrote poems; "Time," "Desert Theme," and

"The Creek's Homeward Journey," which were published in the Vanderhoof newspaper, the *Nechako Chronicle*.

Gradually the weather cleared, and he spent most of his time outdoors with his father, through whose patient instruction he soon learned to drive the jeep, graduating rapidly to driving the new International truck, and Big Red, the tractor. He perfected his shooting skills in target practice and in grouse hunting. He learned to milk, and to chop wood. Soon haying time with long hot days in the meadows and heavy bales to haul, would occupy all of us.

On the creek, 100 feet from the little bridge, was a small wooden structure which George had created as a hot weather cooler. Teeney converted it into his own retreat complete with seats, and christened it Creek House. He was crazy about frogs. His "Catch 'em Alive" campaign was like the pursuit of big game. No conservation measures were in existence to hamper the chase; twenty-seven were counted in a single safari.

Creek House quickly turned into Frog Ranch. It was clear that a boat was needed to get the frogs to and from the ranch. With George's help, he constructed Toad Boat complete with sails and rudder. It was painted green, and after many adjustments was successfully launched, not with champagne, but with orange soda pop and appropriate fanfare.

He took innumerable photographs of ranch life and the animals, including Moose wearing George's old cowboy hat. Now that George had movable teeth, he delighted in making "Pop-Eye" faces, sending Teeney and me into peals of laughter. He had comical ways of walking, all of which Teeney captured in his photos. For recording Teeney in action around the ranch, the camera was handed over to me.

With me also he walked and talked and picked mushrooms, wild strawberries, and pigweed and nettles for vegetables. He was a natural cook—pancakes, fudge, biscuits. But pies were his specialty—lemon meringue, apricot tarts, and strawberry. They all had his trademark on them, a hole which he cut in each one after it was withdrawn from the oven. With a secret sort of smile, he consumed each cut-out piece approvingly.

As it happened, his cooking skills became most useful, for at the end of his first few weeks with us I was lying flat on my front in the hospital in Vanderhoof. While the Jeep's gunny-sack "seat" long since had been replaced, the constantly bad state of our road had finally caused damage to the end of my spine. With only local anesthetic Doc Mooney sawed off my coccyx in true frontier style. I recuperated for a few days at Frontier House. Back at the ranch, Teeney was promoted to chief cook.

In early July we three walked through the knee-high meadows for the last time before George cut the grass—then letting it lie to dry before windrowing it. The continuous rain since the dry spell, although late in coming, had worked miracles, saving the hay crop from failure. Clover that had been dying from lack of moisture was now lush, and its intoxicating bouquet was carried on the breeze for the first time that summer. Saturated with moisture and soaked with the sun, it was as heady as the liveliest wine.

The dogs, who were accompanying us as always on such excursions, suddenly started to bark. Immediately, a crashing sound followed, accompanied by the sound of pounding hoofs. Fifteen feet to our right a cow moose thundered through the undergrowth, swerving as she headed into the more dense growth. We continued on, Moose keeping close to us until the sound had died away.

The feathery stems of redtop were long enough to wave when a gentle wind touched their tips. The ubiquitous dandelions had started to flag and their clocks had blown away, leaving the little button-top and recurved sepals standing starkly a yard from the ground, so rank had been their growth since the rain. The signs said it would not be long until haying time.

🌲 🌲 🌲

George had many friends in Vanderhoof whom he had known for several years. Some were his own particular buddies, and others were also friends of the Hobson family. I knew none of them very well as our visits to Vanderhoof were infrequent and of short duration and visits were infrequent to Little Creek. It was good then when the sons of George's friends, George Steele and Maynard Kerr, visited us to become Teeney's. Sometimes, Menno Voth and the Derksen boys from Braeside came also and brought their horses.

The three of us had a very special friend, Alec Moser, whom George had met in the beer hall. He was an Englishman and had come out to our part of the world inspired by the spirit of adventure after reading Rich's book, *Grass Beyond the Mountains*. We three became great friends, and he stayed with us on the ranch from time to time and helped George. They also hunted, fished, and rode together, and sometimes I went along. Not only did I feel that he was a real friend, but also a link for me between the old country and the new life. A close warm relationship had developed among the three of us. Now Teeney made it four. A friend of Al's, Dave Dennison, had accompanied Al from England, and when haying got underway, they both stayed with us.

I loved those summer days of haying. The highlight for me was when I appeared on the meadow in midmorning or mid-afternoon with a huge jar of freshly-made tea and cookies and we would lie in the shade, sheltered from the hot sun, and look up dreamily into the blue sky. The break was all too short before George would start up the power mower again. Soon the machine, vibrating excitedly at the base of the grass, felled the stalks like ninepins until all were lying in regular rows. In the parts of the meadows where there were grasshoppers, they perched like miniature brown monkeys at the tops of the stalks, and when they sensed the coming of the tractor, they dived to get out of its way, causing the whole area to look like an enormous fishing net full of small sprats jumping in all directions. At another time, the side delivery rake would gather up what hay the grasshoppers had left and place it in billowy waves where the grass had been the thickest and least ravaged by the insects.

Then I would watch as the teeth of the baler gathered up the windrows with a rhythmic precision reminding me of marching armies in movies of that time. Or I would lie on my back and gaze into the blue sky. At times, diaphanous-winged grasshoppers sailed around about me as far as I could see. They had then reached the stage when they spend most of their time flying. They moved with the grace and smoothness of floating thistle down. The baler laid her rectangular eggs at odd intervals on the meadow. I wondered how many grasshoppers had been baled with the hay, thus increasing considerably its protein content.

The men would take bales off the field in the wagon and stack them under the hay shed, or they would build small haystacks on the field about five bales long and four wide, piling them like little houses in order to shed the rain. At other times, they would lean several bales upright against each other, also to shed the rain.

When we were haying in the Prout Meadow, we often took time to fish. Fishing in the narrow creek was intriguing, but not in the same league as lake or river fishing in the area. Trout caught in the Prout ranged from seven to nine inches. Larger ones were the exception. Small as they were, they fought with demoniacal fury. Expert or amateur one fished blind because the extra lush growth of coarse slew grass completely covered

the flowing water. Inevitably, in any fishing expedition
anywhere, George caught the biggest number, Teeney,
the next, and I, always, the least.

One day, Al came with us to fish in the Prout Meadow for the first time. He already knew of the unrivaled
trout fishing in British Columbian lakes and rivers. He
had also fished in the trout streams of England. True
English sportsman that he was, he vanished into the hazy
distance at the far end of the Prout Meadow, complete
with hip boots, special rod, wet and dry flies that he had
tied himself, and a handsome creel slung over his back.

After fishing, George and Teeney got back to the
base first and were already frying a mess of small rainbow trout when I arrived with my little willow rod and
one small fish. Al got back last, puzzled and disappointed. He flung down the creel in disgust. It was completely empty.

Amidst much laughter over a delicious meal of panfried trout, Al's spirits were restored and we convinced
him that the size and number of the Prout creek fish
were unrepresentative of the bounty of British Columbia's
rivers and lakes and that his skill was undoubted.

Teeney's two months on the ranch finally came to
an end. He evacuated twenty-two frogs from Frog
Ranch, and rode Paint bareback for the last time. The
day before he left we had a lunch of wieners roasted in
the fireplace and for dinner, stuffed grouse which he had
shot and plucked and I had cleaned. Mushroom sauce
and strawberry pie topped off the menu.

Teeney said goodbye to Al. We took photos of the
three of us outside the ranch house and then set off for
Prince George in the truck. A tire blew out in the middle of Prince George, fortunately just in front of a
garage. We were able to get the wheel changed and
made the airport in time.

The goodbyes were sad ones. Gone would be the
Pop Eye faces which George had made during the breaks

in haying, leaning up against the sweet-smelling bales of hay, his old cowboy hat shading his eyes. Moose rarely would wear George's hat. I would miss mushrooming, the long talks, and the fun we all had together. There would be other summers, but none could be quite like this one, the summer I had acquired a stepson.

FIFTEEN
Nature's Messages

After Teeney had left and Al and Dave were unable to come so often I was the only regular helper George had. Most of the hay was in, however, and what was left he managed single-handed with his good machinery. As he was finishing up, the dogs and I spent at least part of each day in the meadows.

On the last haying visit to the Prout Meadow I took my little willow fishing rod to drop a grasshopper over the tall slew grass where Teeney, Al, George, and I, had so often fished. I walked through the coarse grass still left standing near the tiny creek. The grasshoppers swarmed several on a stem, consuming the juiciest parts of the blades. Like the sound of a wind rustling through trees, they moved only when I was right on top of them, and then only a few inches, as if they knew they were too numerous to be challenged.

I dropped my line with its grasshopper bait into the narrow creek covered over with slew grass. The tang of peppermint crushed underfoot transported me back to happy childhood days by quiet English streams, and a tiny plop told me that a fish was there and interested in the struggling grasshopper. It must have been a very small one, for it nibbled frequently and not so much as a leg of the grasshopper was missing when I finally gave up. Light mist had formed over the meadow and darkness was beginning to fall as we drove the three miles home to call it a day.

George's feet had taken a beating during the summer as the one pair of tennis shoes he allowed himself each year had fallen apart. As soon as we were in the cabin, George set out an enamel bowl preparing to repair the damage to his feet and went to the cupboard to get a clean pair of socks. Seeing the prepared bowl—thinking to relieve his aching feet, and having nothing else I could think of to put in the water—I emptied a goodly measure of bleach into the bowl before he returned.

The usually voluble George became unusually quiet and serious after his feet had been in the bowl for a few minutes.

"Have you got a little brush, Wangs?" he asked quite casually, breaking the silence.

I offered him the only nail brush we had between us, one which had been round the world with me, but he declined it.

"No, something which can be put aside afterwards—thrown away—maybe a little cloth or something."

I found something suitable, and he gave silent and serious attention to his feet, getting his hands as little as possible into the water. I knew he disliked the feel of lather on his hands, but he seemed to be carrying this aversion too far to be practical.

"Have you a towel—a little towel which can be discarded afterwards?" he asked with unaccustomed quietness.

I gave him one and he wiped his feet gingerly.

"Not badly shaped feet," he observed—rather aggressively I thought. "They seem to be all in one piece and the toes look as if they belong." He stood up, and gazed down on them holding the bowl containing a cake of carbolic soap and the wash cloth well away from him. Where shall I put it?" he asked, looking helpless. "I mean the bowl—well, we use it for our faces, and it should be disinfected and the rag thrown out."

"I'll do all that, but we won't throw the soap out," I suggested. "Do you think the bleach helped any?"

"Bleach!" he exclaimed with relief in his voice. "So that's what it was! I thought I had some awful disease. My feet have been far dirtier but never smelled quite like that before. I wondered how I could have picked up anything that smelled that way just haying on the Little Creek. It seemed as dreadful as if I'd just come in from walking barefoot in the streets of Calcutta." He gave a reassured little sigh, and I could see that his usual volubility was returning fast.

With haying over for the year, there was still time to "one-way" a part of the meadow which had been cleared out by a government bulldozer a couple of years before, but which had become overgrown again with young willows.

We borrowed a huge one-way disk from our neighbors, the Wiebes. Then, when every day was becoming more critical time-wise as the season advanced, the loss of a pin from the "one-way" completely immobilized the five shiny, cymbal-like disks in the half-finished meadow.

George asked me to help with the task of detaching the part which needed welding, preparatory to the undercover operation of getting it past the Wiebes, en route to Vanderhoof to get it fixed. Nobody likes having machinery they have lent being damaged, and we were sure the Wiebes would react that way.

George had gone on ahead to the meadow, and I followed a little later. I had forgotten about our new bull in his enclosed part of the meadow which I had to pass through to reach the one-way disk. He was a young bull with "papers," the first registered animal, except The Ghost, that George had ever had. To get him we had swapped our former bull, a large and beautiful cow who had lost her calves three years running, and two underprivileged cows. George called the new bull Mulligan.

When I first noticed Mulligan on my way to the far end of the meadow, he was gazing disdainfully at the only other occupant of the enclosure, a heifer, the last of the herd expected to calve. As I entered his territory, he turned towards me with a disinterested look on his face if to say, "Is she all you've given me?" He was evidently waiting for an answer, for he got up and in a most determined manner advanced steadily in my direction, obviously to investigate further.

Hereford bulls are generally gentle, but I suddenly became aware that I was wearing a pair of very bright red mitts, and although I was skeptical about the old tales of bulls enraged when they see red, I quickly whipped off my mitts and stuffed them in my pocket. Almost immediately, Mulligan turned and walked off in another direction.

I was to have a double role when I reached the far end of the meadow where the action was taking place. I was a captive audience for the colorful language shouted to the winds, and a stabilizer for the heavy wheel at the end of the "one-way." As it was being detached, I had to hang on to it to prevent it from rolling off suddenly at some unlikely tangent.

A missing pin, the size of a stubby lead pencil, had caused the trouble. With my childhood experience with Meccano building sets, and George's expertise, we detached the 500-pound part, trying to remember how each piece was attached. Then, under cover of a tarpaulin, we secretly smuggled it into town, had it welded, and smuggled it back again. The next morning we put it all together. We smeared some dirt and oil on the welding to disguise its newness and soon finished disking the field.

🌲   🌲   🌲

While driving the Anglican Mission Van in Burns Lake, I had written to the Registrar of the Education

Office in Victoria about the question of putting my teaching credentials in order. I wanted to be prepared for no holdup if I decided to stay in British Columbia to teach after the driving job had ended.

At that time I had written to the Registrar, "I am not anxious to spend a winter where it is too cold or too isolated and I would prefer to be in charge of a small school with a teacherage." Given my current situation, this statement about the cold and isolation seemed humorous indeed.

During the summer we had heard that the position of the one and only teacher for the school four miles from the ranch on the Braeside Road had become vacant. The one-room school served the little community of Mennonites who were our nearest neighbors.

We could not believe our good fortune when, soon after I had applied, we heard that the job was mine. It was difficult for us to realize that we would now have a small, but regular income with which to pay a few bills as we went along, instead of once a year when the calves were sold. Perhaps we would even be able to abandon the barter system of payment forever, as we were coming to the end of things we could barter.

I thought about the negative feelings concerning the cold and isolation expressed in that letter I had written before I met George, and before I had spent a winter in British Columbia. How those feelings had changed since then!

The cold and isolation had been a predominant part of the warp on which the stuff of this part of my life had been woven. Those elements of the environment and the lack of money brought out the best in me; they had sharpened my senses of beauty and danger, had successfully challenged my creativity and resourcefulness, had further developed my initiative, and had considerably heightened my sense of humor.

Would the extra income change the simple way of life we loved, with its intimate personal joys and its growing knowledge, understanding, and love of the wilderness? Would the gain produce any accompanying loss?

Even before I knew about the new job, I had begun to look questioningly at us and our present value system. Now additional thoughts came crowding in. We already realized that we needed to see more materially productive results for such a great expenditure of our energy. Was the present growth phase of our life here coming to an end because we were gradually being freed in our thinking to choose some other kind of life? If so, was this new job a step in that direction? All of these questions needed to be asked at this point.

I was ready to go back to the teaching I had forsaken for the fantasy of becoming someone's executive secretary. Apart from the salary, I was anticipating with pleasure expanding my horizons to include the children of this little community. Would this be a step towards the beckoning world beyond?

The prospect of my new commitment increased the tempo of life around the ranch. There were going to be things I could no longer do around the place now that I would be at school during the day. Suddenly I found some loose ends in our daily living which needed tying together before my job started.

I picked a few late peas in the garden and sat against the picket fence to shell them. A gentle rustling invaded the deep quiet of the afternoon. A squirrel, immobile, sat transfixed as though he was a mechanical toy which had just stopped because it needed winding up. Reactivated by the plop-plop of the peas in the pan he ran back into the weeds on the fringe of the garden, picked up something, and rolling it around in his paws, proceeded to eat it. When he had finished eating, he ran back into the weeds returning to the same place a few yards from me. The sun glinted rosily on his meal; he was feasting on late wild strawberries.

It struck me as I finished shelling the few peas and went back into the garden to look for something to add for a meal, that, like the squirrel, we also lived well from the natural wilderness garden. Our own feeble efforts to make a garden had been outdone by Nature's garden. While our garden had reverted rapidly to its natural state over the summer, nature had provided us with free bountiful meals; pigweed and nettles, far tastier then spinach, crisp dandelion leaves for salads, wild stawberries, saskatoons, and mushrooms. And from her great bounty to go with these, rainbow trout, grouse, and moose.

Ever since we had planted the garden in the spring, I had looked forward to the time when we would fill the root cellar with a variety of vegetables for the winter. George had made the cellar at the time the house was built. It was only ten feet square and six feet high, lined with planks, insulated with sawdust, and supported by eight-inch timbers, with a wooden floor and wooden bins for the vegetables. Now the only big roots in the garden were dandelion roots; they were bigger than the biggest carrot. There would be no man-grown roots in the root cellar that winter.

I examined the row of broad beans for whose ripening I had been patiently waiting. Because they were my favorite bean, I had wanted George to enjoy them, as he had never eaten that kind of bean. There were only five pods in the whole row, with exactly ten beans in all five pods. I threw the beans in with the peas and for good measure, nipped out the tops of the plant and threw them in too. Pulling some midget carrots for the pigs, I set off to feed them before bottling a bucket of saskatoon berries I had picked that morning.

On my way to feed the pigs, I stopped at the root cellar. I was sad at its emptiness. When I opened the door I was confronted with no less a personage than the keeper of the door—a toad with jewelled eyes. He was fat, with a distinct air of authority, and I felt he was going to ask me for my credentials if I advanced further. Having none whatsoever, nor claiming to have grown any root worthy of the name, I closed the door softly and withdrew from Toad Hall.

Passing the barn, I heard loud imprecations coming from the inside and ran over to see what was happening. George was thrashing around trying to roll an enormous compressed tangle of baling wire through the small opening of a stall. The discarded wire from the bales of hay he had fed out to the cattle during the winter months had accumulated into this formless mass. Perspiration was pouring from his face, and he was transfixed in the middle of the tangled mass of wire that was as high and as broad as he was tall.

My help was needed. From the rear I guided the mass out through the narrow opening, while George pushed it through. Soon it was snowballed out through the main barn door and into the jeep trailer, later to be discarded in the woods.

"Let's feed these carrots to the pigs," I suggested, the task completed.

As the pigs had grown older, their noses, formerly straight Roman, had started to turn upwards and they already had the look of aged sows I had previously known.

We fed them the dwarf carrots and listened to their contented crunching. George became more calm as he watched them eat. However, the fighting spirit aroused by the battle with the wire remained as he vigorously scratched their bristly backs, and rather aggressively, I thought, announced, "As far as I am concerned they're straight pork."

In the middle of August the hens suddenly stopped laying. For three days there wasn't an egg in the nesting boxes. Thinking that the pack rats again were the culprits, we set traps and caught three rats.

During the next week, however, the hens produced only two eggs and then there were none. But I was ready for such a contingency. While they were still laying well, I had read in the *Prairie Free Press* that if eggs were rubbed with mineral oil they would keep fresh for several weeks. Secretly, I had treated two dozen eggs in this way, dated them, and hidden them in the corner of a large tin-lined teak trunk which had accompanied me from Australia.

When we were without eggs to collect, I produced triumphantly a couple of boiled eggs for breakfast.

"Have you looked at the date on your egg?" I asked proudly as George took the first mouthful.

"No, but I've tasted it," he sputtered, pushing plate and eggcup to one side. He shoved it in my direction. "Just smell it!"

There was no doubt about it. The egg was bad. Not only was I not to be congratulated on my resourcefulness; I was obviously guilty, for with a note of censure in his voice, George continued, "Did you process the eggs?" seeming to imply that if anyone else had done it they would be all right.

George usually seemed uncomfortable when I tackled something I had never done before; he seemed to think I would fail and was suspicious of my experimenting. But I got excited when I experimented, and I felt an experimenter should be allowed to fail. Yet it seemed I was not supposed to fail. So I asked myself: Had I been trying too hard? Was it worth it trying to economize?

It was just too bad about the egg, I decided, after debating with myself. Undoubtedly, it was not a good beginning for a day, but the incident itself was humorous. However, the feeling of futility irked me when I had tried to do the right thing and it didn't come off, causing my over-reacting husband an unnecessary anxiety which was communicated to me. I guessed the problem was finding the right things to do and not just trying to do things right.

Trying to forget the egg episode, I went outside just after breakfast, comforted by the thought that soon, with our new income, I would be able to buy extra eggs when we needed them. I walked quietly along the edge of the creek. A muskrat joined me to take his after breakfast constitutional; his nose showed just above the water and his tail trailed wavily behind. Stern first, he drew into the opposite side of the creek and surveyed the bank where I was standing a few yards away from him, rather in the manner of an early morning stroller in a city park, sitting for a moment on a bench before continuing his outing.

He started swimming slowly towards me and must have suddenly spotted me, for he ducked under with an exceptionally noisy splash for so small a creature. Then with lightning speed he sought a haven in the shallow water.

Stomaching his way along the creek in a frenzy of movement he looked for cover just below me. When he found none, he streaked off under the water for several yards. He swam downstream, leaving a rippled surface which showed his rapid progress towards the old beaver dam, then rounding the corner rapidly, he vanished out of sight.

A few days later I spotted two hens walking leisurely from the corner enclosure in the barn where George had struggled a few days before with the mass of baling wire. Their mien gave the impression that they had been somewhere important.

Recalling my childhood nest-sleuthing days I looked around in the barn and found a nest with ten eggs in it; they were dirty and covered with broken egg. I collected them all except one which I left so that the hen would continue to lay there and not lay her eggs in some other place where I might not find them. I marked the egg and left.

After washing them I decided to make a cheese soufflé with my lucky find. I cracked an egg on the side of a cup. It exploded in my face with a smell like a stink bomb, the shell shooting in all directions, spattering my face, and sticking to the clean utensils set out to make the soufflé.

The rest of the eggs were good. The bad one must have been an egg laid several years ago by one of George's former hens, and the old, ready-made nest had been moved into by our errant hens. I decided that as far as eggs were concerned I'd had it, at least for the time being. I had more important matters to think about.

Before long, I would be navigating my way to school each day along a narrow, winding, dirt road. Always bad, it was now abnormally so after the late rains, only passable with a tractor or bulldozer. Its state was more like spring break-up than late summer.

For some weeks we had had to park the jeep and truck on the town side of the potholes we called the Deadly Duo and the Terrible Trio. Teeney had given these names to the two-feet-deep twin potholes. They were the last of a long necklace of holes of assorted sizes and shapes which adorned our road. Supplies picked up in town had to be carried from the jeep parked a mile from the ranch. The deteriorated state of the road had prevented George from custom-baling hay for other people during the summer. Now the bed of our new truck had shaken loose, and it had to be welded.

It would not be long before we would be selling some cattle before winter feeding began. The cattle trucks would have to travel the road so that the cattle could be loaded from the chute and then driven away.

George had already written several times during the summer requesting the public works people to grade the road, but nothing had been done. Until the kind winter snows came and gently filled the ruts, it looked as if we would have to continue to walk the mile to and from the house.

Thus life continued in our faraway wilderness valley. As ever, it revolved around the solving of primitive problems; eating, keeping warm, attending to the needs of the animals, and transportation. But somehow or other, overcoming these daily obstacles and achieving even minor goals brought their own exhilarating rewards, giving a clear sense of meaning to the simple cadences of our life.

And always there was the pleasant unexpected event to break the steady rhythm. George's uncle, Lytle Hull, who had learned from me at the elegant dinner party at his estate at Staatsburg-on-the-Hudson that we had no water in the house, sent us a check to pay for piping the water from the creek into the kitchen and to install a hot water system.

George had arranged immediately with one of our Mennonite neighbors who had a bulldozer, to dig a trench below the frost line to take the pipe from the creek up to the cabin. The trench was six feet deep and enormously wide, the width of the bulldozer blade, so that the thin copper pipe, lying at the bottom of the trench, looked like a small snake on the floor of the Grand Canyon.

With enthusiasm and minute technical detail, George wrote to Teeney, telling him about the water project:

> The water system is quite simple and a terrific help to Eve in the kitchen, where the battle of the dishes goes on all too regularly. We installed a motor, pump, and main storage tank in the cellar with a pressure gauge attached. In the kitchen we put in a hot-water storage tank with a two-way pipe system connected to a hot-water jacket in the fire box.

The pump draws water from the creek and
stores it in the main storage tank.

The description proceeded for several pages, but
what it did not tell Teeney was the news about the
change the water had brought in George's fortunes. As
soon as it was installed, he had devised a way to water
the cattle by making a wooden conduit leading from the
kitchen window to a wooden trough in the garden plot.

He had then attached a hose to the kitchen faucet so
that the water flowed down into the trough. The cattle
then had a supplementary watering hole that would not
have to be chopped open with an axe through ice a foot
deep after every cold winter night. The water therefore
was not only a boon to me but also a blessing to George.
George was not averse to roughing it less when the opportunity occurred, although to preserve the image of
ruggedness so important to his son, he did not particularly want Teeney to know that.

The day before school started in early September,
thin ice covered the pigs' water bowl and large flocks of
bedraggled robins, no longer in the fine condition they
were before nesting, gathered in the Home Meadow.

The days had become noticeably shorter. There was
no new growth on the range and pasture, but there was
still adequate feed on the open range for the cattle, although the tenderest tops had been nipped off. Here and
there a leaf brilliant with the colors of fall, stood out
among the tired green foliage of full summer.

The air space between the ranch house and the barn
had become an arena for a conclave of hawks; the tips of
the tallest pines silhouetted against the sky, became both
grandstands and starting-off marks for the participants of
a hawk relay race.

To the wild music of a dozen hawks, bird after bird
sailed down from his treetop deep into the arena and
soared up over the housetop. As pursuer became pursued,

Chickens

notes of alarm punctuated the musical theme before the activity gradually tailed off as if certain birds were counted out of the game until only one solitary hawk remained and flew away alone.

It might have been this hawk, who, after the game was over, spotted the hens near the pigpen, for out of a deceptively kind blue sky later on in the afternoon, a hawk swooped down on the quietly feeding group of hens.

With sudden cries of fear and a desperate flutter of wings, the hens tried to make any place a haven of refuge from the attack of the hawk hurtling down to within a yard of them. I shouted and clapped my hands and successfully warded off the hawk's attack. Its body was as big as the hens' with a wingspan twice as wide.

Only great hunger could have forced it down to within a few yards of a human being.

The season was on the turn. Nature's messages continued unmistakably. As I returned to the house the only snake I had seen all summer was basking in the sunshine on the bridge as if enjoying the last of the warm days. It slithered off under the bridge at my approach, zigzagging through the grass until it disappeared.

Change was forthcoming also in our lives. The next day, we too, would begin a new routine.

SIXTEEN

One-Room School

The first day of the school year was still and misty, redolent of early fall. I walked to the Deadly Duo, our twin potholes, to pick up the truck parked beyond them. The early morning mist had breathed tiny sparkling diamonds onto the innumerable spiders' webs strung between the trees and bushes on either side of the road. What masterpieces of construction they were—little hammocks and Taj Mahal domes, each with its yellowy-green architect waiting motionless to trap the unwary insect.

Ahead, a grouse rose and flew into the bush; two flickers flashed white rumps as they curved away in scallops of flight. In a dip veiled in mist, a shadowy, dark form larger than a wolf loomed up. Unmistakably a black bear, it turned away into the bush.

On reaching the truck I drove the remaining three miles to the small Braeside School, and past the turnoff where Abe and Jake Wiebe lived. In a couple of days I would be stopping there to pick up Abe's son, Gilbert, who would be starting school for the first time. The family spoke German at home. The little fellow knew no English and was very shy; I knew no German. He would comprise the entire first grade in the one-room school. I wondered how we would both get along with *Dick and Jane*, the primary reader set in a typical suburban environment quite unfamiliar to Gilbert and so different from the life he knew.

The rest of the twenty Braeside school children were distributed unevenly in the other grades through eight.

The Derksen family lived nearest the school. Jimmy, one of the older boys, was the school janitor. His job was to keep the school clean, to provide us with drinking water drawn in buckets from Trankle Creek, and in the winter to light the woodburning stove for the school day before taking on his other role, that of student. The powers-that-be provided some kind of chemical tablets to be added to the drinking water. This seemed incredible to me. What water could be purer than the spring waters of Trankle Creek!

The Braeside Cooperative Farm Association was made up of five farm families whose children attended the school. The Co-op had been organized in Altona, Manitoba, in 1951; the families had come from the Rhineland Municipality. They had bought nine quarter-sections of land near the Nechako River, some from the government and some from individuals. They had cleared most of the land before building houses for their families. They grew barley and winter wheat and had their own sawmill. They owned a few Hereford and dairy cattle and some sheep and pigs. Money earned was distributed equally among members after debts and expenses had been met.

They were Mennonites, a Protestant sect originating in Switzerland in the sixteenth century, which bases its beliefs on the teachings of the New Testament, especially the Sermon on the Mount. They are loyal to civil government but will not bear arms or take oaths. They generously support foreign missions. They get their name from Menno Simons, a leader in the movement. One of the boys at Braeside, the son of George Voth, was named Menno. It surprised me that even in one small community there were different branches of their church. They lived simply, the women dressed plainly, and the families helped each other in every way. They were also good neighbors to us. Other Mennonite families of Wiebes and a recently-settled family who were not Mennonites made up the Braeside School family.

When I got out of the truck at school it seemed unusual that no children were around, and the school building was higher than it was the last time I had seen it! I gazed up at the elevated building in astonishment and read a large notice pinned on the front: "Anyone entering this building does so at his own risk" it challenged. What an inhospitable welcome, I thought, and what an unnecessary sign. A first-class burglar with a stepladder couldn't get into the darn place if he tried. There were no steps, and the bottom of the door was higher than my head. The school building had been jacked up on cinder blocks, and there were signs of a permanent foundation having been started under the building.

The one-room frame building with its small windows had previously been on wooden skids the length of the building. Small frame buildings on skids could be easily moved from worksite to worksite where they were needed. The school had maintained a low profile until now as if at a moment's notice it was ready to shoot off to some other isolated clearing in the wilderness. But there was beginning to be a distinct air of permanence about it now that it was jacked up on blocks.

I craned my neck to read the fine print on the notice. It said that school would start in several days when the work was finished. Obviously all the children had known what was going on, as children usually do, and they were probably off playing somewhere. But the Deadly Duo had effectively cut off such news from reaching the new teacher.

The school faced the road and stood in a small unfenced clearing in jack pine and spruce with a play-space at the back that was a series of muddy potholes. The tiny, frame outhouses a few yards from the school building, one for boys and one for girls, stood askew, victims of the heaving ground after the frost had left it at spring break-up. Dead moths' wings in neat pairs covered the seat of the girls' outhouse; a mouse must have used it as a table for his late summer feasting.

Two days later on the way to school, the truck, even with chains, got stuck on the hill beyond the Deadly Duo. Abe Wiebe, waiting for me with Gilbert at the turn to his road, had heard me racing the motor and had come down the hill with his "cat," hooked on to the truck, and pulled me up the rest of the hill to where Gilbert waited dejectedly in his father's truck. He was red-eyed and clutched a bright blue exercise book, a pencil, and a new packet of wax crayons.

I opened the door of their truck and said as sweetly as I could, "My, those are nice things you've got there, Gilbert. Come along with me in my truck."

He edged away to the end of the seat and started to cry. Father Abe arrived, and speaking in German, conducted his son to the seat beside me in my truck. He was too small to see out, and he just gazed silently and steadfastly into my face, wet-eyed, all the way to school.

He recovered somewhat when he saw the other children. The get-acquainted day proceeded, and Gilbert had his own special place close to my desk. It was soon evident that in a unique way he was becoming the school's mascot. He moved around from desk to desk, watching the other children work at their different levels.

By the end of the first week we had found out that Gilbert liked throwing things both in and out of school. He showed particular interest in long, narrow objects that he could handle to hit other things with. Indoors, the board ruler came in handy. Outside, any stick that could be found, sufficed, supplemented by a ragged mat which he threw repeatedly with gusto into the biggest, muddiest puddles, especially when someone was near.

Clearly, his large motor development was proceeding well. When he got the chance he worked on his fine-motor development by performing enormous scribbles on the blackboard. Then he would turn to me, chalk in hand, with an almost imperceptible sly smile as if to say, "Look what I can do."

Evidently the subjects I was teaching didn't interest Gilbert, because at the end of the first week he sneaked out of school complete with cap, which he donned on the way out. Unnoticed by anyone, he herded stray cattle off the school playground until one of the children happened to spot him through the window. He returned to the schoolroom with a look of accomplishment on his face, and from that time on I felt Gilbert had arrived; it seemed he thought of the school as his own territory.

Abe called for us both with his tractor after school on the day of Gilbert's cow escapade. On the way back, Gilbert sat in front of his father and steered the tractor; I sat on the mudguard with my skirts up to my thighs. It had rained and the day was overcast, sad and dripping, with the smell of decaying vegetation.

"He has a different face going home," Abe observed by way of conversation as Gilbert interrupted in German. "He said he drove the cattle off the school playground today because everyone else was too lazy to do it, and he says that he likes school now."

Like a ship on a rough sea, we rolled homeward. If the day outside was melancholy, inside, my spirits soared —Gilbert liked school.

As the weeks passed, pupils and teacher learned from and taught each other when the same idea could be presented more simply to the younger children either by the older children or by me. There was no destructive competition among them. All the children were involved in the life of the school; each helped the other. Creativity, individual initiative, and independence flourished as pupils proceeded at their own pace.

Firsthand empirical observation of the physical world around them was possible at our school backdoor. The children wrote simply in their school books: "The spruce has shorter needles than the pine. They are about one inch long. They don't grow much on gravel. The branch of a spruce usually slopes down. The needles are four-sided." and "The moose weighs 1400 to 1800 pounds and stands about six feet high. On its neck it has a beard."

The children looked at their surroundings critically and wrote: "Can you imagine our land without trees?"; "Erosion is a destroyer"; "What would we do without our soil?"; or, as a younger pupil put it, "Dirt is important. We walk on it. What would we do without it?"

With careful planning, past experience, the professional thought-provoking written word, and thinking fast on my feet, life at school became a joy. I could tell how the children felt about their school by the way they ran in eagerly in the morning and hung up their coats impregnated with fragrant pine smoke.

Over the weeks, Gilbert and I formed an amicable nonverbal relationship. We rode and walked together on our way to and from school, discovering exciting things; rocks, insects, animals, and flowers. When one of us saw something particularly interesting that we thought the other one hadn't seen, we pointed to it. I would call it by its name; Gilbert just pointed. The next time we came to the place where we had seen the exciting thing, even if it were no longer there, Gilbert would point and smile, but still not say a word.

Towards the end of September I went to town in the truck after school to pick up some things that George had left on top of his mother's cupboard five days before and had forgotten to bring home. I loaded them up: a box of china, some fish which were definitely not freshly caught, a pound of butter, the mail and the *Nechako Chronicle.*

George and Eve

Eve and friends in front of an
old cabin on the Telegraph Trail

Indian children in front
of the Mission van

The van, stranded!
Start of a six mile hike

Feeding hay to the snow covered cattle

George, Moose and The Ghost

Entrance to Little Creek Ranch

Hughie Goldie's old cabin where George first lived

Opening the water hole at thirty below

George and Paint   Welcome back

Milking, with a sprained ankle

A cool drink
of Bossy's milk

Bossy

A break from haying—Al, Johnny and George

Al Moser

Teeney, "Look what I caught!"

George, David and Teeney
"Look what I caught!"—
two years later

A moment in the shade

Summer's over—goodbye to Johnny and Teeney

Moose guards the cabin chinked with oakum

Bogged down!

A ride to school

Menno Voth drives the school bus

Some of the Braeside children

The teacherage

Drilling the well at the school

George's aqueduct to water the cattle

Big ditch—little water pipe

Long johns—
stiff as a board

Back from England with
lantern—welcome from
Moose and Wampus

Eve at the cooler—Teeney's Frog Ranch

George and Bumpy

Ronnie Mork
A Real Cowboy

Farewell to the North Country

I drove back in the dark, and even with the wiper working at top speed the windshield became more and more smeared and muddier and muddier until I could no longer see through it. I got out to wipe it off several times before I could proceed; I still couldn't see well and didn't understand why the headlights seemed so dim when we had recently bought a new battery. My head and shoulders ached with peering through the windshield, and I only knew where the bad holes were when I hit them.

Just before reaching the Deadly Duo the truck bogged down completely, unable to move either forward or backward. I got out, slipped into my rubber boots, flung the aged fish into the bush, put the groceries and dog bones into the cab so that the bears would not eat them, and closed the cab windows. Before turning off the switch, I examined the headlights. They were completely plastered with mud. No wonder I couldn't see! It had never occurred to me that so much mud could have spattered onto the front of the truck.

I took the flashlight, bag, and lunch kit, put a couple of candy bars into my pocket for George, and set out to walk the mile to the ranch. The night was cold and dark. Something brushed within inches of my face. It must have been an owl. Moose barked before I got to the ranch gate. I felt increasingly angry about the condition of the roads. George must get some action from the Public Works Department and quickly. But the day hadn't been all bad. Gilbert had said "cow" his first English word, and Wampus had had pups in her kennel.

In October, George wrote again to the Public Works Department:

> This is the third letter that I have sent you regarding the condition of our road and in spite of what amounts to an emergency nothing has been done.

A short time back a body repair job on our 1951 International truck was necessary after the box fell off going over some ruts two feet deep. This meant a complete welding job on both the box and cab, putting us to considerable expense.

I have at present over seventy head of cattle. The other day I made a deal for the sale of thirty calves thinking that you would certainly have our road fixed in time for the buyer to get here and haul them out.

Last night the buyer got as far as the corner where our road meets the Braeside Road. He inspected it for a few hundred yards, then went over to our nearest neighbors and left a message for me that the deal was off because he couldn't get through with the truck to the ranch and had to get back to Ootsa.

Several hundred dollars was lost on that deal alone as he had agreed on a high price, wanting them for future breeding purposes. Cattle buyers cannot get to us and we cannot even truck our cattle to market. The condition of the road is affecting every phase of our living.

It is necessary for us to use a tractor and jeep to get my wife to school to teach each day. Even then we have to park both vehicles a mile away from the house and walk to them in the morning and then one mile back to the house when school is over.

I have to carry our supplies on my back and slip and slide a mile to the ranch. I can't haul in the winter's supply of wood . . . our ranching and teaching operations are about to be wiped off the map.

Continuous hard frosts would have helped the road situation, but still more rain continued to fall, and only occasional flurries of snow darkened the sky then melted away again, leaving the road safely navigable only by tractor. One day in early November, after school, as Gilbert and I were watching for Abe's arrival, I saw him pulling around in front of the school dragging something at the back of the tractor. It was a wooden box on runners about four by six feet with an apple box in it turned upside down and covered with a sheepskin.

"Is that for me to ride in?" I queried, staring at it in astonishment.

"Yes, I thought you'd be more comfortable in this than sitting on the tractor," Abe replied, smiling. He was obviously proud of his creation. Suddenly, I felt like hugging him. I sat proudly on my sheepskin, still trying to look like a dignified schoolmarm as we drew away from the little knot of children who had not yet gone home and who were not quite sure what expression to register on their unbelieving faces.

The little box slid smoothly over the homeward road, tipping skittishly sideways only when we hit the biggest ruts. Great gobs of mud flew up from the wheels of the tractor and whizzed past, missing me by inches. A new dimension had been added to my life at school. Sometimes Gilbert joined me on my sheepskin when he got tired of riding on the tractor, thus creating another bond beween us.

Back at the ranch the time had come for us to part with the pigs, which George had succeeded in thinking of as "straight pork." A friend helped George in Operation Pork, and I added a new pig experience to my repertoire, not one I welcomed. Only the extreme practicality of the whole operation, promising to help solve some of our economic problems, enabled me to tackle the tasks in a motivated, organized way.

Friends had initiated me into the mysteries of coping with butchered pigs. They were versed in such skills as making headcheese, sausage meat, and lard, and curing bacon and hams. It seemed phony to me when George and I rubbed canned synthetic smoke mixed with salt into the appropriate parts of the pig in the stages of converting them into smoked bacon and hams. I thought nostalgically of the natural fragrant willow smoke houses of the Indians at Moricetown.

Soon everything was in hand, hanging in the right places or filling the appropriate vessels. As far as I could see, the only residents of the Little Creek to profit totally from Operation Pork by enjoying it to the fullest, were the Crumb Boys, who feasted royally for days on the abundant meat scraps.

At last, in the second week of November, the Public Works grader came out and graded the road. George immediately went into town to arrange for the sale of the calves, which were successfully transported out on an early morning hard frost.

Bossy was now dry. In order to provide us with a milk supply for the winter, George started to milk a tame black cow that had been running with the Herefords and whose calf had just been sold. The cattle were still eating grass in the far meadow when the heavy snows finally came. From then on, they were fed hay either at the home place or at the Prout Meadow, where the bales had been stacked.

November snow filled in the remaining ruts in the road and the snow plow scraped it clean. But the snow banks narrowed the roads, bringing new problems as the land slept on. In December, just after the snow plow had been out, snow fell at night. With its new layer of four inches the road appeared superficially to be less slippery than when it had just been scraped; Gilbert and I sped along to school in the jeep too confidently and too fast, sliding gracefully into a snow bank where we stopped suddenly, tilted at an angle of forty-five degrees. Gilbert and I clambered out and walked the remaining two miles.

The jeep was still in the same position when we returned from school. No one had come that way since we had left it, except a snowshoe rabbit. The day had warmed up considerably. I stripped off my heavy coat and threw it into the abandoned jeep, and we walked on. With the increasing temperature, great gobs of snow fell noiselessly from the spruce trees to the ground, disturbing the lower branches as a stray wind might do or a squirrel leaping from limb to limb, leaving the snow under the trees pock-marked. When we reached the turn-off to Gilbert's house, he strode out like the little man he was.

"You'll be hungry for supper tonight" I said, as he took the lunch pail I had been carrying for him. Without a backward look he plodded doggedly down his road.

As I neared the top of the ranch hill I heard the sound of an engine racing. Moose and Wampus bounded up. "George coming to look for me?" I asked the dogs as I patted Moose on the head. "I bet he's stuck in a snow bank, too." George saw me as I walked down the hill and waved. I was right. The truck was stuck and he was busy with his shovel. Grinning broadly, he walked a few yards to meet me as I approached.

"Where're you stuck?" he questioned abruptly.

"In the dip; before the hill near the turn."

"Will she come out with the shovel?" he asked, putting his arm around me.

"I think so, but you'll need chains. The snow's even worse farther on, with deep ruts in places."

As George weighed this news, I suggested, "Why don't you wait until tomorrow morning? She's off the road and not in the way."

George returned to the problem at hand and proceeded to lay down chains at the back of the rear wheels for traction in getting out of the snow bank. I could see

by the expression on his face that he was getting very
angry now that his anxiety about me was relieved, and
he was once again focusing on the truck.

"Typical," he announced, "eight years in this goddam swamp. You can't make a move around this place
without getting stuck. I'm even stuck with these things,"
he said disgustedly, getting up and tugging at his pants.

I looked down at his legs. He was wearing a pair of
new jeans which had been given to him as a present.

These are lousy pants—not westerns," he declared.
"They're stiff as a board and too big." He paused,
tossed away his cigarette and got down on all fours.

The crotch of his pants hung six inches below where
it should have been. He writhed under the truck to get
at a particularly stubborn area of snow beneath the
wheels, but the pants kept him from moving his legs
widely enough apart to accomplish his objective. They,
and not the immobilized truck, were rapidly becoming
the cause of his rising anger.

"Made in the East—that's what's wrong with 'em.
You can't work in them. It's like being in a straitjacket."

"They're American made," I reminded him gently,
implying that everything made in his country was necessarily good.

"Not made in the West," he barked.

"Why don't you wear suspenders?" I suggested
mildly. George chose to ignore the question.

"If you don't need me, I'll walk on to the house," I
announced, realizing that at that point I couldn't be
helpful. Besides, I could use a cup of tea.

As I turned to leave, he cautioned, "You'll find the
place a shambles. The icicles finally caught up with us.
The mop broke so I used a bunch of rags and that old
red coat to soak up the water. I chopped the icicles off
the roof so we'll be all right for a while on that score."

The combined frustrations of his day would take a little longer to work off, I surmised, as I set off for the ranch house to continue working off my own frustrations.

George had left off roof gutters when he built the cabin and hadn't as yet added them. As a result, snow would build up and melt on the roof during the day. The mercury would usually plunge far below zero at night, and tremendous icicles would develop in the process, reaching from the roof to the ground. They were picturesque but a great liability, as they too would melt, and in doing so the water would back up, get under the eaves and seep into the house.

The piles of chopped-off roof icicles together with the deep snows that had fallen over the winter accumulated above the rock foundation of the cabin. When spring came and the frozen mound began to melt, more water would seep into the cabin. To overcome the problem, George usually, but not always, carted away the icicles immediately after chopping them off the roof. Otherwise, in the spring, he was faced with chopping away the ice and snow combination on the ground, far more of a chore than just shoveling away a few feet of snow.

When I entered the house, I saw dripping rags of all kinds festooning the walls. A red felt coat, hanging from the big Scottish iron kettle suspended from the mantelpiece, dripped red drops into a widening pool of scarlet on the stone hearth. And the smell! Now I remembered. That was the coat Jiggs had selected for his toilet two years ago, and it had been banished to the closet ever since. I had soaked it in the creek for days, hung it in the sun, and with high hopes had subjected it to all the home treatment possible, but it continued to need isolation. I had never had the courage to take it in person to the cleaners in town or to leave it in secret at the receiving depot.

As if understanding, Jiggs, purring monotonously, brushed my legs with his warm little body. "Why did you have to use that coat as a toilet?" I asked Jiggs as he looked up at me. He purred extra loudly by way of explanation.

George came in later in his long underwear, having dispensed as quickly as possible with the offending Levi's, and joined me in tea for two.

"This is a funny little place," he remarked, as he stretched out cosily in his big chair by the barrel-heater and surveyed his home with evident satisfaction.

🌲 🌲 🌲

Christmas came and friends visited. Neil Wylie, a friend of George's from World War II, lived in Prince George. He and his wife, Anne, spent Christmas Day with us. They had met when George was a World War II paratrooper in the Office of Strategic Services. George had jumped into Yugoslavia to join a group of Englishmen who were working with the partizans opening up airports behind the enemy lines for the purpose of evacuating the wounded. Neil was a Royal Air Force captain attached to the British Balkan Services. Years later, after the war had ended, he came to Canada from England and looked George up at the ranch.

He had spent a previous Christmas at the Little Creek Ranch. George told me that he had cooked one of his geese for that special occasion. He had started it in the morning and basted it at short intervals all day long. In the evening when they ate it, it had shrunk to the size of a small grouse. But Neil, ever the gentleman, had pronounced George's Christmas offering the best, but smallest goose, he ever had eaten.

SEVENTEEN
Baths I Have Been In

The children went to school in all weathers. Below zero temperature was no excuse for absence from school. No heated school bus picked them up; they came on foot, or a parent would bring them in a farm vehicle. Sometimes they came by horse and sleigh.

In the morning they crowded around the cosy slab-hungry, oil-barrel heater. Only when the temperature was thirty degrees below zero did the younger children stay away—and sometimes the older ones. The teacher never stayed away.

One exceptionally cold morning George couldn't get the jeep started for me to go to school, although the heater in the toolshed had been stoked long before breakfast and there was alcohol in the gas line. Even after it had been nosed up against the heater for an hour or more, the gas line to the jeep was still frozen. So with lunch pail, heavy coat, and a woolen scarf I had woven, wrapped around my mouth and nose, I set off to walk the four miles to school at thirty below zero.

By the time I arrived at school, my scarf was frozen solid. No one was there, not even Jimmy Derksen, the boy-janitor, so no fire had been started. It was then I realized that thirty below zero was the temperature when the little Braeside community understandably started to make rules of its own concerning school attendance.

I sat at my desk in the empty, cold schoolroom to eat my lunch before starting back home. I opened the little lard pail in which I always carried my lunch, and as I was thirsty I decided to eat the orange first; it had turned into a frozen-solid orange ball! I scraped up some snow from outside the front door and ate that with my sandwich, and set off to walk back home.

It had warmed up, and the sun was shining brightly. Just before I reached the ranch house gate I heard the welcome sound of the jeep. Evidently George had just got it started and was coming to see how things were with me. I jumped aboard happily and we returned to the ranch.

The next day we were all at school again, but the world outside the school was circumscribed by the locked-in grip of winter.

The day was obviously a "magic carpet" day. We had no films or slides and few books. On these days, in our imagination, we left the narrow confines of the classroom and sailed away on the magic carpet to other parts.

First we visited the Indians on the Stoney Creek reservation. There, we helped Alphonsine pick out tiny, colored-glass beads made in Czechoslovakia for decorating the thick moosehide slippers, gloves and jackets she was making. We rocked her baby slowly in a hammock strung between two walls of the small frame house. An Indian boy leaned against the wall playing softly on a guitar, while we watched a young girl stitch a small birch basket with strands of roots dyed green.

Next, we sped away to Chinlac, forty-five miles east of Vanderhoof and looked down on a pine-covered peninsula and a stream bed—the remains of a 200-year-old Indian village mentioned in Father Maurice's *History of the Northern Interior of British Columbia*. We descended bumpily and joined these early Indians who were preparing for a hunting trip and eating "strong food," little cakes made of dried berries and salmon eggs mixed with water and put on hot stones to dry. They shared some with us.

The next stopping place on our magic-carpet trip was Kitwanga, west of Hazelton. Descending slowly towards the narrow river as the setting sun gilded the tiny white wooden church, the Indian school and humble homes, we came to rest on the village side of a cable ferry. An old Indian with a long pole maneuvered the ferry boat to a grinding halt as we landed. A small family walked off the boat towards the village.

A man with his shirt sleeves rolled up was carrying two buckets of water from the river to the school house. He saw us, set the buckets down, waved, and walked over to us. He was the Anglican priest, the Reverend Hayhurst.

"That water's not too good," he said. "Come and look at the dying fish."

We walked down to the river. The banks were covered with two-feet long salmon with ugly humps behind their heads. They were dying after spawning. Others were carried involuntarily with every movement of the water. The smell of their decomposing bodies filled the still air. How different they were now from the silvery salmon before spawning that the Indians at Moricetown had stood ready to impale with their poised spears.

"Would the children like to see the Cat?" the priest asked. "Come along, we'll take a look at it."

We set off down the village road. Tall, brightly colored totem poles lined the right side of the road, their imagery enhanced by the setting sun's golden glow.

"These totem poles made of soft cedar trees, show the Indians' personal histories and clan customs," said the priest. "They are read from top to bottom," he said, pointing to the creatures carved on them. "Bears, whales, ravens, wolves, and supernatural thunderbirds of enormous power, are all a part of the Indians' natural and supernatural world."

We had come to a large, brightly colored, carved, wooden animal, level with our heads. Its tail was erect and it had a fierce look.

"This is your cat," Mr. Hayhurst said. "But it's really a mountain lion. This is the yard of the late Chief Ak-di-ik. It's supposed to have come into the village at night to steal children. But it was caught at last and here it is," said the priest smiling.

"What does Kitwanga mean and how many Indians are here?" I asked.

"It means, 'people of the place of rabbits.' And there're about 100, I'd say. They are called Gitikshans and have been Christian here for about sixty years. Here, and west of Hazelton, the Indians on the reservations are Protestant and as far as Prince Rupert and up the coast to Ketchikan, Alaska. East of Hazelton, they are Roman Catholic.

"Where should we visit another day?" I asked.

"Kitwancool," he said, "it means 'people of the place of reduced number'. The Indians there are also Gitikshans, but they are intermingled with the Nass River Indians—the Nishgas. They travelled across the country north of Kitwancool by a route known as the Grease Trail. 'Grease' because they carried oolichan oil in cedar boxes. The oolichan is a small fish which 'runs' each spring bringing a welcome change of diet from the smoked salmon of the winter months."

"We have to go now," I said. "The light is fading fast. We will always remember our visit."

"You won't find the totem poles as colorful at Kitwancool, but there's one there that's the oldest in the country," the priest called out as we rose and left behind the white church and Indian school and turned to gaze at the Seven Sisters Range as we vanished into the misty blue. "Next Magic Carpet Day," I promised as we descended into our playground mud puddle, "we'll visit some aborigines I know in Western Australia. We'll go 'walkabout' with them. They'll show us their goanna lizards and maybe they'll roast some witchety grubs for us to eat and show us how to throw a boomerang."

The fantasizing was over. The children had already got out of their seats and were getting drawing materials and writing paper. We looked through the window at the firm blizzard-swept snow. What did they see in their imagination? An Indian, spear poised to transfix a silvery salmon as it swam upstream, or a boomerang as it whirred over the hot, smooth, sand-swept world of the Australian aborigine?

In the world outside the little school, the wind whipped the snow from the pines into inchoate forms or was it blown sand in Australia that swirled away into nothingness as we watched?

🌲   🌲   🌲

In the middle of January, George and I set out to see how the horses were faring. They had been foraging in the Home Meadow all winter, pawing through the snow to get the dry grass; George fed them hay when they came around the buildings.

There were Jack and Paint, our saddle horses, and Carrot, who had been caught in a wolf trap when George was working with his brother on his ranch. George had taken care of her then until she had recovered. Now, she lived with us. There was Bess also, Al's packhorse, that he had asked us to look after for the winter. An old mysterious bay horse had also come out of nowhere and joined our bunch. Earlier in the winter, an old horse we did not know, had died in the meadow and had been left to the dogs and wolves. Severe winters were very hard on old horses, and sometimes one failed to make it through.

As we left for the meadow the squirrels in the spruce tree by the cabin signified by no change of movement

that they realized we had passed beneath their home
tree. I bent my head backwards to sight the top of their
forty-foot spruce. At the very top, a squirrel bent over
the delicate tip, gathered it in its paws and nibbled busily. The dogs ran on ahead as we paused. The snow
had built up so high that we had to bend down to get
under the little picket gate to escape the horsehoe nailed
there from jabbing us.

The curly head of a white-faced calf lay on the
ground—a gift to the dogs from the Vanderhoof butcher.
One little horn was missing, and the face was eaten
away. A chickadee flew up from it and came down
again a few yards away. Moose wagged his tail and lay
down beside the skull, looking up at us with an air of
proud possession; he was not hungry, and after claiming
his stake, he and Wampus followed us along the trail and
across the bridge. Bossy and Black Cow looked up from
their hay as we passed through the barnyard. It was
easy walking there. The snow had been trodden down.

The snow was deep along the wagon trail to the big
meadow; forest was on both sides, and we broke trail in
long strides. I followed George, sometimes finding it
difficult to keep my balance. A squirrel had recently
been taking an airing and had left its footprints—a
dainty trail of inverted commas on their side crossing our
path and leading from one towering spruce tree to
another.

We paused at the gate to the meadow and looked
around us. Behind a screen of willows at the far end of
the meadow, the sun was sinking in a backdrop of gold.
A black hump several hundred yards off showed us where
the dead horse was. As we drew nearer, a cloud of
crows arose from the carcass and flew heavily in different
directions, cawing mournfully. Horse trails criss-crossed
the sparkling-white expanse of snow, and a narrow band
of mist rested on the far boundary of the meadow. The
horses were probably beyond the mist foraging in the

dead grass. We took up a horse trail, but the hoof imprints proved too far apart to make walking easy, so we crossed to the dogs' trail, a shallow well-beaten path which they had used to get to the carcass ever since the snow had come to stay.

Frost crystals of varied forms carpeted the deep snow. Myriads at a time trapped the light of the sinking sun and set the wide expanse of meadow dancing. The dogs pranced through the powdery snow, throwing it up like sea spray. Nearer to the carcass the snow was trodden down, and individual tracks became indiscernible except where trails led off from the area. The clearest tracks were parallel curved lines in threes where crows had alighted or taken off.

Although it was already the third month of winter, the carcass stank. The hoofs were buried in the snow, and the neck was outstretched as in pictures of horses slain in battle. Both head and tail had been eaten, and the innumerable exposed sinews looked like dried wisps of hay. The dogs paraded around the carcass as if to show off their prize. Moose tugged for a few seconds at what was left of the tail, straining every muscle in order to tear off one small piece.

The horses spotted us and trekked slowly to the edge of the rough grass protruding above the packed snow. They stood looking around before curving out in single file in our direction. The five horses were there, a bunch of three—with Carrot, an odd name for the big black who was in the lead—and two trailing behind.

The narrow band of mist between us and them created spirit horses walking silently with measured tread through white Elysian fields. We called to them; they curved around in our direction. As they drew nearer, they looked ancient, with frosted whiskers and faces. They renewed acquaintance with us and as we turned to go, followed us closely to the gate of the pasture. As we left, the sky was afire with a lower layer of pink and blue topped with a red so brilliant that as we struck the wagon trail its reflection suffused the whole dome of the heavens.

🌲   🌲   🌲

After our new hot-water system was finally completed, Jake Schroeder of the Braeside Farm Co-op and father of the twins, Alvin and Kenneth, who attended Braeside school, made some new cupboards and shelves in our kitchen. Then we painted the new woodwork a beautiful color which George called "robin's egg blue." We were very proud of them.

Al was staying with us for a few days at this time. I had taken coffee into the living room after supper upon hearing an unusual commotion going on. In the middle of the floor, with a wash cloth carelessly draped over the side, a cake of soap and a bunch of flowers on the bottom, sat a galvanized bathtub looking like a surrealist picture by Salvador Dali. Al and George flanked it, grinning broadly.

The tub had been bought for $5.00 as a present for me from a neighbor who was returning to the prairies doubled up with rheumatism after two unusually wet years. It was to celebrate the completion of the hot-water system. The men had secreted the tub in the warehouse until the time came for its official appearance and my appraisal before its final testing when Al had left.

Baths, like pigs and chickens, have a special meaning for me. Before leaving England for Australia after the war, my first husband and I had accepted the invitation of our local rector to stay at the rectory the night before our departure. The bathroom had two doors, as it served two bedrooms. Entering from ours to take a bath, I found the rector already occupying the bathtub and seriously intent on his evening ablutions.

He was small, and the bathtub was large enough for two. However, whirling my towel nonchalantly, I thought it better to depart hastily to await my turn alone. The next morning at breakfast, I realized that an eleven-year-old harmonious relationship with the rector had been completely shattered in the few seconds' encounter of the previous evening.

On another occasion, our water supply in the back blocks of the wheat-and-sheep-growing area in Western Australia where my first husband and I were living, was collected from the roof in the wet season and stored in an underground tank for the rest of the year. So baths were a luxury—one a week at the most.

Water was heated for a bath by means of a "chip-heater." In it we burned our week's accumulation of kitchen rubbish—paper, eggshells, twigs, and anything else burnable. While the rubbish was burning, the water was running and being heated.

My husband and I shared the water in the tub because there was so little of it and then we drained it out through a pipe to the outside where it trickled into little trenches around the tomato plants. As the summer baked on, the plants became completely leafless, but the tomatoes grew to the size of small red balloons.

At another time in British Columbia when driving in the van along hot, dusty roads, baths were luxuries. Fortunately they were frequently offered and an offer was much appreciated. In return for a bath, my travelling companion and I baby-sat for a rector and his wife while they went to the local movie.

The water was hot in the stove reservoir long before we were able to find the tub hiding on the back of an outside dark wall. The back door of the house opened directly into the kitchen and apprehensive lest the clerical couple should return early and walk in on one of us naked, we decided to put the filled tub into the rector's study.

With much shoving, pushing, and spilling of water, we finally made it, feeling relieved and secure knowing that at least one door stood between us and discovery. We bathed in holy splendor surrounded by religious books, and by the time our hosts returned, we were renewed physically and spiritually, the tub had been replaced, and the watery evidence on the floor removed.

But perhaps the most memorable bath I have ever taken was also during my van driving period. A farmer's wife we were visiting had informed us cryptically that as the menfolk were all attending a local market that afternoon it would be a good time for us to take a bath.

The water for the bath was heated outdoors. A wood fire burned under a large galvanized container standing on a few bricks in the farmyard. The container was filled by a hose attached to a tap in the yard. We had no idea at that time where the tub was. When the water was hot enough we learned that we were to carry both hot and cold water in buckets several yards to a designated place behind the hen-house, where a long galvanized tub sat with a plug in it.

I have never enjoyed a bath more. I had a feeling of complete abandon. Hidden from the house, and relaxing at full length, I gazed up through a cloud of one-stepping mosquitoes to the trees above. My eyes roved lazily from the doorless privy, where I could see that the Eaton's Catalogue was down to the pink pages, to the few hens pecking around, and from my sunburned legs to the apple box at the foot of the tub which held my clean clothes.

Now I was about to have a new bathing adventure. After Al had left, George brought in the thoroughly chilled tub from the warehouse, carrying it before him like an ancient shield.

I had kept the fire well stoked. George had already brought from the toolshed the only bucket that had survived cracking from water freezing in it; it had recently been used for filtering water from gasoline and was to be used now to transfer the water from tap to tub.

Gleefully I dragged out from under a pile of unused linen an elegant green-and-white bathmat with hollyhocks and a birdbath on it—a survivor of my more sophisticated days—and laid it lovingly by the side of the tub.

All preparations for bathing made, we surveyed the scene and discussed how we should empty the tub when we had finished. Since it needed cleaning, we put it through a trial run by washing it out and trying out our proposed drainage plan.

George had assembled odd bits of hose lying around that might fit onto the projecting pipe under the bath where the plug was. We tried to remove the plug, but it was stuck in so tightly that he had to use a pair of pliers to loosen it. The hose didn't fit properly and water swooshed out all over the kitchen floor and not a drop went into the catching vessel.

We mopped up the water and wryly contemplated the prospect of having to carry both bath and bath water out bodily through the back door to empty it, but that thought rapidly generated a new round of creativity.

"Why didn't I think of it before?" George exclaimed, "Guess what!" I suddenly got the idea.

"Why the cellar, of course," I said. "We'll open the cellar door and drain it down there."

"Yes, that's right," agreed George. "When we've finished taking our baths we'll pull out the plug, empty the water into the cellar and then pump it out."

That is just what we did. It was the most luxuriously wallowy bath that either of us could remember ever having, and actually inside our own four walls.

At the beginning of February we brought Mulligan back from the Prout Meadow where he had been living on slew hay all winter. He was a shaggy registered bull with distinct possibilities. His name belied his birth, for unlike his namesake the stew, Mulligan was already showing that he was not the product of diverse elements. All George's energies were now dedicated to feeding him for his future role in life.

Every day George said; "Come and look at Mulligan to see if he is any bigger and fatter." This noticeable growth was supposed to come about as a result of his being fed with chop and pellets, priced at $9.00 a sack from the elevator in town.

When I couldn't honestly say that he looked any different from the day before, George would rationalize, "Of course, he grows long, too, so you can't really notice the fat."

At the same time George was also fattening Wobo, the pup we had kept from Wampus's litter. We had given the rest of the pups away to our neighbors—one to the Derksens, that they called Wolf and another to the Co-op. There was always a certain amount of risk connected with having large dogs when there was livestock around, especially dogs which might have some wolf blood in them, because of the tendency of some dogs to kill chickens and sheep or worry the cattle.

We didn't entertain that fear where Wobo was concerned; George's efforts to give Wobo special food had resulted in his growing a big behind and an unimpressive little front. He turned out to be a most unintelligent dog, not a bit like either his father or his mother. His sole asset was social; he had learned how to sit up on his big behind like the little celluloid "Kelly" dolls, weighted at the bottom, that I knew as a child.

A few days later, George was preoccupied. He had that cattle look.

"How's Mulligan?" I asked.

"I don't think he looks well. He hasn't been looking good for the last few days." He deposited a small sack of pellets on the kitchen floor. Mulligan wouldn't touch them and we couldn't waste them so he was going to grind them up in the meat grinder and perhaps hide the broken-up bits in the "chop" or mixed dry feed he gave to him.

Poor Mulligan, I thought, George is going to stand over him several times a day to see that he eats that stuff when all he wants is sweet-smelling clover hay.

"He's all sweaty, and none of the other cattle are," George said thoughtfully. "On second thoughts, I think I'll take him off chop and pellets for a while. I think it's too rich for him."

"Yes, I think you're right," I remarked. "Remember Wobo when you fed him all that special stuff; it didn't do much for him."

Mulligan recovered as most animals will when they are fed a reasonable diet, without "special" food. He became fat and glossy. Things seemed to be going along at an even tenor both at school and on the ranch until one day George was driving me to school. The little winding dirt road had become extremely treacherous because over the winter the snowplow had built up high and wide banks of snow, leaving the road extremely narrow. In addition, some of the snow had melted, and the road was wet in some places and icy in others.

As we rounded a sharp curve, a car suddenly appeared and ran into us head-on. It was driven by a young man who lived in the area and had no license as he was learning to drive. When I was thrown forward, my left eye hit the knob of the windshield wiper—the knob was on the inside of the jeep. I began bleeding profusely and suddenly couldn't see out of that eye. We were worried. Instead of going to school, we drove to the Vanderhoof hospital where several stitches were put in my eyelid.

Fortunately, I was out of school for only a few days. But my thoughts about the roads were long and serious. It would soon be spring break-up time. How was I going to get to school during the worst of that period? Of course, I could live in the little teacherage near school during the worst of the break-up. I had always wanted someday to live all alone in a tiny teacherage. Perhaps that day would come.

EIGHTEEN

Mud and the Visiting Inspector

The day school closed for the Easter vacation we needed food from town for the weekend. As Abe was going into town in his brother's logging truck we had asked him to bring our food back with him. But he returned to school at ten o'clock and gave me back my food list, saying the road was impassable. They hadn't made the first hill past the school. There had been no freezing at night for seven days, and rivulets of water flowed down the sodden road. Our Easter feast was a continued Lenten fast. The Monday after the ten days' Easter vacation I wore a dress instead of the pants I had worn most of the winter. I chose a brown dress so that the mud wouldn't show up on it. Stockings, too, would be easier to wash than muddied pants.

George drove Gilbert and me. Frost overnight gave the road a fudgelike consistency. The guts would have been torn out of the jeep if there had not been a metal plate underneath to keep parts from being jerked out. We proceeded slowly in the deep ruts. Few springs were left in the gallant jeep. How often I had wished it were a completely padded cell! Its motion was like that of a train on a narrow gauge railway in Western Australia. I seem to remember the rails were four feet, six inches apart; one could beat two-time quite rhythmically in either train or jeep. Proceeding monotonously in this rhythm, I suddenly noticed that at the starboard side the ruts were getting bigger.

"Hold it!" I yelled, but it was too late. We could go neither forward nor backward. We were becalmed. There was too much fudge to shovel away and the only thing Gilbert and I could do was to walk to school the rest of the way; we had done it often enough before. George walked with us. At the top of the next hill we spotted some movement ahead. It was Klaas Wiebe with his team of white horses. How slowly he plodded along toward us. George turned back when he saw him coming, as Klaas would be able to pull the jeep out for us.

"You need a helicopter," Klaas observed, smiling, as Gilbert and I met him.

"I'd be satisfied with hip boots," I replied. "We're sure glad to see you. You'll be able to pull the jeep out back there. How's the family?"

All thirteen of the family had been sick a couple of weeks before, and several of his good-looking blond childen were still away from school.

As Gilbert and I trudged onwards, the fudge on the southern slopes of the road was rapidly becoming chocolate pudding. My rubber boots had plenty of space between the top of the boot and my legs, and great gobs of mud, thrown up as I walked, were caught neatly in the space between boot and leg. The sticky mud stuck to our boots, building them up to twice their size, making the going extremely rough.

"What the jumping jiminy, Gilbert," I exclaimed, as I was aroused out of my trudging trance by mud flung on my face. His feet had grown twice as large with the sticky mud so that he could hardly lift them, but in sheer frustration and with one Herculean effort he had thrown a leg up as if to cast it away and the mud had flown in all directions.

"Let's go and wipe it off on the snow bank and start all over again," I suggested.

For him, it was a good idea; he stayed on top of the snow bank, but I being much heavier, sank into three feet of snow and the icy crystals mixed with the mud already inside my boots. By the time we reached school the snow and the mud had mixed to a consistency which, when warmed by the heat of my legs, baked and enclosed the lower part of my legs in a mud cast.

The next day we managed to get all the way to school in the jeep, but on the way back she behaved like a flirtatious filly feeling her oats. She frequently left the well-wheeled part of the road, going off at tangents without the slightest provocation. After side-stepping the Deadly Duo, we reined her in suddenly at the Hill Bump where the road had given way entirely, revealing a bustling underground stream which we just couldn't get across. That time the walk was at the home-end, and I had a particularly heavy load of school books.

My mind was finally made up. The time had come for me to take up residence in the teacherage until the roads improved. My patience was rapidly coming to an end. In addition, my ire had been aroused by a recent circular sent from the Department of Education proclaiming, among other admonitions: "Teachers are apt to become slack in appearance when they live in rural areas." Pondering the neat mud amulet plastered on my throat that I had worn unknowingly in school that day and surveying my mud-stained clothes, I yelled my most colorful expletives to the only mirror in the house.

We packed the things I would need during my stay at the teacherage. The next day we got up at six to stow away the bedding, clothes, utensils, and food in the jeep. We made a couple of trips to load up, wrapping the typewriter in the comforter to protect it. Abe and Jake were waiting at the end of their road with their tractor and trailer. They were on their way to town to meet their brother in his truck on the main road. They

were going to haul him back through the worst parts of
the road.

We got stuck in a rut just outside the school playground, but a passing tractor pulled us out. George put all the things into the teacherage and departed rapidly in order to get back to the ranch before the sun softened up the road too much. Later that day one of the school neighbors ploughed up the road near the school to help it dry out and to get rid of the biggest ruts.

I was excited all day thinking of my new temporary home and could hardly wait until school was out to walk the few yards over to it. Several large black flies greeted me as I entered the teacherage. I was glad the mosquito season hadn't started, for there was a gap of one inch on the badly fitting screen door.

The building was twenty-four by sixteen feet. It was divided into two rooms by a partition; the bedroom occupied a third of the whole. At the back of the house a small woodshed was used during the winter for a make-shift stable for the horses that drew the sleigh in which the Co-op children sometimes came to school. Its front was partly closed at the top with large pieces of corrugated cardboard, and three poles were driven into the ground across the opening. There was a small manger in one corner. Some poplar banches, cut to fit the teacherage stove fuel box, were stacked neatly at the back. A roughly-made meat house which could only be reached by a giant stood at the back of the house on the north side, but close by was a crude ladder which I supposed was to storm the meat house to grab the Sunday roast.

The bedroom faced west. I could use the space beween the window and the window screen as a small refrigerator. The mattress on the bed had been there since the teacherage had last been occupied; I hoped it wasn't damp. The little shack had been hopefully prepared for electricity at some distant period in the future;

empty holes gaped vacantly from the two ceilings. A
couple of boards nailed in suitable places, with four-inch
nails driven into them, served as pegs to hang clothes
and towels on. An odd chair or two, a small table, and
a picture of the royal family completed the interior
decoration. Not quite the Ritz—much more exciting.

The heart of the teacherage was the combined
cooking and heating stove. Moulded into the stove was
the name Ruth. Ruth had lost a leg, giving her the appearance of a peg-leg woman, but in spite of this incapacity, she was a hot babe, temperamental, and, on occasions, uncontrollable. A couple of dry poplar sticks in
her firebox heated her up enough to make the shack
stifling hot and the thermometer on the oven door registered 600 degrees in six minutes flat. One of the holes on
her top was covered with a rusty tin lid which fitted
perfectly, but jumped out of place at the slightest
movement around her.

She was fascinating—so primitive and hot to handle.
To get into her oven, I had first to assemble my courage,
then a knife and two thick cloths. One cloth was to
clutch the handle, which was merely a thickening of the
middle metal part; the other was to move aside the
metal catch which held the oven door to the rest of the
stove. To get it closed again the reverse complex procedure was followed. The meals I cooked were simple
but triumphantly shared with Ruth.

I had hours of extra time at my disposal. I lay in
bed at night by the light of an oil lamp and looked over
the children's work: "When I grow up I would like to be
a rancher and farmer in Northern British Columbia. I
would have two sections of land. I would have my own
shop to fix the machinery. A small shed would do for
my living quarters. Every year I would butcher a small
bull for meat."

The writer's fourteen-year-old brother, Richard
Derksen, the oldest in the school, and the eldest of the

Derksen family, wrote with unusual insight:

> Star of the North! Thou seest all
> The grief and dismay on this earthly ball.
> Man claws for wealth with greedy hands
> And strives to conquer neighboring lands.
> Each day brings new and changing care
> Oh why do we no better fare?

I hoped the children were learning basic economic concepts in addition to those I knew they were learning at home, as we all belonged to a credit union run by the children with their own elected officers. It was a branch of the Vanderhoof Credit Union.

At its annual meeting the children had exhibited their own posters. One of ours was a winner—a $5.00 share in the credit union. It depicted a man upside down in a bramble bush accompanied by the following lines:

> There was a man in our town
> He was so wondrous wise
> He jumped into expensive debt
> Just like so many guys.
> But when he saw the harm he'd done
> With all his might and main
> He joined the Credit Union
> And jumped right out again.

I had time to plan our handicraft exhibit at the May Handicraft Fair in Vanderhoof. We were proud of what we were making in school; bound single-section books with the end-pages designed by the children; sheep's wool gathered by the younger children and spun by the older children on primitive wooden spindles, then woven into mats and blankets on looms made by the older boys; doormats made from gunny sacks and hooked with

Mud and the Visiting Inspector 209

discarded pieces of binder-twine cut from bales of hay; baskets made from willow; and a fully furnished doll's house for the younger children everybody joined in making.

I pondered what and how well the children were learning and in what ways they were beginning to understand the environment, its richness and its dangers. I wondered if some children would go onto high school and college and which pupils would leave school as soon as they could.

I had time for my own dreaming, too. Enclosed cosily within the four rough lumber walls, I felt the lonely spirit of the place. I was moved deeply and hauntingly by my new experiences. I treasured them greatly; they were being transmuted into something rich and strong, becoming an inseparable part of me.

Feeling an increased self-awareness, I forgot the mud, the bad roads, and the confining physical difficulties. I recalled anew the spirit of the early pioneers I had met and felt a unity with them and with the little Braeside community. Were not George and I also battling to make our dreams come true and in doing so, changing, and becoming better able to cope with our future problems? I slept each night a dreamless sleep in the brooding silence.

The drying spring winds blew, and the road became passable. My uniquely happy stay of two weeks at the teacherage ended. The giant Winter awakened fully from his long sleep, wiggled a toe and tilted the boys' outhouse crazily at an angle of forty-five degrees. He gave a final kick, heaving the ground so that the front door of the school would only half open. Spring had been born again, and I returned to sleep with George in our cozy home.

Strings of geese winged over, their arrowheads pointing north. A ray from the westering sun, trapped behind a curtain of dark clouds escaped and singled out

two of the birds, turning them dazzling white. Or were
they really white? I watched until they were out of
sight, but I could not tell. The formation wheeled; four
geese broke off from the strings as if uncertain of their
way. I could no longer distinguish the individual beating
of their wings, but there was a moment when the whole
string pulsated with life like a flickering cinema screen,
and then they moved on in a liquid-flowing, ever-changing
formation.

    At the ranch the creek had overflowed its banks, and
the thin coating of ice from the night frost was breaking
up rapidly. Crack followed crack in the warming sun
and the ice broke off and sank. Such rapid movement
was unusual in this brooding land and stirred one's
senses with a feeling of momentous happenings to come.

    I was seized with an extreme busyness in the house.
I shook the dust mop out of the back door on a tiny soft
breeze. Balls of fluff rolled away under the tree of our
friendly squirrels. One of them scampered after a ball of
the fluff, caught it, rolled it around between his paws
and mouth, and placed it carefully in a special spot.
Each time I shook the mop he gathered the balls until he
had three of them all in one place, then off he scampered
up his tree with all three, tail held high in the air, like a
playful kitten. What luck, he must have thought, that
those strange humans throw out of their house just the
stuff I need for mine.

    The day for the annual handicraft show at the
beginning of May finally arrived. It was raining for the
first time in nearly a month. Two boxes under a tarpaulin at the back of the jeep were filled with the children's exhibits; the doll's house was wrapped around with
a large piece of corrugated cardboard.

    With us inside the jeep were two big bags of handicrafts, a box of eggs for Frontier House, and a small
loom wrapped up in the old mattress cover that was still
stained with blood from its previous trip into town when

it contained the nibbled remains of our last quarter of beef.

The road was dry in most places, and bumpy, but one spot was a morass, quite impassable with an ordinary vehicle, but we had chains on all wheels. A detour had been slashed in the bush at that place, and half a dozen assorted vehicles had been parked on the near side of the same place. Farther on, frost boils in the road were numerous; everything slid around in the jeep like unlashed objects on the deck of a ship in a storm.

When I unfolded myself at our destination, I discovered that I had been sitting on the eggs. The back of my newly-pressed dress was smeared with raw egg, and the chimney was off the doll's house. With a flash of genius George collected the spare egg from my dress, before I cleaned it all off, and applied it to the old glue on the chimney. It stuck there for the hours of the exhibition. Afterwards we stayed the night with George's mother as the next day was Sunday.

The heat we generated inside the jeep on our return trip to the ranch caused two small pieces of beef which had been frozen solid when we started, to thaw and drip blood all over our prize handicraft cushion. After turning off the Braeside Road, we got to the first dip on our road without incident. Then we saw a vehicle facing us canted at an angle right in the middle of the road. As we got nearer we saw little heads popping out of the truck cab on each side and recognized Mary Wiebe and her family. Ironically, the truck was loaded with sawdust to put in the next bad spot.

The family had been penned up in the house for a month because of the condition of the road, and this was the first day they had all been out. The children were dressed in neat little checkered coats and were on their way to visit relatives who lived only a short distance away.

We hooked on to the front of the truck and pulled them clear. By this time, Abe Wiebe had appeared over the brow of the next hill with his tractor. He greeted us with a wry smile, turned around, then hooked on to us and pulled us home.

The school year was nearing its end. An Inspector of Schools for the Department of Education of the Province of British Columbia was expected any time for his first visit. The school projects were being completed and the children were finishing up their work on the ecological plots they had pegged out in the bush near the school.

We had participated in the sports day of the whole school district, bringing home one solitary point won by the long-leggedness of a young Wiebe girl. In the mathematics test for thirty-eight schools in three school districts we had brought individual and group success for Braeside school, with third place.

In May, G. E. Johnson, Inspector of Schools, arrived. He stayed two days and looked at the records and the children's written work. A couple of weeks later he sent the following report:

GROUNDS:
> The school grounds have a rather desolate appearance. The large field which has been cleared should be cleaned off and seeded to grass. Driveway and walks should be marked off and gravelled. It is difficult to keep the school clean under the present muddy conditions.

CLASSROOM:
> The classroom is adequate for the enrollment. It and the entrance hall are not as clean as they should be because of the condition of the grounds.

Mud and the Visiting Inspector

LEARNING SITUATION:

This is Mrs. Hobson's first year of teaching in British Columbia and she has had to face the problems of new courses, new methods and procedures. She has done this well.

For the most part pupils are making satisfactory progress. Senior students did particularly well on an arithmetic test given throughout the inspectorate. Written work of the pupils is of fair quality. It has been well-checked by the teacher.

These children have done some very good work in the field of practical arts. Mrs. Hobson has a special ability in this field which should be encouraged by supplying extra teaching equipment and materials of this nature.

Pupils have good work-habits. There is a friendly and co-operative teacher-pupil relationship. I am satisfied that Mrs. Hobson has given good service in this school. The children are being intelligently and effectively taught.

The report pleased me, and I was glad that the visit was over. It had been a good year. The school curriculum for the year had been completed early, so during the short time remaining we spent whole days at the children's secret places—at beaver dams and at the canyon where the Nechako River runs deep and where gigantic fish were said to lurk in bottomless pools. We ate lunch at tumble-down log cabins built long ago, telling tales of hope and despair.

A pipsissewa flower plucked from a sheltered spot, a string of pan-size rainbow trout, the sturdy shoulders of the oldest boy carrying the youngest girl, a memory of picking berries and looking down the clearing to see a bear doing the same, and then the little school family broke up and disappeared along the small back trails leading homeward, and the past tilted towards a future day.

In a few days' time we were expecting Teeney and his cousin Johnny Scholz, for the summer, and now that the school year had ended I was free to prepare for their visit.

NINETEEN

Fishing Summer

At the Little Creek Ranch four happy people relaxed after dinner with steaming mugs of coffee round the big table. We had met Teeney and his cousin, Johnny Scholz, at the Prince George airport earlier in the day. It was Johnny's first visit to the ranch. He was a little younger than Teeney, who was fourteen. He was dark and good-looking, not yet as tall as Teeney.

The boys were telling us about their experience on the last part of the trip from New York—Vancouver to Prince George.

"At the airport in Vancouver a little man was waiting for the same plane we were taking," Teeney began.

"Yes, and he hadn't shaved for weeks," chimed in Johnny. "He kept drinking out of a flask in his hip pocket and he was smoking cigarettes from a package labelled Export—I think they were doped," he added seriously.

"When we got on the plane, we thought we'd better tell the hostess about him," continued Teeney, "so I wrote her a little note telling her we thought that liquor and doped cigarettes were being smuggled into Canada."

As they told their story, I imagined the boys closely observing the little man's every move. To the boys, well-dressed and carrying expensive cameras, the little man must have seemed incongruous, a fictional character

remote from their experience. No wonder they were
curious about him. They couldn't be expected to know
that he might have been a trapper returning to his lonely
cabin, or perhaps a prospector and drinking away the
last penny of a large stake or a logger, seeing life
through a bottle.

"The stewardess was very pretty," Teeney observed.
"We waited until the passengers were seated and she
wasn't so busy, and then gave her the note. She smiled
and then said, 'This will be attended to,' and vanished
into the part of the plane where the captain was. I wish
we had given her our address," Teeney remarked a bit
regretfully. "We might have got a reward."

By the time we went to bed that night George had
covered thoroughly the subject of the rugged individualists of this world, their differing ways of life, life's disillusionments, and the importance of trying to understand
other people's values and their way of life.

The arrival of the two boys stimulated us and
changed the texture of our lives and our consequent
behavior, as had Teeney's visit the previous summer.

People play a number of roles during their lives, and
our behavior differs in shifting from one role to another.
We have our public and our private selves and variations
of each, and it is difficult for an individual to know
which and how many of the different role behaviors
belong to the real person. The behavior of my husband
when he was with his Vanderhoof friends was quite
different from the George I knew when we were alone.

With the arrival of the boys and with effortless
transition, George added to his roles of husband, rancher,
and being "one of the boys," those of father, mentor and
buddy to the two boys. While this change enlarged considerably the map of his emotions, it also caused a colorful kaleidoscopic shift in the relationships among all four
of us. I also took on new roles, less well-defined perhaps
and only peripherally related to most of the new action

around the ranch—which was distinctly masculine in character now that Teeney was a year older and also because Johnny was with him.

One of my roles was a combination mothering-mentor role. It was somewhat objective, a kind of extension of a teacher's nurturing style, but with some opportunity for the subjective warmth I had been denied by the loss of my own child; I had found that warmth the previous summer during Teeney's visit, when I had learned to love the thirteen-year-old boy who had become my stepson.

Relating to an adolescent, together with my new adventure in living, combined to enable me, in a curious way, to assume a kind of second adolescence. I came to believe that this second adolescent stage had characteristics of what a well-spent decade of my forties would be, in order that the decades of my future life could also be well spent. I found myself cheering symbolically from the sidelines as I looked in on their masculine activities. At other times, I felt I was a real part of the total action in the life of the ranch.

During these new experiences I reappraised my husband and appreciated again, through these new eyes, his tanned good looks and rugged physique, his curly, prematurely gray hair, infectious enthusiasm, excellent sense of humor and of the ridiculous, his quick temper when frustrated, and his strong personal code of honor.

I thought again of his years in Yugoslavia during the war, which he had discussed with me only occasionally. Teeney was a very young child then. I wondered again about his chosen lonely life on the ranch before I had arrived and about the money and effort he had sunk into it in his idealistic and romantic search for a particular way of life. I wondered also if the ranching life had been a subconscious desire to escape from continued full involvement in the world in order to find his real self. If indeed George's life on the ranch was such a search, it seemed to me he might be looking for a protagonist of gigantic proportions against which to pit himself physically—maybe Nature herself.

It was very evident that the new roles he had taken on since the boys' arrival were streamlined into a concerted effort to enable his son to continue to experience and maybe to understand a way of life which George believed had considerable merit. Such an experience could then be added to Teeney's other life experiences to balance the more sophisticated way of life to which his son was accustomed. It was obvious to anyone who knew us well that we were not laying up material treasures on earth as a result of our life on the ranch, and this certainly must have been very evident to two intelligent boys who were accustomed to many material privileges.

Our own lack of such privileges at this time undoubtedly raised questions in the boys' minds, which they sometimes expressed openly. But George and I both felt that in our living among the perpetual wonders of the natural world we had found treasures of a different kind worth laying up for ourselves and also sharing with others.

Sharing our life with both the boys and their reactions to it, both covert and overt, provided a sounding board for a recognizable conflict in my own mind. I was living a simple life, happily, far away from the mainstream of life, whereas at various stages in my life before, I had been fully involved with people and events in the world around me. I had found happiness in both patterns of life. Here, a destination I had arrived at completely by chance, my life revolved almost entirely around one person except for the children at school. Which way was really the way for me to live? I asked myself. Did I need a bigger world?

How to live one's life is one of the toughest questions we have to answer. Both George and I had already passed many different tests in living in our respective pasts, patterns of living very different from the present one. If anything had died in either of us during those life phases, later births had compensated us—new loves and new lives. Each of us, however, had clung to that early love of nature we both had, and we continued to grow in that pattern of life. Life is movement. The life we were presently leading had a pattern that was ever-changing. One should not live in a life pattern that has ceased to shift.

It struck me how well developed my adaptive and coping devices had become throughout the years. My sense of adventure, always acute from the time when I was a little girl tingling with excitement whenever I had to go to new places alone, was still characteristic of me. In addition, I enjoyed life wherever I happened to be. But could one be too unquestioning about the life one was leading, too adaptive, forgetting the existence of other patterns of life? From time to time little incidents occurred during the boys' visit that caused me to continue to ask myself these questions.

Teeney asked me suddenly one day, seemingly puzzled: "Why do you always wear the same dress and stockings with seams down the back?" An insignificant concern one might think. But I did remember that I had worn the same dress both years when I had met him at the airport.

I was somewhat taken aback by the question. The charge about the dress wasn't strictly factual, as I did have more than one dress, but I did, at that time, have only that one I saved for special occasions.

Before I had become a Little Creekman I had a normal wardrobe and enjoyed good clothes, but it had become eroded with time and extensive traveling, and I had not been able to replace it. Until this rather disconcerting question was asked, the shortage of personal clothing had seemed quite unimportant to me, and I had felt no sense of loss of such material things. As for the stockings, I didn't have any seamless stockings because I still had many with seams to wear out. Evidently to Teeney, however, "seams in" were at that time "out."

That simple and apparently unimportant question had quite an impact on me at the time. I suddenly wanted a pair of seamless stockings. I very much wanted to be "in." I had to laugh at myself when I realized that I very much wanted to belong to the boys' world, to gain their approval, while at the same time belonging to George's and my own little world on the ranch. Is this the real me, with my peaches and cream complexion, dressed in shrunken jeans and an old shirt, or am I really a Dresden doll or Santa Claus's youngest daughter, as I had sometimes been called? It was the adolescent in me asking, and I could not give an answer.

And so a series of new personal relationships was formed in the heretofore relatively uninterrupted isolation and simplicity of our life, adding new and unaccustomed dimensions to all our lives. These relationships developed throughout the summer, both through the real everyday events of daily living and also through fantasy. The times when, figuratively speaking, we had our feet on the ground, were both bad and good; there were the everlasting mosquitoes and the black flies, which actually bit out pieces of flesh, leaving hard red bumps; and there were the nettle stings, the misunderstandings, the voices raised, the tempers lost, and the silences. But the bad times were forgotten in the good times which were more frequent.

There were the chores out-of-doors; trying to find Black Cow in the dark and milking her, haying, and wood cutting. Then there was the playing: fishing, riding the horses, target practice and camping, all to the accompaniment of great laughter, tall tales, and more Pop-Eye faces when George took his teeth out. Inside,

there was the cooking and the jubilant eating. Teeney
was an even better cook than the year before.

Always there was the jeep, often with the brakes
gone, rattling along with the men staring through mud-
specked windows at oceans of bumps and mounds of
heaped earth. And this is where the fantasy began.
When the boys were in the jeep and I an observer, what
had previously been reality to me when I myself was
riding in it suddenly seemed to become an illusion in
which they were all playing parts, and I was a detached
observer given to introspection concerning the recent
past, the very real present, and the possible future.

Until the boys arrived, George and I were, to me,
real people in very real situations, taking our life very
seriously. Somehow or other, after their coming, the
reality and the fantasy became difficult at times to tell
apart. This feeling was fostered by the spirit of Wetsel,
Zane Gray's frontiersman, a popular character with the
men. He haunted the ranch during the summer with his
superman's attributes. The boys' physical prowess and
woodsman's skills were measured by Wetsel's standards,
and his presence amongst us could even be felt at meal-
times, fostering gargantuan appetites difficult to satiate.

Furthermore, Daganaw, a real trapper on the Nechako River in earlier times, a giant of a man whose cabin
still stood on Grouse Trail, was promoted by the boys to
Giant Daganaw. His cabin, rotted by time, was regard-
ed by the boys with awe and surrounded with mystery.
The rusty cans, open cupboards, and old tables in the
cabin took on an aura of hallowedness, and where his
bones might rest became a subject for serious surmise.

Fantasy invaded our sleeping hours, too. George
dreamed dreams: "There was a big hole in the jeep and
the gas came pouring out," he recounted to an attentive
audience one morning at the breakfast table. "I got a
ride to town to get some gas. When I got back to where
I had left the jeep, it had gone, so I started to hoof it

home, getting down on all fours every so often, like an Indian does to try to sniff out the jeep—you know you can smell it a mile away.

"Well, I traced it to Fort St. James and found it with a big hole in the roof lying upside down in a ditch. I turned it over and set it facing in the right direction for home. All went well for a while and then I had a big blow-out. If you remember, I had no spare tire as it had dropped off one day. Now guess, boys, what did I do to mend the tire?" he had asked.

"You used your head," said Teeney, laughingly.

"No, that was too small to go in the hole. Now use your resourcefulness. Guess what I did. I had a sling shot. Yes, I used the rubber of the sling shot to patch the tire. But it didn't work, and then I saw a horse and wagon coming down the road with no driver. I whistled twice and the horse heard. I stripped him from the wagon and harnessed him to the jeep and he pulled me home."

The next night George had another dream: "I dreamed that Johnny had the idea of building a raft, but we only had the large saw and our penknives with the little saw on each. The tree we picked was eight feet in diameter. It took us a long time to saw it down with our knives and it fell in the wrong direction. We cut it up into eighteen-foot lengths; Johnny's end was overhanging the river. He sawed off the wrong end and he fell in the river. When we had rescued him and had sawed up the other pieces we tied them together with our shoe laces."

Some intuitive leap must have taken place in the boys' minds at that point because during the next two weeks at every available opportunity they were off in the bush doing something top-secret.

One day Teeney said to George: "Daddy, come with us and look what we've made."

"What the hell's that?" said George, having arrived at the scene.

"It's a raft."

"What's it doing up here on the top of a hill in high, dry, bush country five miles from water?"

Deflated, each said it had been the other's idea.

"Why, it would need a bulldozer to drag it down to the water and besides that, we'd have to cut down the trees at the sides of the trail and take down the barbed wire to get it to the river."

George told me later that a shocked silence had followed his appraisal of their handiwork, only to be followed by hysterical laughter by all of them with Teeney rolling in the woods, clutching his stomach. Crushed egos were boosted later by their constructing a practical lean-to where they camped out overnight.

Apart from my much expanded role of chief cook and bottle washer and the cosy times we had all together in the house, I liked best to go on fishing trips either to the Nechako River or to Ormand Lake. The Nechako River is about four miles from the ranch. Grouse Trail, as the boys had named the trail to the river, was easy to find as far as Daganaw's cabin and then it became more difficult as the windfall made the going rough, but when we saw the Great Tree rising above all the others we knew we were at the river.

Turning left along the bank and hiking another mile, we came to Crystal Canyon, a name the boys had given to that part of the river where the beach was sandy and rapids ran in a deep gorge. In summer it was placid, but at spring break-up it became a raging torrent. A few years before, an acquaintance of George's, finding an old Indian dugout canoe in good condition on the bank, had thought he could run the rapids in it and had lost his life.

On reaching the canyon George and the boys plunged into the river, slipping through the cool water, swimming easily, laughing and wallowing in it and kicking up the spray in glee while the silent pines pointed upwards unmoving towards the infinite sky. We didn't stay overnight at the river but made a campfire and ate the trout we had caught. George was the best fisherman by far and invariably caught the most fish, much to the boys' envy.

Teeney was exceptionally well-organized, and it carried over into outdoor life. He had complete control of everything: no uncooked fish ever dropped off his forked stick into the fire, his tea never tipped over, his toast never burned. Everything he needed for a delectable meal was always at hand when he needed it; his marshmallows were always toasted to perfection. From his own little world of eating, with a faint smile of amusement, he surveyed others less organized.

When we went to Ormand Lake, fifty to sixty miles away we usually stayed a couple of nights. Sonny Weinhardt, the son of Herman and Margaret Weinhardt and around the boys' ages, went with us and lent us his homemade boat. Ormand Lake is a small lake only a few miles long—tiny, compared with Stuart and Babine Lakes. The larger lakes, when whipped up by the wind, could suddenly become little seas.

To compare Ormand Lake with a jewel would be trite and sophisticated. It is rather otherworldly, transcending the senses. It reflects the dark mystic hills, often through a mist rising vertically, veiling the tall spruce trees along the shores. Such beauty in the profound silence of the wilderness was an experience that entered one's soul. Only the gentle lapping of the water on the shore, a faint rustle through the trees, a coyote's call, or a loon's mournful cry could cause me to return to the rational world and the people around me.

It was always the same on each visit. The whole world of beauty was manifested in that first glimpse of Ormand Lake. At these moments I found it difficult to admit to myself that a man is more than a mountain, the stars, or even a lake.

Then the business of the camp began; a canvas lean-to was erected; fishing rods were readied; we made our way in Sonny's little boat towards Rainbow Creek, at the far end of the lake. The edge of the boat seemed to be only a fingernail's breadth from the water when we were all riding in it.

Coyote Ridge stood out bare on our right . . . a canvasback duck dived thirty yards in front of the boat . . . a baldheaded eagle sailed overhead . . . we had safely reached Rainbow Creek. The water there tumbled in foam. A wet fly, a dry fly or a little spinner? Perhaps a Royal Coachman? More rainbow trout for supper than we could eat. Afterwards, Teeney singing in his deep voice as the campfire flickered hypnotically.

Back at base camp, we spent the night in our sleeping bags under mosquito nets. There was wind and rain. Then, after a breakfast of eggs, bacon, and hot coffee, we again crossed Ormand Lake to Rainbow Creek. The second day's fishing was good. We fished pool after pool as we worked our way downstream until each of our forked carrying-sticks grew heavy with fish. Across the creek we saw the deserted fish-nets and smokehouses of an Indian fishing camp as with a half-filled gunny sack of rainbow trout we pushed off from the shore and starting our motor, returned to camp.

The afternoon of the following day we removed the lean-to stakes and folded up the canvas in preparation for breaking camp. After we had packed the camping gear into the truck, together with the damp gunny sack of cleaned fish, I went down to the water's edge, where George and the boys were skidding the boat up the steep bank toward the road. Feeling rather useless as I watched the heaving and pulling, I told George I would walk on ahead down the road and he could pick me up.

The day's end was gray and still. The wind of the night was hushed and spent, except for occasional convulsions in the tops of the trees when patches of small pines swayed rhythmically to the wind's dying outbursts. From the base to the top of each pine a group of trees swayed with the accuracy of a metronome. Then coming almost imperceptibly to a stop, the rhythm was taken up by another group a few yards away as the vagrant wind stumbled, tattered and tired, along the tree-top highway.

I walked on. A moan broke from a group of trees. I stopped, listening intently. There it was again—the same moan, but fainter, and again a rhythmical repetition. But it was only the interplay of trunk on trunk as the trees crossed and recrossed. A friendly black-headed Oregon junco, white bars flashing, darted across the path. Mounds of earth had been thrown up years before along the sides of the road when the way was first bulldozed. They were covered with asters and yellow and white daisies, and in the wetter places, with the strangely delicate mimulus.

Roots torn ruthlessly from the ground clung tenaciously to the stones which had lain buried deep with the growing trees. Fireweed grew prolifically in the rich earth around them.

An adult grouse poised on a root was indistinguishable from the background until I drew up level with her. She did not fly but faced me bravely. Her little brood fluttered to safety on the dead lower branches of the nearest pine. She had stayed to distract me until the little birds in the covey, each no larger than a hen's egg, were distributed in safety. Then she raised her head proudly, uttered agitated maternal mutterings, and flew off to join her offspring.

Huckleberries grew prolifically and would soon be ripe. An occasional shiny, dark-blue berry stood out at the top of the branch where the sun had caught it. Others farther down the stem were green or various shades of claret, but all were shiny, and the little well at the top of each berry held its fill of the night's rain.

"One Mile" printed on a pine where a slice had been slashed out just above eye level advised me how far I had walked from the lake. Tall, emaciated pines came down to the road's edge so close that those which had been struck by the bulldozer leaned haphazardly across the others, looking like a giant's game of Pick up Sticks.

As I walked on, the trees became thicker. They cut out the light and it was dreary to walk. No birds sang. It was as if the day were already dead. Mosquitoes, which earlier had been encouraged by the sun's pale rays, had gone, and I, a pygmy among the silent pines, walked on. I was becoming anxious about the truck and stopped to listen for it, but I heard nothing.

I emerged from the gloom where a little spring welled up in the middle of the road. It snaked its way downhill to meet a small creek flowing under a primitive bridge. There, moss with delicate fernlike fronds carpeted the moist earth and higher up on a dry bank, handsome stag's horn moss trailed. I picked some to take back with me and thought again of the man I had watched take down his stag's horn moss from the wall of the cabin he was leaving forever. I would be hanging this moss on our cabin wall. How long would it be before I took it down?

At last I heard the truck in the distance. My lone adventure was over. The truck caught up with me. I jumped aboard, and we drove on towards home. With the last trip to Ormand Lake the boys' vacation was soon to end. With their help the hay was nearly all in and the winter wood had been buzzed up and stacked, but there were no more bottles of pop cooling in the creek under the bridge.

When the boys left, the spirit of Wetsel departed and the fantasy faded. The tall tales were told no more. The summer had gone.

TWENTY
Cattle Roundup

Much summer work remained to be done, but there was still time for fun. Al returned to help George with the last of the haying. At the end of the day he joined George for an hour or two of grouse hunting before dinner.

On these occasions they fanned out in different directions, each letting the other know which direction he intended to take as Al was not yet completely familiar with the rough country around the ranch. One cloudy day in late September, Al chose to cross the main meadow and head southwest. George went due north at the main gate into the heart of grouse country where ripe berries were plentiful.

It was raining steadily and the night hung inky-black when George returned a couple of hours later with five grouse. Halfway through the meal Al had not yet returned. The rain had decreased to a steady drizzle. George went round to the side of the cabin, and facing west, cupped his hands to his mouth and yelled into the night. He listened intently for an answer, but the silence was broken only by the steady patter of rain on the leaves. He repeated this performance several times but to no avail. He returned to the cabin grim-faced and announced that Al was lost. Before I knew it he had taken his gun and lantern and stepped into the darkness.

George told me the rest of the story several hours later: He had reached Daganaw's cabin an hour after leaving the house when he heard a faint faraway cry and then a shot. It had taken quite a time with several more shots spaced at intervals for Al to get a bead on George's position. Sometimes Al's answering shots grew fainter and all but died out. Because the whole area round Grouse Trail is interlaced with deep ravines and willow swamp, the shots from his gun ricocheted around from one ridge to the next like a bouncing rubber ball.

Finally Al drew closer, but George began to hear strange wild screams. He finally entered the light of George's lantern dripping wet but grinning from ear to ear with a wild look in his eye, moss and brush on his head in place of his hat, and carrying a half-cooked grouse.

"What the hell did you interrupt my dinner for?" Al had exclaimed vehemently. "I was just getting settled down and comfortable for the night."

"All right, you old swamp-jumper, but how the hell do you explain those weird shrieks I heard a few minutes ago?" George had asked, as they hit the homeward trail. In answer Al pulled a wooden goose-honker from his pocket and had blown on it several times.

"I was trying to save on ammunition," he explained.

🌲   🌲   🌲

In late fall, George, with a friend, Walter Erhorn, was gone all day. After a hearty breakfast of pancakes, bacon and coffee they had picked up the lunches I had prepared and gone to the barn to saddle up. I had watched them with the binoculars as they rode across the clearing. George was riding Paint, and Walter, Jack. Before disappearing into the bush George rose in his stirrups and waved his ubiquitous beat-up cowboy hat. He had won that hat in a crap game with a Mexican vaquero on Governor Stirling's cattle ranch in Texas when he was sixteen.

It was round-up time and the men had gone out to drive the cattle home from the range. The next couple of days were busy ones. They drove the herd into the large main corral which was connected by gates to several smaller corrals with a cattle squeeze and a loading chute.

The chute, often used for loading the cattle on trucks for market, would not be used this fall. Instead, George and Walter would be driving the cattle to the railhead in Vanderhoof. From there they would be shipped to Edmonton where we hoped they would fetch a better price than they would locally.

After the men had rounded up the herd on the range and driven them home to the ranch, they spent two days working the cattle. From the cabin window facing south, between house chores and with the binoculars, I was the sole spectator of a little rodeo, or stampede—as a rodeo is called in British Columbia. There were some events my miniature rodeo did not have, like bronc riding and bulldogging. There was plenty of cutting-out, however, with good in-and-out fast riding and turning. There was calf roping and some nonrodeo events which I purposely did not watch, such as branding and castrating the bull calves and dehorning the odd cow.

The day of the drive broke damp and cold. I crossed the meadow to see them leave. In the dim light I watched the shadowy forms of the riders as they worked to get the timid uncertain herd moving down the little road toward Vanderhoof. It was a colorful sight accompanied by some profanity as the men darted in and out of the bush bringing back strays, waving their big hats, and yelling and whistling.

The men had slickers rolled up and tied in back of their saddles; their sandwiches were in their saddle pockets; and they were wearing chaps and jackets. George's jacket was an old moose-hide job he had won in a poker game with a trapper in Vanderhoof. It had quite a history. One winter he thought he had lost it. Then while cleaning out the barn in the spring, he had found it buried in a manure pile with only the fringe protuding. He had dropped it in a barrel full of rainwater beneath the roof outside the cabin. Two weeks later he had retrieved it, but it never quite lost its unflowery-like fragrance or its subtle earthy tones.

The cattle were beginning to stretch out down the road; soon they were swallowed up in the gloom. Their bawling grew fainter and then finally died in the distance. Suddenly, I felt an overwhelming loneliness. I looked across the little meadow to the beckoning light in the cabin and heard the welcoming sound of the dogs barking where George had shut them up in the warehouse before he had started the cattle drive. I retraced my steps hurriedly and let the dogs out of the shed. They greeted me with joy, running in circles and jumping up as they followed me into the house.

It was the afternoon of the third day after the cattle drive. I was picking saskatoon berries in the woods on our land about one mile southwest of the barn. I was beginning to grow anxious, as George had not yet returned. I held up the quart jar of saskatoons admiringly. "Not bad for half-an-hour, boys," I declared to Moose, Wampus, and Wobo lying under a tall, blue spruce tree. The dogs thumped their tails on the mossy earth, then rose and followed me as we started for home down the narrow game trail that needled through a poplar grove. Suddenly, they charged ahead of me enthusiastically. A little later when I arrived at the gate, I knew why. Both Jack and Paint were browsing contentedly in the little meadow pasture below our cabin—the men had come home.

That night, over steaming bowls of Mulligan soup or "intert" as I used to call the same kind of culinary masterpiece in England because everything went "into it," we discussed the dismal state of our financial affairs. On a cattle drive eight years before when George was working on Rich's ranch they had received eleven cents per pound on the hoof for yearling steers. The check George had tossed with disgust near the sink when he washed before dinner, represented an average of twelve cents per pound.

"Not bad," George said sarcastically. "Ten years in the swamps, and we have a penny a pound raise for cattle. At this rate, if we live to be a hundred we might have just enough saved up for a week's vacation before they put us under the sod."

I made no comment but went over to the oven and took out a hot saskatoon pie I had made from the afternoon's berries. It was oozing purple juice. I broke off a piece of the crust and ate it. "Nearly as good as Teeney's pies," I pronounced to George, smiling.

Later that evening we let the dogs in for a treat and settled down in front of a brisk log fire. With Jiggs purring contentedly on my lap, we talked further about the ranch life we both loved and what the future in this wilderness might hold for us. We had to be practical. Last year we had made a profit of $768.00 on the cattle, and that was our best year. How were we to get ahead at this rate? In the past, as far as I could tell, George had lived on spirit, hope, and his physical strength. But we were not getting any younger.

I watched George heave a heavy pine log onto the fire with no effort and wished it were as easy to make money as that. George had built his herd slowly and successfully over the years even though the price of cattle had stood still, but this could not offset the unbroken rise in the price of machinery, maintenance repairs, gasoline, labor, food and clothing. It was time for us to face our present financial situation as it really was.

As the night wore on, we fell silent about living costs and cattle prices. I watched the fire slowly fade and the thrust of the flames become less vigorous. Something in the dying of the flames was depressing.

George got up, stirred the logs with the long iron poker, then, calling to the dogs, he opened the front door and let them out. He then went into the kitchen and put the coffee pot on the stove.

When he returned he held up the cattle payment check. "I'd frame this if we didn't have to eat," he said, and went back into the kitchen.

"Tell me about the drive. How did it go?" I called out.

George brought back two cups of coffee. He removed Jiggs from the chair, resumed his seat, rolled a cigarette and blew a column of smoke towards the ceiling.

"Everything went fine until we were about a mile from Vanderhoof—halfway down the hill where that logging mill is with all the shacks on the side of the road. All the family laundry was hanging out. By the time we drew alongside it, the cattle were really edgy. I was riding in front, and Walter was on the tail. Suddenly, a wind came up and the logging camp whistle blew. The whole clothes line seemed to come alive, with the long underwear doing a rhumba with the girdles. The cattle went crazy. We almost lost the herd. It took forever to reach Vanderhoof, only a mile away. The horses were streaked with sweat and our voices were so far gone we could only motion with our hands and speak in a whisper."

It was a relief to laugh at the scene George had conjured up. It was a needed tension breaker to live vicariously through the cattle drive with George and Walter, at the same time feeling relief that we had finally admitted to each other we were not making a go of it financially and we needed to look seriously at some alternative way of life.

Ideas came crowding in on us as we began to plan during other evenings of the fall and winter days.

TWENTY-ONE
Change is in the Air

We settled down in the fall and winter evenings to hours of research into where we wanted to live. Our books were: the *Strout* real estate catalogue, *How to Make a Living in the Country, Today's Lands of Opportunity, Reploge's Atlas,* an atlas of the world, but so obviously printed in the United States, as each state had a page to itself—the same space accorded to the whole continent of Africa, and an out-of-date book of climate and population statistics.

"Read some more," George commanded as I tackled each book in turn, reading it aloud. "Read everything that's for sale. Where it is. How much it is and what part down."

I read everything: rock farmhouse in Arkansas, rich farmlands in Ohio, fruit and juice stands in Florida, trout farms in Oregon, and starred business opportunities in every state.

George sat back with his feet on a stool listening carefully. From time to time he transferred a cigarette from a relaxed, outstretched hand to his mouth, where it hung contemplatively in a forty-five degree angle droop.

Idaho's Coeur d'Alene, the Rogue River Valley of Oregon, the western slopes of the Rockies in Denver, Colorado, a mile-high lake where the biggest rainbow trout in the world was caught, and of course, Las Vegas, where there was always the chance of winning at dice.

He might be lucky again! After all, George had slipped unobserved over the border from San Diego, when he was sixteen, and had made twenty-one straight passes at the dice tables in Tijuana.

Yes, it would have to be the West. But it rained a lot in Oregon. It was too cold in Colorado, and real estate prices there and in California were too high—in Arizona, also.

Then we found Huckleberry Finn country, where the Mississippi and Missouri flowed. Frogs croaked in Louisiana—George liked bull frogs—and there were turtles and marshes—George had an affinity for turtles, also, but it might be too hot for me.

How about Arkansas? A good part of Arkansas was stippled in black in Norman D. Ford's *Lands of Opportunity*. Arkansas was definitely on the march: attractive rock dwellings with fireplaces—George's dream-house had several rock fireplaces. "Yours for a song," it read. "$2,000.00 down." Where was the catch? Somehow we didn't choose Arkansas, and we continued steadily and systematically to work our way towards the East.

At the beginning of the war after the 101st horse cavalry had been mechanized and was going south on maneuvers, George had ridden a motorcycle at the head of the column. He had looked down into the spectacular Rockfish Gap in the Shenandoah Valley of Virginia and had thought that he would like to live there sometime. Maybe we should live in the East and not in the West. Perhaps the Southeast. We began to study Virginia.

🌲   🌲   🌲

School life continued to be filled with simple pleasures and Eva Wiebe, aged eleven, wrote in her composition book:

The school has been painted recently. The inside, Mr. Bradley painted green around the windows and doors and the walls are a cream color. The ceiling is white.

Then we got some supplies from the School Board, including a table-tennis set and some other small games with which we often play. We got two baseball gloves and a stove in which we we can burn coal. Two loads of coal were brought to the school. We got two pails, one for water and the other one for getting in the coal and putting it into the stove.

We got some scissors, protractors, tape, compasses and other little things to help us with our work.

The really big school news was the drilling of the school well. Klaas Wiebe, aged ten, wrote a diary for a week in January:

January 7. It was ten below zero today. At noon it started snowing. Mr. Nicholson started working on the well again today. The machinery is about thirty feet high. The well is forty-four feet deep now. Our calf always sucks so we put on the calf weaner. We had to draw the machinery for digging the well. We had to draw Mr. Nicholson's Ford truck, too. We saw a coyote on the river about a quarter mile from our water hole. We went sleigh riding on the ice.

January 8. It was twenty-four below zero. The river has a layer of ice fifteen inches thick. We are doing some wool weaving now. I saw a cow moose today.

January 9. It was fourteen below zero in the morning. But in the daytime it was very warm. Mr. Nicholson has dug seventy-five feet now. My dad fixed the harness for our horse.

January 10. It was pretty chilly this morning. Mr. Nicholson has dug ninety feet now. We couldn't get our car started so we got our horse. We pulled the car backwards. I had to steer the car.

January 11. It was ten below zero. Mr. Nicholson has now dug 130 feet. My mum made soup. We are deciding on a school magazine now. Mr. George Voth bulldozed our mill road.

January 12. It was twelve below zero. it was snowing until four o'clock. The well is 170 feet deep now. At dinner time when I was giving our pigs food I saw a big yellow aeroplane that was just about twenty feet above the trees. And also today my mum all of a sudden noticed that it was very smoky inside the house. She looked all over the place but couldn't find a thing. All of a sudden she saw a stick burning between the frame and the stove.

January 15. It was sixteen below zero today. The well is 180 feet deep now. When I was coming to school this morning, I heard a woodpecker pecking on a spruce tree.

After punching through 328 feet of earth and rock, Braeside's first deep well was dug; the school could now get its water from a pump instead of having to crack open the creek with an axe each day in winter.

Like many other ranchers in the area, in the winter George let his horses forage for themselves on the wild hay and slew pastures. Horses paw through the snow right down to the grass; cattle do not paw and cannot survive on their own and must be fed. The exception, however, is when cattle mix in with the horses. When this happens, the horses do the work and the cattle get a free ride.

On the whole, the winter was pretty rough and to conserve on our diminishing hay supply, in January George drove the cattle to a thrashed-out oat stack that he had bought near to Vanderhoof.

In March, after the cattle were driven back to the ranch, an Arctic blizzard swept down from the North, and the temperature dropped to forty-five below and held between there and thirty below for a week. It was tough on all the animals.

Jack, Paint, Carrot, and the Mysterious Bay came up from the meadow. Al's packhorse, Bess, that we were looking after for the winter, wasn't among them. After throwing some hay to the horses, George filled a packsack with hay and some oats, stepped into his snowshoes, and set out in search of Bess.

George found the places in the snow where the horses had recently bedded down. He combed the whole meadow for her, but she was nowhere to be seen. The worst had probably happened, he told me on his return, unless she had pulled for new country, which was unlikely. Somewhere under the thick blanket of snow, Bess lay buried.

The other horses were doing well, except for the Mysterious Bay; she was thin and gaunt. The next morning George distributed their hay in four bunches so that they would eat without fighting over it and then went over to the barn, where he was feeding a weak calf with a bottle.

Hearing a racket coming from the horses, he saw Paint strike out at the Mysterious Bay. She reared up and fell over backwards and off the beaten path into a deep snow drift. She foundered in the snow, unable to rise. George grabbed a shovel and ran over to her shovelling the snow out from under and around her, letting her rest while he cleared the ground.

Then he got at the back of her and pushed and yelled. As she made the effort to rise, he threw his weight against her hind quarters to brace her and keep her from buckling. She was too weak, however, went forward only a few steps and collapsed again.

He worked on her for several hours, bracing his body under her neck to prevent her from lying on her side. He tried to get her to eat some oats but she didn't have the strength. Finally, her eyes closed, her breathing became almost imperceptible. She sank back on her side and died.

It was a dismal time. We had already lost several calves during the cold spell; and one old cow that we had hoped would make it through to spring finally died.

An uncanny silence hung over everything, and there was no wind. It seemed to have petered out as the flickering spirit of the mare was snuffed out. No birds or squirrels ate at the bird table.

Everything was desolate. Crows sailed over the tops of the spruces and I knew they had sensed the presence of death. Snow floated slowly to earth with the same inevitability which had overtaken the Mysterious Bay, and now it was covering her gently and decently with a soft white shroud.

Back in the cabin that night I listened to George's assessment of the past, of our shared great love for our animals and wilderness home. These and his love for his mother, brother, and his many friends were assets on the balance sheet. But I also knew that ten years of slugging it out on this far northern frontier without a break, had been no picnic. Also, recent economic problems and frustrations had left their mark. When green grass reappears in the spring, I thought, and the birds start to sing their love songs, this time we may be seeking new horizons.

George wrote to Al to tell him the bad news about Bess. A short time afterwards, Neil Jackson, an Englishman who was working with one of George's friends in Vanderhoof, spent the day with us; he was interested in ranching and packing. George and he had tentatively discussed making some sort of a deal on the machinery and cattle whereby he could live at Little Creek, run the ranch and eventually buy it if he liked it.

When he left, the idea was that he would write to England to find out about his finances and then contact Al to see if he might be interested in buying a half-interest in the cattle and machinery and in becoming a partner.

In the meantime, we continued to build castles in the air about our future. How about Florida?—a goldfish pool and air conditioning . . .

"And all we've got in our pockets to buy anything with," concluded George, after several minutes of such self-indulgence, "is two bits and Wittman's got his hands on it."—Wittman was the bank manager in Vanderhoof.

Early one evening during the worst of spring break-up, the dogs started to bark. No vehicle could get across the wash-out unless they had come provided with material to make their own bridge. It had to be someone on foot.

We looked out towards the road in the direction the dogs were running. "Better get some pants on," I suggested to George who was comfortably clad in long

winter underwear and dressing gown. I could see two
men coming toward us over the snow. As they got
nearer we could make out that one of them was Al and
the other, Neil Jackson.

"Hello, you old mudhoppers. How are you?" George
yelled from the front door. The greeting was apt, and
before coming into the house they discarded their muddy
boots. They had walked four miles after being stranded
on the road in Al's truck.

The men made the rounds of the ranch before supper, and it was late before they returned. When I first
went to the door I could hear their voices way off down
the meadow. Then I heard the tractor start up. George
must be giving a sales talk, I thought.

Still later I went to the door again. I could hear
them talking on the bridge, although I could not see
them, as it was already dark. I caught words that
sounded like final inevitable words. I closed the door.
How I wished they would come in! They finally came.

"Well, darling," George announced, "Al and Neil
think they would like to buy the ranch." I mumbled
some words which I thought would be appropriate, but
all the time I was thinking: How about us? We do want
to sell the ranch, don't we? We had said so to ourselves, to each other—and to them. Then what was this
numbness I was experiencing?

There was no answer to my self-questioning that
night. Everything went on as usual as in a visit from
friends. But there was a difference. George talked
noticeably more than usual, and I talked less. George's
dark eyes appeared bigger and more sunken, more otherworldly. Something had happened to him also in those
few hours since I had seen him.

The men stayed up until dawn philosophizing over a
bottle of whiskey. There had been a heavy frost that
night, and George had driven me to school the next day

without any trouble. But when he picked me up after
school and had parked the jeep as usual at the wash-out,
walking was particularly difficult because of the extra
sticky consistency of the mud.

"We couldn't do this for the rest of our lives,
Wangs," said George, putting his arm comfortably round
my shoulder, knowing how I felt about the possible sale
of the ranch even though with every step I took I lifted
pounds of clinging mud so that I could hardly move one
foot in front of the other. "It's the roads that hold us
back."

We went into the house the back way—the first time
we had used that road since the snow had deepened. The
shades of the back windows were down, as if the house
was in mourning. We entered and looked around as if
seeing our home for the first time. It seemed quieter
with a different quietness from its habitual brooding,
loving, possessive peace. It was as if it was deep in
thought.

"If Al and Neil take the ranch we will be leaving it
in good hands, Wangy," George said comfortingly.

We brewed our usual cup of tea, sitting close together, deep in two armchairs. Such times as these have
made up the sum total of our happiness here, I thought.
It's not the highlights that count so much but the everyday innumerable moments of deep peace and calm in the
great silence.

I thought of the winter I might not see there again.
The tired earth being covered with the first silent snowflakes followed by the depthless mid-winter. How we
had grown in stature in the long wilderness winters and
had been strengthened in our love for each other.

"Never let a different environment affect our love,
George," I said, my face crumpling like a child's in
distress as the true meaning of this home swept over me,
and I wept, remembering also how a change of environ-

ment had contributed to the break-up of my first marriage.

"It's strange," observed George, turning away to hide his face from me, "how tears seem to squeeze through, though one is not crying. I guess it's crying inside."

We walked over to the big window and looked out over the ranch. "I guess we'll have to leave Mulligan after all, 'Mulligan Without Portfolio.' It'd take a lot to ship him to the States."

He paused, listening; we could hear the thrilling talk of geese flying low and opened the door to watch as they winged their way farther north, talking excitedly. As they passed overhead, the strong beating of their wings became louder, and we watched until they had vanished out of sight. We said nothing. We might be going south with them in the fall. Then in the spring, only they, and not we, would come winging back.

We closed the door and went to the window again. "We'll be leaving The Ghost and the animals buried here but they will sleep well and we shall see them again." George spoke quietly, gazing over his land. "This ranch has been a father to me and I have been a father to it. Hughie cared for it for forty years. I have loved it for ten, and sometimes cursed it. But this little ranch has made a better man of me, and I have spent the happiest years of my life here. If Al and Neil buy it, they will care for it, too."

We sat down. If we once leave, I thought, we will never come back to the cold northland so brooding and so still, so rich and cruel, so secretive and inscrutable. It hurt to think of that possibility. I recalled the first day I had visited the ranch and later when George had offered his home to me; it had been winter then.

The earth here, I pondered, is not prodigal with her riches, and when she gives, she gives abundantly bringing forth in painful birth all her hidden reserves, strong beyond measure because of the long period of winter resting. But when she takes, she takes relentlessly and without remorse. Her victims struggle ineffectively and the land settles back again into an abiding watchfulness.

I felt the need to do something physical. I got up, picked up a rake from outside and raked some of the winter's debris from around the front door. A log was still embedded in dirty ice and I uncovered two colored plastic icicles which had fallen months before from the beautiful blue-spruce Christmas tree while it was being carried outside. Near to them a green soda bottle, left out to cool at the festive season, had frozen and burst into a dozen pieces.

Wobo was busy, too. I could see him from the front door trying to catch the toads which were spawning in a flooded area near the house. I should have penned him up because he spent the rest of the day churning up the water and frightening the toads and he was still splashing around in the dark long after we had gone to bed.

TWENTY-TWO

Ranch for Sale

We were asking $25,000 for the ranch including everything; land, stock, hay, machinery, buildings, etc. With the Prout Meadow sold to the Co-op, we had a three-quarter section remaining, with ninety acres in hay, ten in oats, seventy acres of virgin land broken up, and another sixty acres of willow and poplar uncleared; the rest was pasture and timber.

Al and Neil had decided at first that they could only muster up $7,200, with $500 a year on the balance at five percent interest. George's remark to me after he had heard the offer was brief and to the point: "Why, the pay-off would come at the time of my funeral." He could not accept the offer, although he would have liked to as Al and Neil were friends of his. We had to have more capital than that to start over again somewhere else.

We then listed the ranch for $25,000 with George Ogston, a local real estate agent, asking no less than $15,000 down. In the meantime, Al had spotted an advertisement in the *Prairie Free Press* for the sale of a well-known St. Bernard kennels in Saskatchewan.

Knowing George's love of all animals Al had discussed with me the idea of our raising St. Bernard dogs instead of cattle so that perhaps we would not have to leave the Little Creek. He wrote to the advertiser and asked them to address their reply to me.

Oddly enough, the letter from the kennels and the letter containing Al and Neil's final offer for the ranch arrived in the same bunch of mail.

While George was getting a gas-barrel filled, before we left town for the ranch, I opened the fat, three-page, beigy-brown letter from the kennels in Saskatchewan. It had the heads of St. Bernards all over it. I scanned it hastily, skipping excitedly from page to page, noticing only what seemed to me at that time to be the phenomenal income which could be derived from breeding these wonderful animals and only casually noticing the price at which their business could be bought. We returned to the ranch to study further the two important letters.

In their letter, Al and Neil said that they were willing to pay $22,500 for the ranch. The down payment of $7,200 was to cover the cattle—forty-two head and one bull—and the machinery, with an additional $2,000 trade-in value for the truck.

If we kept the proceeds from the fall calf-crop, Al and Neil had estimated we would then have $10,400 all together. They were asking for 150 tons of hay as a bare minimum for the eighty head of cattle which they hoped to winter over. The $500 a year minimum to be paid off in not more than twenty years, remained the same as their first offer.

But George wanted a minimum of $15,000 cash. "Read the dog letter," George said, and I did: "We have twenty-four St. Bernards in our kennels. We have been selling from 175 to 216 dogs per year for the last five years. Most of our pups sell for $135 each. Our yearly intake is around $17,000. You could have our fencing, kennel buildings and any other equipment along with the dogs. I imagine our big sleeping houses could be pulled down and sent either in box car or trucks."

At this point I had strange hallucinations of gigantic dogs peering sadly through barred boxes on trucks stuck fast in the Deadly Duo, followed by a long convoy of trucks laden with enormous sleeping boxes also stuck in the mud along the whole road from Vanderhoof to the ranch.

"Read on," urged George, as I returned to reality.

"As for the price, I think the kennels would be a good buy at $25,000, but I'll make the price including equipment $15,000 cash." Cash was underlined heavily. If you think you want to buy at $15,000 cash, you shouldn't wait too long."

"Jumpin' Jiminy," exclaimed George. "Just think, out of forty brood cows a fellow should be able to sell thirty-five six-to-seven-month-old calves by the fall at $50 apiece, which equals $1750. It costs $600 without labor to put up the hay to feed these forty cows. Therefore, $600 off $1750 leaves $1150. That doesn't include my labor for putting up hay or feeding the cattle over the winter, nor does it include depreciation on machinery, the cost of salt blocks, etc. Now if I were to sell these forty brood cows and one bull at beef prices this fall, I would realize close to $4,000.

"That same $4,000 invested in St. Bernard dogs would buy about six bitches and one male, according to the letter we have just read. Each bitch would average, say, two litters of five puppies per year, which would bring sixty puppies a year at $135 apiece, which comes to $8,100, or about four-and-a-half times what we're making in cattle." George continued. "It costs about $50 a year to keep Moose. Therefore one bitch, which would cost us $50 a year to feed, would produce twenty-six times its cost of keep in two litters of pups at $135 apiece, whereas one cow which costs us $15 to feed, produces only one calf at $50, or a little over three times what it costs to feed."

I felt like saying "Quod erat demonstrandum," after this masterly proof. I too was becoming caught up in this new idea and George's enthusiasm which knew no bounds. Choices and options were fast appearing as if out of nowhere with the arrival of the three pages of beigy-colored notepaper covered with large St. Bernard heads. If the ranch didn't sell, we could stay and raise St. Bernards and sell our cattle to buy the dog-breeding stock; if we did sell the ranch, we could move to a more suitable place to start raising St. Bernards.

George loved these dogs. He had told me all about his St. Bernard, Teddy, which he had in California and which had looked like a lion because in the hot weather he was shaved all over except for his neck, face and the end of his tail. And wasn't his beloved Moose also half St. Bernard.

"Why," George continued, his voice raised more loudly than ever with eager enthusiasm "the ranch is the most perfect set-up for dogs you've ever seen; it's at the end of a dirt road; no cars to run over them and no neighbors to complain of noise. There's no telling how far we could go in this business. I've got to go as soon as possible to see the kennels before it's too late." The question of whether we could afford the plane fare never came up for discussion.

But George wanted to show Al and Neil's letter to George Ogston before he made any moves. George Ogston had been a friend of the Hobson family for a long time and we invaded him at his home the next day, completely unexpected, just as he and his wife were starting on the first pineapple cube of their dessert. I had not met George's wife, Beatrice, and while the two Georges got into a huddle over Al and Neil's letter, she and I had a lively conversation.

The Ogstons were moving into a new home over a recently modernized office. I learned that if one wanted a decently renovated hardwood floor, it had to be alternately scratched with steel wool and varnished three times. I thought thankfully of my once-a-year floor effort, when I spread liquid wax over the Little Creek pinewood floors after the mud of spring break-up had dried up outside.

The Ogstons must have thought us a strange couple because when the discussion about Al and Neil's letter was over, George, who seldom can keep any good thing to himself, brought up the subject of St. Bernard dogs and asked me to produce the letter from the kennels for George Ogston to read. George told him that we were seriously considering going into the dog business and not trying to sell the ranch at all.

We voyaged in "dogdom" all the way home. The next day I typed out a list of fifty-six questions which George wanted to ask about the dog business when he got to Watrous, Saskatchewan, and which ran the gamut from: "What degree of cold can puppies endure without dying?" to "Do rats or weasels or any other kind of animals bother the puppies at night?"

I also typed a letter to Al and Neil. George dictated:

> Eve and I have been giving your offer a great deal of thought. We honestly feel that our place, less the calves, is worth $23,800. We realize the necessity of a substantial down-payment on any property we would wish to buy.
>
> The twenty or thirty-year payment plan has its obstacles. Two or three decades is a long time and so many things could happen.
>
> I look back with no little wonder at the day when you were both here and I wanted practically to give the place away . . . My

only regret is that I was not wealthy enough
to have done it and that I misled you into
thinking that it could be done.

The roads are good now and you can get
all the way to the ranch. We are looking
forward to seeing you as soon as you can
come out.

He then packed a little bag, and with no cash, only
a checkbook, and clad in his oldest ranch clothes, he left
at midnight to drive to Prince George to catch a plane
the next day for Watrous, Saskatchewan.

As the door closed behind him, he said, "If I stop at
the gate for a while, I'm not seeing a man about a dog
but shoveling out a hole so that you can get that gate
open without breaking your back." And he was gone.

Large dogs padded through my dreams the rest of
that night. Meals without George were empty affairs
eaten on the prowl. And as for the business of the
ranch: Had he said the bull drank only three buckets of
water a day? Of course my buckets were not full ones
like George's. Before school in the mornings I gave him
three with a slice of baled hay. At four o'clock when I
returned, his nose was covered with large watery drops
the size and beauty of the moonstones I once had in a
bracelet. He heard the bucket clink as I picked it up
and ran to the creek to fill it. He watched me through a
space in the rails of the corral as I returned and emptied
it into his large tub. He swayed rhythmically from side
to side while I poured it and then drank deeply. I knew
he wanted more. He drank nine of my-sized bucketfuls
each day.

Then there was the cellar to pump out. We had
been pumping water out of it steadily for the last two
years. I donned rubber boots and descended into the
cellar twice a day to change the belt from the pump to

fill the water storage tank to the one to pump out the cellar.

I had developed a cold since George had left, and in an effort to get rid of it I enveloped my head in a towel and put my face over a large jug of boiling water with friars balsam floating on the top. I was inhaling deeply, all set to breathe in the first breathful of the healing vapors when I heard a knock at the back door, opened it, and there stood the Rawleigh Man.

You always ask the Rawleigh Man to come in, even if you are alone in the house and also can't think of anything at all that you need at the moment. The image of the original Mr. Rawleigh, whose picture fronts his bottles—a benign, bewhiskered man of middle age with a high white collar, of upright and astute mein instills in the user, or the mere beholder of his products, a feeling of absolute trust, not only in the products themselves, but also in the representative.

Additionally, if he had walked from the nearest mud hole carrying two heavy bags of his products, you not only asked him in, but you also asked him to join you, if not under the towel, at least in a cup of tea. You also asked him to recount the latest local news which he invariably knew.

The outward appearance of the bottles and containers had always fascinated me. By the time the Rawleigh Man had left, a bottle of anti-pain oil (which had been marketed for fifty years, the bottle said,) and had saved the feet of the daughter of a woman on the prairies from frost-bite, a bottle of cold tablets, and one of a pink liquid called Pleasant Relief had been added to the miscellany of bottles on the kitchen shelf.

When he had left, I took two of the cold tablets, reheated the water for the inhalation, and breathing deeply, self-hypnotized myself by murmuring "Pleasant Relief" over and over again until my face ran with perspiration and I emerged from the towel, my hair in small ringlets from the steam and my spirits in a state of spiralling exhilaration. I went to bed immediately and rose the following morning completely cured.

George returned from Saskatchewan after having spent several days working at the kennels with the owner and asking his fifty-six questions. He had picked out four dogs he liked—Big Clara, Esme, Merri-Joan, and Giant Rambler in case we decided to go into the dog business either on the ranch or elsewhere. Then he took a long look at the old barn and all the other buildings on the ranch and a longer look at the road and announced dramatically, "I must have been building kennels in the air. It isn't at all practical to breed St. Bernards at the Little Creek Ranch."

So in the middle of June, we put an advertisement in the *Prairie Free Press* and the *Sunday Oregonian*: "FOR SALE, cattle ranch in tiny valley in heart of moose, deer and fishing country . . . good road . . . ," and waited. It took up thirteen lines. It was a masterpiece of salesmanship. After all, we had been reading other people's advertising blurbs all winter. But why on earth did George say "good road?"

The oat seed should have been planted already; it was still in sacks and was being visited daily by the friendly pack rats. The weather had been just right for sowing when George had gone to Saskatchewan. On his return there had been many days of heavy rain. He got with it as soon as the weather was better and I was nearly ready to take tea and cookies down to the meadow on this first long-awaited occasion when I heard the ominous racing of a motor coming from the direction of the barnyard.

I walked dejectedly from the house. George wasn't in the meadow at all, but on the tractor on the bank leading out of the barnyard to the meadow, completely stationary, except that with each revving of the motor the tractor disappeared a few more inches into the stinking mud. The disk and harrows which he had already disengaged from the tractor were already completely submerged.

He had stuffed slices of baled hay under the front wheels, but it had been swallowed up in the mire. A stream of expletives, intermingled with interrogations and aggressive statements to the wide open spaces greeted me: "Why did I buy a tractor mounted on rubber? If I had one with steel wheels I wouldn't be here." and "If you gave this country back to the Indians, they wouldn't take it." The wheel of fortune had come turnabout. At that time, in my spouse's mind, we were due for an immediate take-off, if not to greener pastures, at least to dryer ones.

That evening as a special treat to counteract the day's frustrations we were each munching happily on a bar of Cadbury's nut chocolate when George's top denture split neatly down the middle. We tried to glue it together with some kind of quick-drying "Wonder" glue but it didn't work and we knew we would have to mail it away to be mended.

The next day, I took it into the post office in Vanderhoof after school, and on the way back I picked up several of the Derksen children who had stopped off at their uncle's to collect their dog, Wolf, the son of Wampus and Moose.

Wolf had turned out to be a magnificent specimen with a black muzzle, built stockily, "right on the ground," as George termed it. But he was in disgrace; he had been chasing their uncle's cattle and had slashed the legs of one of them.

The next day the Co-op children came to school with the sad story of the killing of three of their sheep and four lambs. Their throats had been slashed, but none had been eaten. It was a great loss to them coming on top of other stock losses throughout the winter. The children told of tracks like large dog tracks and suspicion had fallen on Wolf.

The next night the sheep were corralled and the Co-op men kept watch all night. The children had nothing to report the next day except that large fresh tracks had been seen all round the carcasses.

There were four large dogs around—Wolf, a brother of Wolf, who belonged to the Co-op and our two, Moose and Wobo. We no longer had Wampus. A few weeks before, she had vanished into the darkness one cold winter's night after we had heard a wolf pack howling nearby, and we never saw her again. We often wondered if she had joined the pack, as we knew she was reputed to have some wolf blood in her. We decided not to pen our dogs up or to restrain them, as none of our dogs had been accustomed to wearing a collar.

George had gone over to the Co-op the day following the killing and had heard of it firsthand. He had thought the culprit sounded like a wolf, the pattern of the killing and letting it lie. The following day the children told me that a farmer living at Fort Fraser had given them some ear tags to tag on each sheep's ear. These had an unpleasant smell which was supposed to repel wolves and the farmer who had invented them had used them successfully on his sheep after an attack by a wolf. We heard no more until the following Sunday night when we were sitting at a late supper. I saw a man approaching the back gate. It was George Voth.

"Hello you old swamp-jumper," yelled my husband from the kitchen door. Moose was in the kitchen with us, and let out a series of staccato barks as George Voth entered, and Wobo, who was outside, joined in.

We were always pleased to see George Voth. He had walked from the Deadly Duo which still lay in wait

for the unwary, and he said that he had not dared to
drive through, as the hole in the road looked bottomless,
so he had left his little Austin on the far side of it. He
sat down on a stool with his back to the wall and
George told him about getting stuck in the barnyard with
the tractor, disk, and harrows and how swearing had
done no good.

"You should have found that out long ago," said
George Voth smiling. Then he added in a more serious
vein, "I've got bad news for you. Wobo is the killer.
We've kept watch for four nights. The first night our
two dogs turned up and prowled round the corral and
went away, but the next night, Wobo jumped into the
middle of the heap, scattering them in all directions and
overthrowing a lamb onto its back. Moose didn't join
in."

The men had had guns and could have shot Wobo
but did not because their sheep were all around. Although the culprit was our dog, I felt less troubled now
that the truth was known. I had noticed at midnight the
day after the killing had happened, and just before we
were going to bed, that our two dogs had vanished and
were not within calling distance. I had been awakened
by their barking at four-thirty the same morning, so
they must have been away for four or five hours, time
enough to travel the three miles between the properties.
The killer had been found. George Voth took Wobo with
him when he went. Alas, poor Wobo, you had to pay
the price. You will never play again with the spawning
toads.

🌲   🌲   🌲

A light postal package the size of a pound of butter
lay on my desk at school the next day. It had been left
there by Abe, who had brought it from Vanderhoof. I

opened it expectantly, then remembered that George's upper denture must be nestling under the white tissue paper. All in one piece again, it was joined together neatly as if the plastic had been heated and drawn together with a needle, scraping a piece first from one side and then the other. The join looked like a zip-fastener. I was glad it had arrived at this time, as I would be able to give him a pleasant surprise packet after the lamentable happenings of the last week.

George picked me up in the truck after school. We were to stop at George Voth's on the way back home as he was repairing the jeep for us. Just before we got there, I produced the denture triumphantly. George examined it gingerly.

"Now I shall be able to have a decent meal again," he said, slipping it into his mouth as deftly as slipping off a raw oyster from the shell. He flipped it around in his mouth in a most professional way, talking all the time. He had only been without it for a week, but when it was in his mouth again he suddenly looked a little like a pack rat. The timbre of his voice changed, and the teeth slipped.

"Wangy, I don't want to have anything to do with it, put it in your handbag."

Not another dismal failure, I thought, but secretly held out hope that in the serenity of our home and with the help of Fasteeth, the repaired denture would at least be half a success.

George's spirits recovered with the repairing of the jeep. When we got home he announced, "Now I'm going to treat myself to a cracker." I reissued the teeth and left him to the trial run. When I returned, he was holding the denture in his left hand in exactly the same position as he holds a piece of celery eaten before a meal. He was carefully tapping on Fasteeth with the same precision as he would put salt on the celery.

The teeth back in place, he surveyed himself in the mirror and then considering it more of a challenge, he decided on Shredded Wheat instead of a cracker. The whole operation was a complete success. Things were looking up in the Little Creek household.

The two ads had produced sixty-eight letters or postcards of inquiry from British Columbia, the Prairies, Washington State, and Oregon. Some were short, a mere inquiry; others were all business, asking pertinent questions as detailed as the ones George had asked when he went to Saskatchewan.

The "open range" on government land aroused great interest. What was open range? many asked. Others inquired "Are you related to the *Grass Beyond the Mountains* Hobson?" "Are there any wild fruits?" "Is the water soft?" "Do people up there speak English?" "How many cattle? Your ad says only two milk cows."

Trades, renting, and terms were proffered as alternative propositions. A few indicated why they were especially interested: "a place off the streets for the kids," "a second place," "a place for my son."

I answered them all in a letter of two-and-a-half pages, describing in detail the ranch and the cabin chinked with oakum and enclosing a brochure about Vanderhoof.

On receiving a copy of our letter of reply, one woman wrote back: "It sounds like the Garden of Eden." We surmised, however, that she was not about to enter the Garden, for she added, rather apologetically, it seemed to me, "Money is scarce up here." How well we knew what she meant! And how odd that she wrote "up" when she lived south of us when I had always considered south "down," and north "up."

Now the genuinely interested prospective buyers started to arrive.

TWENTY-THREE
Goodbye Little Creek— Farewell to the North Country

They came by road in cars old and new; by train, and by commercial and private planes. Their visits coincided with Teeney's third summer vacation at the ranch. A good friend, Dave Noble, came with him, and although the hard work and fun of the summer before were repeated, we were all aware that this summer might be the last on the ranch.

For prospective buyers and with great ingenuity, George developed the obvious disadvantages of the ranch into positive pluses: "A dirt road is not up to concrete or gravel," he informed prospective buyers with great enthusiasm, "but we are not bothered by our cattle getting run over by cars or trucks." Or, "There is a completely modern one-room school four miles away." I had never thought before of any one-room school being modern until I heard George say this, but he almost convinced me. After all, I thought, the school does now have the only deep well in Braeside, even though outhouses are our only bathrooms.

George would also say: "We have natural refrigeration and no cattle diseases. Ticks and pests are almost unheard of here, and for people, why, it is one of the healthiest climates in the world." "And," I would add, bringing up the rear and getting into the spirit of things, "the cabin is chinked with oakum, and that keeps the bugs out."

Teeney and David accompanied George when he took the visitors to the main meadow. "Let me do the talking," George would say in preparation; while he talked, the boys spent several minutes trying to open each gate, most of which were still held in place with tangled baling wire intricately entwined like a "cat's cradle."

One particularly grave, self-important sort of fellow was unimpressed with all the talking. He also took a dim view of the gates and everything else he was experiencing. The ill-suppressed laughter of the boys as they tried to undo the wire didn't help.

George attempted to save face by remarking that it was seldom that anyone other than he passed that way, and since he had always been the leader in obstacle courses in the paratroop division when training for the Office of Strategic Services, he announced, "It means nothing to me at all, boys, nothing at all." Then he added, "Hopping over them keeps me in good shape." The total experience evidently caused the visitor considerable distress, for he didn't stick around long and was never heard from again.

Not so R. L. Mork of Cheadle, Alberta. With his pretty wife, Velda, he visited the ranch in the middle of August. They both fell in love with it without reservation, and we sold it for $20,000 cash.

Ronnie Mork was an original. He was tall and lean, used colorful language, and not only looked and acted like a cowboy—he was a cowboy. When he entered the cabin, it seemed to grow smaller. He took down the swords, knives and guns, from the cabin walls and amidst great hilarity, decorated himself with them, quickly transforming himself into a cross between a pirate and a backwoodsman. We knew at that moment that the Morks would make perfect Creekmen and carry on the tradition of all Little Creekmen. So they returned to Alberta to sell their farm.

Between Ronnie's visits we all went to Ormand Lake. We had recently acquired a boat of our own. It was part of the $5,000-deal we had made with the Co-operative when we sold them the Prout Meadow. George Voth had made the stoutly-built boat; we christened her "Little Creek."

The timelessness of the wilderness held us again in its spell. The last streak of color left the sky as we watched on our last night there. Again, the dark lake mirrored the mystic mountains . . . a mist settled . . . a trout jumped . . . a loon cried.

For centuries that had all been happening before, and it would happen again for ages to come; there would be other beholders and the lake would then belong to them. That night was mine, and although my feet would leave it and I might never return, my spirit was captured forever in the invisible net of that wilderness night.

On the ranch, with the help of the boys, work proceeded at an increased tempo. The pain of the realization that our wilderness life must soon end was lessened by knowing that what we then worked at would benefit the new Little Creekmen, Ronnie, Val and their children.

The baler hammered out the bales for the winter feed. The boys dug a new hole for the "Little House." Before we left, it was skidded over the new hole. After the digging, the hole filled with water and with a lacrosse stick David had brought with him, the boys rescued careless toads from drowning. Bossy had a new calf.

Many people came and went. Friends and acquaintances I had seen previously only in Vanderhoof came out to the ranch to visit us, to hunt grouse, to fix machinery and to look over the things for sale. Black Cow was bought and went to a new home. Everybody stayed for something, coffee, tea, lunch, supper, or for the night. I was cooking continuously.

Our friend, Neil Jackson, cut off two of his fingers when he was mowing hay for Jack Andros, and we went to visit him in the hospital. Dave Noble had to leave the ranch at the beginning of August, but Teeney stayed on a little longer, very much aware that it was a last goodbye to the Little Creek. We went to Vanderhoof more often and visited friends. Suddenly I realized how many friends we had. We stayed for coffee, tea, lunch, supper, or for the night.

A stay for the night took place after we had been to a movie. On returning to the ranch, we got stuck on the road just beyond the Nechako Bridge. We trudged back and took a room, most appropriately, at the Vanderhoof Hotel, where four years before my adventure had all begun, and where it shortly was to come to an end, at least with the land.

Ironically enough, the movie we saw was *Quo Vadis*—whither goest thou? The glib answer to the question that night was, "Not very far." As to our future destination, I was still asking myself that question on the day the first snow of the fall flew.

In the meantime, Ronnie reappeared after having sold his farm in Alberta. Leaving his horse-box with two mares in it by the old cabin, he strode over to the ranch house. In one hand, he carried Wendy, a little dog with hair all over her face, and in the other, he waved a bottle of whiskey.

George spent the next few days introducing Ronnie to "the boys" in Vanderhoof.

In the meantime our search in the Strout catalogue had ended up in the Shenandoah Valley of Virginia: "Surrounded by lovely river—here is an unusual home, picturesque and steeped in history—large central hall with walnut staircase—four fireplaces . . . (This is not the house we bought—that is another story.)

This was it; the four fireplaces did it for George. Would it still be for sale? All our activities became geared towards getting as soon as possible to Staunton, Virginia, to meet Jessie Anderson, Strout Real Estate representative.

Our plans were to fly to Detroit, buy a new car there, and then drive to Virginia. We would not be able to take much baggage with us, so we decided to send our personal belongings, our treasures, and the manuscript "Back Tracks," on ahead of us by rail to Richmond, Virginia, to await the day when we settled down again and could pick them up. We did not know anyone in Richmond, but we liked the name. George's father and his brother were named Richmond, and, of course, it was the state capital. In an inexplicable way we felt comfortable consigning all our worldly belongings in care of that old, historic city.

We couldn't send on everything we owned. My loom, George's western saddle, his snowshoes, and Bumpy the Moose were among the things we regretfully had to leave behind. But we did crate the Rocky Mountain sheep to go over one of the fireplaces in our new home.

A huddled heap of once fashionable New York trunks and suitcases and an odd assortment of packing cases and boxes labeled "George Hobson, Richmond, Virginia— to Await Arrival" lay forlornly on the platform of Vanderhoof station. No one knew which way they would travel to Virginia or how long they would take to get there and the bill of lading for the eighteen items was sketchy.

We bid goodbye to the miscellaneous assortment, including a plywood tea chest, an old teak chest, a heavy jarrahwood box from Australia, bound around with the ubiquitous Little Creek baling wire, a duffle bag of laundry, and a frail little black hat box. A tall, well-traveled Royal Robe trunk which had spent most of its lengthy life in India was the guardian of the heap and kept look-out on the station. Oddly enough, from the label inside, it was returning to the very Richmond where it had been manufactured decades before.

It had belonged to my former husband, and on his return to England from India and the Middle East after World War II, it had contained, to him, a most precious cargo. I did not share his enthusiasm for it—a huge stone jar of highly-spiced Indian bazaar pickles. To keep it safely anchored in the trunk, Indian saris and lengths of Damascus brocade for me had formed a mummy-like wrapping around it.

I had eaten a piece of the pickle, a tiny fragment of carrot no bigger than the size of my little finger nail, and had immediately broken out into a cold sweat; I ate no more. The present contents were less volcanic. But the trunk itself lent an unmistakable social dignity to the otherwise ill-assorted and plebian collection.

🌲 🌲 🌲

When our Mennonite friends heard that we were leaving, they planned a party for us in the school. We played games, and they gave us presents and a book, *We R Going with You*. It had been made by the children with the help of their new teacher, Jake Schroeder, of the Braeside Co-op and father of the twins, Alvin and Kenneth.

The signatures of the twenty school children prefaced the book; Gilbert's was large and bold. A collage of airplanes, gloves, a weathervane, and a couple carrying air baggage, encircled the message: "The four winds will carry our best wishes to you around the globe wherever you may happen to go—until we meet again."

A map followed, entitled "Your Braeside Neighbors, 1955." Divided into numbered sections, it pinpointed our neighbors' homes, the roads, railway, and the Nechako River—"Beautiful Queen."

The book was so truthfully and simply expressed that it brought tears to my eyes as I turned the pages. "Trankle Creek (we called it Little Creek) stops in at the Hobson's, bubbling and singing as it goes happily along, cheering you with its songs in times of trouble and strain," it read, accompanied by a picture of a man and a woman looking towards the sunset.

It continued: "May the beautiful warmth of the evening skies at Braeside remind you of the warmth of your fireplace on the ranch—may these sunsets often come back to you and say, 'That was a perfect stay.'" How well they knew that the fireplace was the heart of a home.

A picture of the children coming to school by horse and sleigh was accompanied by: "Our imaginations run wild with things we see as we go along, with conversation of fishing, swimming, camping, following bush trails, watching the beavers at the canyon, chasing a squirrel up a tree. The 400 trips to school while you were our teacher have given us many experiences long to be remembered."

"The Workhorse of the Ranch"—the jeep, Cadillac of the slippery, muddy and rugged roads of Braeside, had a page to itself, as did the Little Creek Ranch: "The log house is furnished with rustic furniture, game heads and skin rugs. Paint, the saddle pinto is grazing close by. In your dreams, Mr. Hobson, you may often be mounting the saddle and sound forth with a loud and booming Huppa! Huppa! as you urge the cattle on and pick the strays out of the bush."

The older children wrote with enthusiasm about the crafts they had learned, the walks we had taken, and the wild flowers we had found. There was a photo of a pet baby fawn, a whole page about Moose, and photos of most of the children. One photo was of most of the Klaas Wiebe family—all blond and all under twelve. Under it: "This is a photograph taken two years ago. The children are: Eva, Klaas, Anna, Gertruda, Tina and Willie. Joseph and Justina are the twins."

The book of mementoes ended with individual letters from each child in the school: "The time has come to say goodbye, so we will wish you good luck all your life. You have been a good teacher. When we found work hard, you helped us with it. We will write to you in our spare time."

I was still misty-eyed when I had finished reading. The children and their new teacher had captured so well a true vision of our life, its happiness, its challenges, the quality of our individual existence, and the integration of our experiences. What sense they had made of it all!

"May the sunsets often come back to you and say, 'That was a perfect stay,'" the children had written. In a way the stay had been like a fairy tale. In all good fairy tales the chief characters, after experiencing many problems, end up being changed people, better and wiser.

That is what had happened to us; the mirror of our little world was giving back to us what we had become from our experiences in tackling these problems. When Nature had challenged us we had met the challenge with courage and spirit. We had used our skills and shown our love for her. We had fought her at the times when she was cruel and capricious, but we had also lived with her in comforting harmony.

From this direct and personal contact with the things which were the source of our material life and our close contact with each other, we had gained a greater knowledge of and a more complete understanding of the wonder of life. We had also acquired additional life-coping skills which would hopefully carry over into the future.

In late October, four years after I had first arrived at the Little Creek Ranch, the time had come for us to slip quietly away. Moose, our beloved friend, and now the only dog we had left, was going with us. We would provide our own crate for him from Prince George to Vancouver, but at Seattle, the United States airline would provide one. On hearing this, Al volunteered to make the crate. While Moose lay unsuspectingly full length on the kitchen floor, George stalked him with my tape measure.

"Four by three by two and a half," George sang out, emphatically. "That should give him plenty of room to move around."

The time of departure had come, and the crate had been made. Moose evidently liked his new home. He lay in it lionlike in the back of Al's truck. Al was to drive us to Prince George where he planned to entertain us at a farewell party before we left on the following day.

Gently we closed the front door of the little cabin for the last time and walked over the meadow to Al's truck. I did not look back, as I did not want to prolong the leaving. We drove off quickly. I kept my eyes straight ahead on "Pothole Road." We had been through a lot together, that road and I, and it seemed as if I were forsaking a comrade-in-arms as it rolled back behind us. I clutched my stag's horn moss from the cabin wall tightly as we drove on.

For the first couple of miles two Canada jays darted ahead of us in and out of the trees that hugged the side of the road. I hoped they were the Crumb Boys escorting us into the future. We passed the Braeside School and the tiny teacherage and continued on through Vanderhoof without stopping. Good-byes had been said earlier; they had been quick and sudden, which was best.

We rode on new smooth black-top for the first thirty miles of the road to Prince George and then for

the rest of the way we bounced from pothole to pothole.
Good old sturdy British Columbian two-by-fours I said
to myself as I looked through the back window of the
cab at Moose's tarpaulin-covered crate. A pity he isn't
a Chihuahua though—twenty cents a pound to get him
to Vancouver and eighty cents after that—and there's a
lot of dog.

We walked into the lobby of the Prince George Hotel
where we had planned to stay. Rusty Campbell was
there just as he had been on our last visit. He told us
that beds were unobtainable at the hotel without booking
ahead, which we had not done.

"I know a place. It's called Rose-something-or-
other," he was saying, "though heaven knows why.
There aren't any roses around here. But it's an autocourt—a motel—on the main drag. You ought to get in
there."

So we threw down at the Rose-something-or-other
autocourt and chained Moose to the bed. Then we went
with Al to a chicken and champagne dinner party. As I
drank a pre-dinner cocktail, a strange feeling of déjà vu
overwhelmed me. It was as if things distant were being
brought back into the present and combining with the
unknown future. Sadness and joy mingled as we ate
together celebrating good-byes to the past and hellos to
the future.

On our return to the room after the delicious feast,
we were unprepared to see the bed stuck in the doorway
between the bedroom and the bathroom. While we were
away, Moose had evidently made a beeline for the bathroom and had dragged his jailer with him. We unchain-
ed him and righted the bed. I went into the bathroom
closing the door. George went to the autocourt office.

A blood-curdling growl a few minutes later just
outside the bathroom door startled me. Convinced that
our backwoods dog's primitive spirit was already showing

severe strain after a few hours in a town, I flung open
the door and confronted a ferocious, snarling animal with
his hackles raised. It was our beloved, gentle Moose,
confronting eyeball to eyeball in the mirror on the front
of the bathroom door, the biggest, hairiest dog he had
ever seen.

The next morning, allowing ourselves thirty minutes
to get everything fixed up at the airport, Al, George and
I passed through the swinging doors of the airport with
our baggage and coats.

"There's the dog, too," George reminded the harassed young man behind the ticket counter. "He's outside in his crate."

"Where's his certificate? His rabies certificate?" the young man asked resignedly.

"Certificate, certificate?" queried George, looking at me. "Wangy get that paper which told us that we needed no papers to get the dog over the border." I promptly produced the document from my bag.

"Yes," continued the flurried young man—there were many passengers and little time. "He can go across the line but not out of this area without the permission of the Royal Canadian Mounted Police. I'll see that he gets to you on a later plane and have his certificate fixed up for you."

"He's got to go with us and we've got to go on this plane," George asserted decisively. "We've got a big deal on which means thousands of dollars to us," continued George with a dramatic gesture which took in all the waiting people clustered around in little knots.

A bespectacled man calmly stepped forward. "I think I can help you," he said, "I am the agricultural representative here."

He looked vaguely familiar; I connected him with raspberries and suddenly recalled that while drinking coffee in a Vanderhoof restaurant at the time we were making our garden, he had told me how to grow raspberries on ridges.

He walked to the phone and a few minutes later, two Royal Canadian Mounted Police officers, one a corporal and the other of higher rank, entered through the swinging doors. George walked over to them and told his story. The higher ranking officer took over at the phone. In a few moments he had arranged everything satisfactorily.

"Bring in the dog," sighed the young man at the counter. George and Al vanished rapidly through the swinging doors. All eyes were turned in that direction and a few seconds later George's rear appeared parting the swinging doors, followed by the crate and Al. They staggered across the floor with it and eased it down in front of the harassed young man.

"My God," he said, clutching his forehead.

Moose surveyed the scene nonchalantly. He was not sure what the fuss was all about. He felt secure enough with his master's and mistress's high rubber boots to keep him company. We had to wear the boots up to the last minute at the ranch because of the mud, and so we had thrown them into the crate, as there was nowhere else to pack them.

A young man with a yard stick appeared from nowhere.

"Too long to get it into the plane, much too long," he announced flatly.

The crate suddenly appeared much larger as it sat there on the floor. It had occurred to me earlier that it was on the heavy side and might cost a lot, but that it would be too big to go in the plane never entered my head.

Dismayed, Al, George and I looked first at each other and then at the fabulous crate made of good old

British Columbian two-by-fours with "Good Luck, Moose" printed on it.

Without a word, George opened the crate door and Moose walked out with the self-assurance of a movie star appearing before his public. George attached the chain to his collar and handed him over to me.

With great dignity George and Al lifted the empty crate and solemnly backed off with it, out through the swinging doors and onto the truck again.

The plane was due to leave at any minute. Moose was on the scales. By now the waiting young man wore an air of complete resignation.

George had difficulty weighing Moose properly. He could not get all four of his big paws on the scale platform at the same time.

"Sixty pounds," sang out George. How he must have shrunk, I thought. George had always said he was "a 100 pounds stripped."

We said a sad goodbye to Al and took our places in the plane. Moose was chained in the space between the passengers and the pilot—a privileged dog indeed and probably a first for the airline. We took off.

A few seconds later, the captain said: "Ladies and gentlemen, we are returning to the airport for a check on our weight manifest. There will be a slight delay."

"It's Moose that's making the difference. What a dog!" George proclaimed for all to hear.

At this latest turning point in my life, the return of the plane to the airport afforded time for a quick backtrack of my own. For me, a second four-year span of living had just ended, and for George, British Columbia had been home for ten years. Materially, he had slipped back; in other ways he was wealthy.

Where our new home would be we did not know with any certainty. It did not concern me that this was so as it struck me that one's destination is not necessarily a specific physical place. It could be a way of looking at things, an attitude. For us we would be taking the experiences at the Little Creek Ranch with us wherever we went. The intensity of them in our little world would enable us to look at the bigger world with wider eyes. We were looking forward to the new experience with an enthusiasm heightened by a sense of adventure, a real joy of living and the excitement of a new challenge.

Whatever the extent of involvement with the world that our new life would bring, I felt that we would be able to build a firm foundation, to create, design, and direct our living successfully, even though there would be forces at work pressuring us to conform.

I felt good about the last four years so soon to be known as the past, except that my father had died shortly after my trip to England. He had lived his life sensitively and courageously, although he had died at too early an age, for he loved life. Although I was far away physically from my mother and sister, in reality we were closer than ever. It was good that I had been no stranger to my family. Nor had George been a stranger to his; they too had been close.

George's mother still lived in her comfortable home in Vanderhoof, where we were always welcome. Rich and Gloria had a little girl, Cathy, and my former husband and his wife had a girl, Mary. Rich's second book, *Nothing Too Good for a Cowboy* was hot off the press.

Al and Neil intended to make the Central Interior their home. Teeney, Johnny and David were still at school and would be able to visit us again when we had a new home. The Braeside children were in excellent hands with Jake Schroeder as their teacher.

Jack, Paint, Carrot, Bossy, the herd of cattle, and all the other Little Creek animals would continue to live on their own familiar stamping ground and they would be happy with their new owners. The Crumb Boys would fare well—they had well-developed survival skills.

The plane took off after the short delay. We nosed southward towards the unknown future. Our new dream cast its shadow before us on the clouds. Coleridge put it better: "In today already walks tomorrow," and the children of Braeside had put it their way: "The clouds are writing promises in the sky."

A rift appeared in the clouds. Through it I glimpsed the olive-green Fraser River flowing south beneath us. I thought again of the man with the stag's horn moss whom I had met several years before. He too had journeyed south. I wondered what his tomorrow had been. As I thought of him, I felt a part of some mystic composite dream. My own dream had merged with those of the countless others who had dreamed their dreams in the Central Interior of British Columbia.

I put my arm through George's. The roughness of his coat and the warmth of his hand were very real. We were both silent, each thinking his own thoughts. I saw again the cabin chinked with oakum, our wilderness home in the wild little valley; the front door was open. In the years to come, in our dreams, hand in hand, we would wander again through the meadow, over the bridge, and into the cabin through the ever-open door.

Epilogue

For thirty years our home has been at the edge of George Washington National Forest in the Shenandoah Valley of Virginia. From our windows we watch the sun set behind the blue Allegheny Mountains, ancient guardians of the Valley.

Built of two-hundred-year-old broad-axed chestnut logs, our home has a massive rock chimney with three fireplaces. Black walnut, sycamore, weeping willow, hickory and maple trees enfold it. Another "Little Creek" runs through our land. Muskrats nose across a pool where wild mallard ducks swim. In the spring, American Mergansers make flying pit stops on it. Tall blue herons stalk the edge searching for fish. Little green herons are hard to spot in the undergrowth.

But the pull of life in even wilder places is always with us and in our imagination we often walk hand-in-hand across the Little Creek meadow and through the cabin's open door. In our memory, all is still the same; in reality much has changed.

Vanderhoof is now a town of 5,000 and 50,000 Canada geese stop over at the Nechako Bird Sanctuary. Prince George is the third largest city in British Columbia.

Visitors travel regularly to the Kenney Dam along the road through the River Ranch made famous by Rich Hobson's trilogy of books, *Grass Beyond the Mountains*,

Nothing Too Good for a Cowboy and *A Rancher Takes a Wife*. These true pioneering stories of penetrating into that land of lakes, mountains and wild hay meadows have inspired many. It was fitting that Mt. Hobson was named after him.

Rich died on his River Ranch in 1966. Grizelda Hobson died a year later. Rich's wife Gloria and daughter Cathy live in Vanderhoof. Al Moser, attracted to Central British Columbia by Rich's first book, still lives in Vanderhoof with his wife Rosa. Neil Wiley and Anne live in Prince George. The Morks eventually sold Little Creek Ranch and the farm Co-operative families went their various ways.

Teeney and his wife Victoria have a home in France and are working on advanced degrees at Oxford. Johnny Scholz is an architect. He, his wife Jane, and daughter Lucy live in Maine. Dave Noble and his wife Ruth live in New Mexico; author and photographer, he writes about the ancient ruins of the Southwest.

As for us, we built our kennels. We sent for the St. Bernard dogs George had picked out on his visit to Watrous, Saskatchewan. Big Boy, Esme, Merri-Joan, and Clara arrived by Railway Express, sitting up straight in enormous wooden crates. We raised registered puppies for twenty years and at one time had over 100 puppies and dogs.

Moose's life in his new home was brief. It ended suddenly in hunting season on the road near our home. We buried our northern dog under an ancient southern sugar maple tree.

I continued to teach—in high school and college—to work professionally in the field of human services, and I studied. I received a doctorate in education from the University of Virginia. George makes our home and land a place apart, an oasis for us, Rags, our old English sheepdog, Tiger, our cat, and the wild birds and animals which also make it their home.

Epilogue

Canada Geese

The Rocky Mountain sheep, instead of Bumpy, the moose, keeps vigil over another rock fireplace. My lantern glows in a different window, linking a new country to the old country. It lights our personal dreams until they finally merge with man's composite dream.

Churchville, Virginia
August 1986

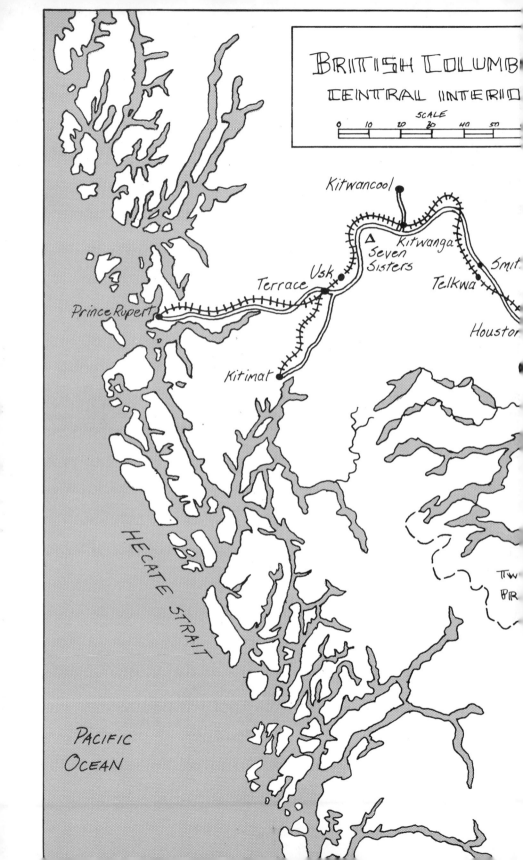